MY TWO CHINAS

The Memoir of
a Chinese
Counterrevolutionary

MY TWO CHINAS

Baiqiao Tang

with Damon DiMarco

Prometheus Books

59 John Glenn Drive
Amherst, New York 14228–2119

Published 2011 by Prometheus Books

Inquiries should be addressed to
Prometheus Books
59 John Glenn Drive
Amherst, New York 14228–2119
VOICE: 716–691–0133
FAX: 716–691–0137
WWW.PROMETHEUSBOOKS.COM

15 14 13 12 11   5 4 3 2 1

Library of Congress Cataloging-in-Publication Data

Tang, Baiqiao, 1967–
    My two Chinas : the memoir of a Chinese counterrevolutionary / by Baiqiao Tang with Damon DiMarco.
        p. cm.
    ISBN 978–1–61614–445–6 (cloth : acid-free paper)
    1. Tang, Baiqiao, 1967– 2. Political activists—China—Biography.
3. Counterrevolutionaries—China—Biography. 4. Student protesters—China—Biography. 5. China—Politics and government—1976–2002. 6. China—Politics and government—2002– 7. Human rights—China. 8. Political refugees—United States—Biography. 9. Political activists—United States—Biography. I. DiMarco, Damon. II. Title.

DS779.29.T36A3 2011
951.05092—dc22
[B]   2010048472

Printed in the United States of America on acid-free paper

To my father, Tang Rentong,
my mother, Luo Huaying,
and my wife, Felicity Lung—

Because of your unconditional love
I have never felt lonely
as I walk along this road.

Also to Pan Mingdong,
my brother in arms.
Your tireless spirit continues to encourage me.

A Note on the Text

In traditional Chinese culture, surnames come before given names.

With the exception of Baiqiao Tang, we have preserved that tradition in the pages that follow.

The Anglicized form of Chinese names and words is open to debate.

We have adapted spellings as we deemed most appropriate.

You will note that many names in this book bear asterisks when they're first introduced. The asterisk means that this person's name has been changed for the purposes of this memoir. In some cases, details about the person's life or appearance have also been altered.

On a separate note, Baiqiao Tang feels deeply indebted to the men and women with whom he worked during the 1989 democracy movement.

Some fought to advance the cause of freedom. Some helped to hide Mr.

Tang when the Chinese government hunted him. Some ultimately helped him escape to China.

These people deserve the highest recognition for their actions. But many still live in China, and no hero should be punished, persecuted, or imprisoned twenty-two years after Tiananmen Square because of details released in this book.

We thank you for your understanding.

Contents

CONTENTS

Foreword

Following the Tiananmen demonstrations of 1989, many Chinese democrats began to look at the Tibetan issue from a new perspective that differed from the official version of Tibet that they had been taught by the Chinese government. Many of them sympathized with the Tibetan people and could understand the Tibetan people's grievances against the Chinese government. Among them is Mr. Baiqiao Tang.

His Holiness the Dalai Lama is pleased to learn about this book that details Baiqiao Tang's experience. His Holiness has always admired the efforts of the Chinese people working toward a more democratic and open China. His Holiness believes that it is important for them to tell their story to the larger world.

His Holiness hopes that this book will encourage other Chinese to

strengthen their democratic aspirations and put the spotlight on the weak-
nesses of the attitude of some of the current leaders in China.

Tsegyam
Secretary to His Holiness the Dalai Lama

Preface

Courage and bravery are things in the movies. As a kid growing up in Southern California, I loved watching World War II films and fantasized about landing on the beaches of Normandy with John Wayne and Robert Mitchum. No matter what the action, they never got injured, their shirts were always pressed, and they always got the girl. I wanted that kind of excitement, so in the fall of 1987, I found myself sitting in the first-class cabin of a 747 jumbo jet bound for Thailand. I had just accepted a position in Bangkok as the Associated Press Southeast Asia photo editor, and I couldn't get there soon enough. But I wasn't fooling myself; this was to be a very dangerous posting. In fact, the more I thought about it, the more I wasn't sure if I had the courage to risk my life. The truth is, I am scared of guns and even spiders. It's ironic that fate landed me in some of the most dangerous news assignments in the world. I am no hero, but I would soon come to know many heroes in China. Many like Baiqiao Tang.

Tang and I have never met, but it seems we share some common traits. We both believe in justice, and neither of us likes to be pushed around. He was one of the most active student leaders during the 1989 pro-democracy uprising in China, and I would end up documenting his movement. It is possible, even likely, that we crossed paths during one of the 100,000-strong marches that took place in Beijing during that time. Fate proclaimed that we both had our jobs cut out for us. Both our lives would soon be changed forever.

Born in Hunan Province, Tang believed that China could be a better place to live, that her people deserved better than what they were getting. Many Chinese felt the same. For a brief moment during that spring of 1989, I saw a wonderful thing happen: everyone in China became excited by the dream of a better world. Police and soldiers were singing along with students. Strangers were helping each other. A new sense of pride was in the air. Direct dialogue with the Communist Party seemed possible. But in the end, everything came crashing down.

On June, 3, 1989, everything seemed calm in Tiananmen Square, Beijing. But something bad was in the air. Bystanders were standing rather than sleeping. Some had blocked off the street with road dividers. Looking back, it's as if everyone knew that something terrible was about to happen.

Then, out of the shadows, a very old man with a heavy coat and a toothless grin approached me, eager to share something. The old man excitedly opened his tattered garment and showed a large hatchet dripping with blood. He smiled proudly, as if he'd just bagged a giant tuna. The fate of the soldier was clear. Shocked at the sight, I smiled weakly and quickly moved on. The military crackdown had begun.

An armored personnel carrier suddenly plowed through the protestors' barricades and came tearing around the corner with sparks flying off its treads. I dove for cover and started trembling. I felt nauseous. The movies had not prepared me for this. Everyone started chasing the APC down the street until it rolled to a stop in front of the Great Hall of the People. At this point, the demonstrators climbed on top of it, waving flags and cheering.

I had used up most of my film and flash batteries, so I decided to head back to the AP office to transmit the images I'd made. The situation was getting out of control, and I felt lucky to be uninjured. It was a false sense of security.

In the distance, another APC lurched toward me. It was having engine problems; its chassis was completely engulfed in flames. I was terrified that the soldiers inside might panic and start firing their front machine guns. The swarming students shoved pieces of steel pipes and barricades into the treads. The soldiers were roasting alive inside. I couldn't believe what I was seeing.

By midnight, it was clear that I'd somehow landed in one of the biggest news stories of the century, but my dying flash was taking forever to recharge. One picture a minute was all I could take. This is the kind of nightmare every news photographer fears.

People began screaming all around me. My camera was grabbed by the mob. I raised my passport and yelled "American!" figuring I would either get killed or someone would help me. Fortunately, it was the latter. A leader approached me and the crowd went silent. They cleared a path to show a dead soldier lying sprawled on the ground. The leader returned my passport and barked, "You photo . . . you show world."

I then noticed that another protestor had caught fire. People were trying to help him as he rolled on the ground, flailing his arms and screaming. It was a shocking scene, but all I could do was swear and wait for another minute to pass. How could I have been so stupid? Why hadn't I brought more flash batteries? Little did I know, that mistake would save my life.

With the flash recharged, I raised the Nikon F3 Titanium camera to my eye. But at the same instant, a terrific blow snapped my head back. Blood flowed over the remains of my camera. Everything was in a daze. It took me a moment to realize what had happened: a stray brick had hit me straight on. My flash and the entire top of my camera had been sheared off, but the Nikon had absorbed the blow that I'm now convinced would have taken my life.

Then the back door of the burning APC opened and a soldier jumped out, surrendering with his hands held over his head. The protestors regarded him for a moment before closing in with steel pipes, clubs, and knives. I still remember the look of terror on that soldier's face. There was nothing I could do. This was nothing like the movies.

After what seemed like an eternity of weaving past burning buses and dodging large-caliber machine gun fire, I reached the AP office located at the Diplomatic Compound. With tears in his eyes, AP photo editor Mark Avery used a pair of pliers to extract the film from my shattered camera. Mark was upset because one of his Chinese friends had been killed in the crackdown. The soldiers were killing civilians! He cautioned me not to return to the streets.

It was one of the most difficult professional choices I've ever made, but I decided to stay inside my hotel. I was suffering from the flu, had a major concussion, and was just too scared. I hated myself and felt like a coward. I couldn't stop thinking about the bravery and courage of all those protestors down in the streets. I barely slept that night.

The next morning, I returned to the AP office. A directive from New York headquarters had arrived, saying: "We don't want anyone taking any unnecessary risks . . . but if someone could please photograph the occupied Tiananmen Square, we would appreciate it."

This message was almost comical, but I thought I could get the right kind of shot from the Beijing Hotel, which offered an excellent view of the square. The problem was the secret police. They were everywhere, using cattle prods on journalists. So I hid my camera in my clothes, grabbed a bicycle, and left.

I avoided soldiers by weaving through streets clogged with smashed bicycles, broken rocks, and burned buses. At the Beijing Hotel, I could see three white-coated security police standing guard at the entrance. But I also saw a young American student standing in the shadows. He had long hair and wore a dirty Rambo T-Shirt. I had to think fast.

I approached this kid and said, "How you doing, Joe? I've been looking for you." Then I whispered, "I'm from Associated Press—can I come up to your room?"

The security police left us alone. I guess they thought I was a guest. The kid's name turned out to be Kirk. He nodded and ushered me into a darkened elevator where he told me that two tourists had been shot by Chinese soldiers mere minutes before, their bodies dragged back into the hotel lobby.

Kirk helped me find a secret way to the roof, where I made my images of the occupied square. And later, I photographed events on the street from the window in Kirk's room. But I soon found myself running low on film. Kirk said he'd see what he could do about that and went downstairs. He managed to grab one roll from a hotel guest he met in the deserted lobby. Exhausted, I sat down to nurse my aching head and quickly fell asleep.

The sound of approaching vehicles woke me with a start. Back on my feet, I looked out the window and saw a perfect image. A long line of tanks was rolling up from Tiananmen Square. But then I complained to Kirk that some guy had jumped in front of the column and was screwing up my composition. I blame the concussion I'd sustained on my initial inability to see that picture for what it was. But reality clicked in a few seconds later, at which point I realized that—technically speaking—the scene was too far away for my lens.

I rushed to the bed where my teleconverter lay. The instrument would double the focal length of my 400 mm lens and make for a closer, better shot. I slapped the teleconverter onto my camera and set the auto exposure. Returning to the window, I clicked off three quick frames before, horrified, I noticed that the shutter speed was set too slow. But before I could address the error, onlookers ran to the lone man standing before the tanks. They picked him up and swept him away.

Later I realized that the film Kirk had given me was less sensitive than the kind I normally used. It seemed like everything was working against me.

The secret police were still outside. Trying not to dwell on my blunder, I worked it out with Kirk that he would smuggle my film from the Beijing Hotel in his underwear. It was a risky plan, but I felt the police were much less likely to suspect some young hippie kid wearing shorts and a T-shirt than me. Watching from the balcony, I almost laughed out loud as Kirk, laden with precious cargo, painfully peddled his bike past the security guards, heading toward the AP office.

Five hours later, I called Mark Avery at the bureau. He asked what shutter speed I had used when I'd snapped the images. My heart sank. The pictures, I thought, had not come out. But Mark said, "It's OK. It wasn't very sharp, but we moved an image on to the newspapers."

I felt a mild sense of relief but was still unhappy about the botched photo. Disappointed, I returned to my hotel.

Apparently my image was sharp enough after all. The next morning I was flooded with congratulations from around the world. Newspapers everywhere were prominently displaying the tank photo on their front pages, heralding it as iconic.

That picture, and what I went through to get it, changed my life forever. I felt a new inner strength from having participated in such a historic event, but I also felt a great sadness.

I will never forget watching the state-run black-and-white video of tanks toppling the student-built Goddess of Democracy. That statue was symbolic of everything the young protestors had been fighting for—and there it was, being crushed under the heavy treads of soulless metal tanks. And I never found out what happened to the unknown rebel. In some ways I think it's better that way. That faceless man is my unknown soldier. He will always inspire me to stand up for my principles and beliefs.

But as my story ended, Baiqiao Tang's fight was just beginning. He and hundreds of other pro-democracy activists were about to be hunted and thrown in jail by their own government.

My Two Chinas is a very personal and insightful story about one man's struggle to be free. I consider it a must-read for anyone encouraged by stories of hope and the good fight. Author Damon DiMarco brilliantly leads the reader through the maze of Baiqiao Tang's life as he runs from secret police, survives torture and imprisonment, and eventually escapes to the United States. But perhaps best of all, reading this book helped me to answer many questions I had regarding the events that transpired in the crackdown that followed Tiananmen Square.

Many pro-democracy activists are still imprisoned in China today. I admire the courage and bravery shown by Baiqiao Tang and thousands of other Chinese like him who shined during those dark days.

As for me, though I was injured that day and my shirts are rarely pressed, I did end up with the girl. Twenty years later, I returned to China for a BBC interview. While there, I met a pretty young German girl who was sitting on the Chang'an Boulevard. After we introduced ourselves, she commented on having once seen my famous *Tank Man* photo in a Berlin museum. I think she was impressed. The following year we married. That's a beautiful kind of reward.

I guess heroes come in all different shapes and sizes after all.

Jeff Widener
Pulitzer finalist, nominated for the acclaimed Tank Man *photo*

Introduction

I read this book in what seemed a timeless sitting—I couldn't put it down, I found it so incredibly moving. It is a vivid record of human courage and uncompromising intelligence, full of the life of China over the last few decades, with its sufferings and its triumphs, its villains, and its kind and hearty heroes.

Since Baiqiao Tang's story is so utterly real and concerns what is happening in our world in real time, it holds us in the greatest suspense of all—how are the deaths and lives of China's true patriots going to turn out? I assure you, their success is vital not only to China, but also very much to us all! If China's leadership continues to act out of fear, aggression, and violence, the whole world will face a huge danger! Tang's book records nothing less than his "act of truth," as it was called in ancient India: the absolute holding to the principle of goodness in the face of whatever odds.

We begin by meeting Baiqiao Tang as a youth—*Xiao* Tang, or "Little Tang," as he was called. The vivid, poetical portraits of his family members are unforgettable, especially his remarkable father, a schoolteacher, a reluctant Communist Party member, and a pillar of the community. We follow Tang's struggles through school and admire his growth of character as he turns from his budding brilliant career as abstract mathematician and physicist to political engagement. We see him bravely extending his father's commitment to justice and sanity by determining to live his ideals, and to change China by pushing beyond the oppressive "dictatorship of the proletariat," toward the vibrant democracy that liberates the creativity in all people.

We see how Tang gets swept up in this ethic, becoming a leader in the China-wide Tiananmen Square revolution of 1989. And we can understand from this account—described here better than ever before—how the 1989 pro-democracy movement was inspired by the great Hu Yaobang, how it was led by students and workers against the cruel dictatorship maintained by Deng Hsiaoping, who too closely held to Mao's legacy.

Then we follow Tang through excruciating ordeals. He suffered his share of agonies in the violent suppression of a peaceful revolution that ultimately ruined Deng's name, who ruthlessly implemented his notorious dictum that the Chinese Communist Party (CCP) should "kill 200,000 to rule for 20 more years"—200,000 for 20! Tang gets caught and tortured for years in dehumanizing prisons. His vivid and detailed descriptions rival Solzhenitsyn's chronicles of the Russian gulags. I am inspired by his determined integrity. His clarity about the right side of life and history keeps his spirit from being broken by the horrendous cruelty he endured.

Miraculously, he wins release due to a shift in CCP policy. Then, the daring support of some compatriots who secretly admire his stand enables him to travel the country. He does business while touching base with the many individuals all over China who survived the purges and now wait for the moment when they can realize their dream of justice, human decency, and democracy.

Tang is alerted in the nick of time to another shift in the winds of power, the signs that indicate he will once again disappear into the *laogai*—horrendous "reform through labor" concentration camps that have swallowed up millions of dissidents—so brilliantly described by Harry Wu as a relentless system of human slavery, the ground level of China's supposed "economic miracle." And Tang's story evokes for us the human reality of these horrendous happenings that engulf China, a nation comprising one-fifth of all human beings on earth.

After his escape, he discovers the modern world, America, New York, and he describes with keen accuracy the problems of the Chinese democratic student exiles. He shows in his own case how the long arm of the CCP reaches out both seductively and threateningly, even into his new life in Queens, where he falls in love, does not sell out, and works steadily to change China from abroad. Though Tang lost his beloved father under very suspicious circumstances—he was probably murdered as punishment for his son's dissidence—he sticks to his personal integrity and power in a way that would undoubtedly have made his father deeply proud.

Clear-eyed, Tang records the subtlest details of the cruelty and hypocrisy practiced by various "authorities," yet he concludes with hope, not hatred. And this is what makes this book so remarkable. Throughout his whole movement to change China in a more positive direction, Baiqiao Tang and his generation have pursued a peaceful revolution. They have responded to Mao's demented "power from a barrel of a gun" philosophy with nonviolent resistance and endurance.

Tibet is usually a sensitive subject, even for Chinese democracy advocates. But Tang does not mince words in describing the CCP's behavior on this point. He calls China's Tibetan policy imperialistic, cruel, and self-defeating, declaring that the same holds true for the Chinese oppression of the Uyghurs in Xinjiang. In other words, he totally gets that the CCP's internal oppression of the Chinese people is inextricably linked with its imperialistic policies with its neighbors. Indeed, Tang's determination to change China—to push it free from the iron fist of the CCP's one-party domination and its massively militarizing dictatorship—is no less than a determination to change the world.

This book is especially timely since, as I write this introduction, Liu Xiaobo was recently recognized as a Nobel Peace Prize laureate. No doubt, Xiaobo is suffering the same kind of dehumanizing abuse that Tang did; he is now two years into an eleven-year prison sentence imposed for his peaceful expression of dissent as expressed in his historic Charter 08 manifesto. China is the only "world power" in the top six or seven that does not allow democracy and does not honor its own constitution's enshrinement of freedom of speech and opinion. This is extremely dangerous for peaceful prospects in the world of the twenty-first century, extremely dangerous for China herself, and absolutely intolerable for the Chinese people.

Baiqiao Tang is a heroic patriot. He opposes the violent nationalism that the CCP whips up in the Chinese masses to conceal its own oligarchic practices, as well as its unjust and inhumane governance, in order to maintain its power. In the past, such unstable and immoral dictatorships, puffed up with wealth and emboldened by weapons, have catastrophically disturbed the peace of the world.

Our planet has become so fragile through environmental imbalance and the destructive power of war. This system can no longer work. So Baiqiao Tang is therefore a hero for us all—for the whole world, not just for China.

I am humbled by his persistence against extreme odds and honored to write this introduction. Welcome to Baiqiao Tang's world of hope through the power of constant truth!

Robert Thurman
Jey Tsong Khapa Professor of Indo-Tibetan Buddhist Studies
Columbia University

part one
Youth

1

While I was a prisoner in Changsha Number One Jail, my fellow inmates told me this story. It happened in early 1977. Winter gripped the city of Changsha with talons of ice. A drunk spent the night in a city park. He was shivering, hungry, and high on cheap wine. Exhausted, he made a bed for himself by unfolding scraps of old newspaper and spreading them out on the ground. Then he lay down and went to sleep.

A couple of policemen found him the next morning. They laughed and kicked him awake and told the drunk to hop to his feet and get moving, so he did. Wiping sleep from his eyes, the drunk staggered a few feet away. Behind him, a policeman shouted, "Stop!" The drunk turned around to see what the problem was.

The policemen were standing over his makeshift bed and staring at the ground. The drunk looked too and his eyes went wide. A crumpled picture of Mao Zedong looked up from the scraps of newspaper left on the frozen grass. The drunk must have been lying on it all night.

"I'm sorry," he blurted. "No! Please! I'm sorry! Don't!"

The police ran toward him. They beat him, cuffed him, and took him away to Changsha Number One Jail, where he was befriended by prisoners who, many years later, became my cell mates.

"Mao had died a few months before in September 1976," said one of my fellow inmates. "In order to keep the people in line, the Party ran Mao's picture in the papers all the time. *Remember Mao Zedong!* said the articles. *Obey the Party! Uphold your Great Leader's legacy. Do it for society. Do it for your province. Do it for your family. Do it for your country!*"

I took a good look at these men. They were old and toothless. Their arms and legs were stringy, their bellies bloated. They suffered from malnutrition and stayed alive on cigarettes. Most hadn't seen their families in years and knew they would die in prison. Honestly, some had died already even though their bodies lived on. Chinese prisons can have that effect. They empty you out, tossing the kernel of life aside, leaving nothing but hull and shell. Some of those men had lived through Mao's Cultural Revolution. They had the scars to prove it. On their bodies, livid welts, and in their eyes, furtive glances. Like beaten dogs, they shied away. Their gaits were crippled, movements crabbed from broken bones improperly healed.

"What happened to the drunk?" I asked.

"Oh," said an inmate. "You know. He was taken to court and found guilty of being a counterrevolutionary. After which they took him outside and shot him."

For a moment, our cell went quiet.

"You know," began another old inmate, "I think that drunk was lucky. They would have treated the bastard worse had Mao Zedong still been alive."

He grinned at us, revealing a smile of gums.

2

I grew up in Hunan Province, a region known for its outspoken people. In China, you will often hear, "The Hunan food is spicy, but her people are even hotter." True. We Hunanese take pride in our strength of will and character. We drink strong wine. We argue and fight. We do not hold our feelings in. Some people like to call us *juelu*, a Mandarin word meaning stubborn donkey. In Hunan, this is a compliment. Why not? We call a person stubborn when he stands up for himself. Fights for his convictions. Elevates his ideals.

Take my grandfather, for instance. He died when I was very young but I still remember his pride. He was old and blind, and he used to say, "What is a person who will not fight? Who cannot make a stand? Show me that person, I'll show you a dog! There's no one like that in Hunan! What comes from Hunan is good for China!"

Then he would ask me to fetch his pipe, which I would always do very fast since I loved to watch the old man smoke. His withered lips would form an O, and scented rings would pop forth smelling of cloves and cinnamon. The rings would travel a certain distance, undulating wreaths of smoke. I loved them but learned not to grow too attached. I knew that they lasted only a moment. After that, they would disappear, as my grandfather soon did. As all of us do.

My grandfather's favorite poem was "Li sao," which means Sorrow of Departure. It was written by the famous poet Qu Yuan (ca. 340 BCE–278 BCE). Sometimes the old man would pick up his chin and quote in his trembling voice.

I gaze afar, oh! 'mid clovers white and wait for our tryst, oh!
  in the twilight.
Among the reeds, oh! can birds be free? What can a net do, oh!
  atop a tree?
White clover grows, oh! beside the creek; I long for you, oh!
  but dare not speak!

I remember being so young that I didn't know what a poet was. I asked the old man to tell me.

"A poet?" asked my grandfather. He smiled and laughed. His dead eyes stared straight ahead like twin silver coins set into his face. "Well, my boy! A poet is a person who speaks the truth. Who appreciates things. Who looks for beauty everywhere. And of course he smiles a lot."

"I don't think I know any poets," I said.

My grandfather sighed. "Of course you don't. We don't have many around anymore. The Party does not like them."

Even though I was very small, I knew what the Party was. *Zhongguo Gongchan Dang*, otherwise known as the CCP, or the Chinese Communist Party. I remember noticing how adult people's faces always changed when they spoke the Party's name. Their mouths would compress into tight, bloodless lines. Bright eyes would fall at once to the ground, losing their luster like pearls cast in dirt.

The subject caused me confusion since my father was in the Party. He worked as a teacher and a principal of schools, a very wise man who was greatly respected. I loved him very much. But I noticed that even his attitude changed whenever he mentioned the Party. A garrulous man, his body would stiffen. The tone of his voice would grow hard, more reserved. It was a frightening transformation, and one I cared not to ponder much in childhood.

"Tell me more about Qu Yuan," I said.

My grandfather laughed and tapped his old knee, as thin as a withered branch. This was my official cue to climb gently into his lap, so I did. "The poet Qu Yuan," he said. "Another great man from Hunan Province! Qu Yuan lived a long time ago. He was a minister to the king. In fact, that's where all of his troubles began."

"Tell me!" I said.

My grandfather stared into space for a moment. "Well," he said. "The king had many advisers, you know. Most had gained their positions by telling the king what he wanted to hear, a common tactic in government.

One time, the ministers told the king to oppose the neighboring state of Qin. Qu Yuan alone objected. He thought this notion was foolish. Opposition would lead to war, for which there was no cause. 'Oh King,' said Qu Yuan. 'Do what is best for your people. Ally with Qin and be happy!' The other advisers were not very pleased. A war can generate profit, you know. Lots and lots of money. The advisers hoped to get very rich, so none of them changed their positions."

I remember being breathless. Wide-eyed. All this talk of kings and wars was acting on me like wine, boiling my blood, making me want to hear more. "So what happened next?" I asked.

"The other advisers drove Qu Yuan from the palace and chased him into the wilderness. The king did as they said and went to war with Qin. There were many great battles and thousands of people died. Qin soldiers went to Qu Yuan's village and slaughtered many of his relatives. But worse: Qin won the war. The king was killed, but his ministers got promoted. Yes. The king of Qin gave them piles of gold and nice, new uniforms to wear on holidays and special occasions. And that, as they say, was that."

"But what about Qu Yuan?" I asked.

"He was so upset that he found a great big rock and held that rock to his chest when he waded into the Miluo River and drowned himself."

"He died?!" I started to cry. "But why, Grandfather? Why?"

"He did it to protest corruption, *Xiao* Tang."

"But why did he have to *kill* himself? Why not continue to live and fight?"

My grandfather's face turned very sad. His dead eyes focused on nothing. "Because, my child," he said. "When no one hears the truth anymore, or looks for beauty everywhere. When no one appreciates things, or smiles a lot, the world is simply not a place for poets anymore."

3

My father's name was Tang Rentong. In Mandarin, this means "Mercy United." As a teacher and a principal of schools, he believed that knowledge was heaven's gift, more precious by far than gold or jewels. "In this world, *Xiao* Tang," my father would say, "knowledge has no price."

Xiao means "little" in Mandarin. My father was Tang. Therefore, I was Little Tang, ever his diminutive. Though sometimes he would call me *zaofang*, a word that means "rebel," and more suited my nature.

I loved him more than I have skill to communicate. Quite often, to earn my father's attention, I would recount the opinions and stories I had learned on my grandfather's knee. My hope was that my father would see how worldly I was becoming, that even at five or six years old, I was a facile conversationalist. For instance, one time I told him, "Father! Hunan is the greatest province in China!"

My father was seated behind his desk, writing a letter. His pen stopped moving. He peered at me over the rims of his glasses. "Oh?" he said. "And why is that?"

"Because," I said. "Hunan has given birth to many great men, like the poet Qu Yuan."

My father regarded me for a moment. Then he returned his eyes to his letter. His pen started moving again. New characters lined up in rows on the paper. Meanings couched in contortions of ink. "That's very true, *Xiao Tang*," he said. "Hunan boasts many great heroes, and the poet Qu Yuan is one. Qu Yuan loved his country like no one else."

"I know! He drowned himself!"

"That's right, because he knew right from wrong. Qu Yuan was a patriot of ideals, rather than country. But have a care, my son. There are other sides to this story."

I frowned, sensing a lecture approaching.

"Hunan gave birth to many great men: the poet Qu Yuan. Cai Lun, the man who invented paper. Qi Baishi, the famous painter. Zeng Guofan, the famous general. But Hunan gave birth to other men, too. Some who were not so good for China."

I was young and bold and very proud and itching for a debate. "Who?" I demanded. "Who from Hunan was not so good for China?"

My father smiled and kept writing. "Mao Zedong," he said.

4

Two men standing side by side like signposts guarding the mouth of a road. As I look back, it's clear to me how my father and grandfather shaped my thinking. My grandfather showed me the fire of passion while my father preached wisdom, temperance, and reason.

And yet he was no less courageous. If anything, Father's principles made him a hero in our hometown of Yongzhou.

Everyone knew who he was. He was everyone's favorite uncle, the town's unofficial mayor. He treated one and all like family. If he walked down the street and saw two people arguing, he stopped and said, "Now, now. What's this? Tell me what's going on!" No one ever told my father to butt out or mind his own business. He had a special way about him. People saw him as an impartial judge. They asked him to mediate their disputes.

Since I didn't know any better, I began to accept that this was the normal way for a man to behave. To put others before himself. His neighbors. His family. Utter strangers. This is the way of the world, I thought. By then I was learning lessons in school. My teachers had taught me how Mao Zedong said all the people in China were equal. That's why communism worked, they said. Father treats everyone equal, I thought. And Father is a communist. But why, then, does he act so tense whenever he speaks of the Party?

I was still very young. I thought in youthful terms. Simple avenues. Simple reasons. Nothing overly complicated, as life so often turns out to be.

5

Father lent money to anyone who asked, whether friends or neighbors or far-flung kin. They were all alike in his eyes. He hated seeing a person in need, so he got the money however he could and gave it to them with no strings attached. "Pay it back when you can," he would say. This was quite an incredible feat if you knew how poor we were. Doubly impressive if you knew my mother, whose quiet seething could turn flesh to stone.

"How can you do this, Tang Rentong?" She would always speak softly. She never shouted, preferring to wield guilt like a whip whose lashes were razor sharp. "Charity must start in your home. You barely know that cousin's name and yet you sent him two hundred yuan! Don't you see that your daughters need shoes? Soon they will walk in bare feet and get blisters!"

Looking back, I can see she was right. Our family had needs that went unfulfilled. However, in my father's defense, he never gave anything to himself, nor spent a single yuan for his own sake, nor allowed himself any luxury.

The principal of a Chinese school was expected to look the part. But my father wore the same clothes year after year. They would have disintegrated right off his back had my mother not intervened to buy him a new pair of trousers or a shirt. He wore shoes whose soles had torn loose from the uppers and flapped like clogs whenever he walked. The worst part of all: he carried a tattered old courier's sack that was surplus from the People's Liberation Army. I can still see him with that sack. He carried that bag wherever he went, slung around one shoulder, the finishing touch to his threadbare attire. He looked like some kind of refugee. A derelict with a smile.

My mother would hound him ceaselessly to at least get a nicer, normal bag. A briefcase befitting his office, perhaps. My father would never fight with her. He would smile a little awkwardly and shake his head, resolute. He said he liked his old army bag. "It's sturdy," he said. "It will last. You see? Look how they've stitched it here. Feel how strong that strap is, wife. That's durable canvas they used!"

Sometimes he attended conventions for principals in his district. Rich foods were often served at these meetings. Apples, for instance, a delicacy. But Father would never eat his servings. Instead, he'd slip them under the table, hide them in his courier's sack, and bring them home for his children. He did this with other treats as well: cookies and cakes and packets of tea intended for cultured pallates. All had been given as gifts and favors, but Father never consumed them. He would pass them around the table at supper, eager to have us taste fine foods and develop appreciation of them.

"Try this," he would say. "It's a chocolate truffle. Now what do you think of that, hmmm? No, no! Don't chew it. Just let it sit. It melts on your tongue. Like that. You see? What do you *think* of that?"

He was always happiest seeing us happy. And I started to see he was always right. About chocolate truffles. About everything.

I remember one summer it was very hot. So humid it was hard to breathe. The air was like a thick, wet towel tossed on top of the city. My friends and I were nine years old, maybe ten. To stay cool, we would roll up the cuffs of our trousers and wade out into a man-made canal that lay in a valley behind our school. Cattails waved on the shorelines. There was the smell of mud and clay. The water was green and impenetrable, a strip of jade that was tossed on the ground. The canal ran past where we often played for another hundred yards before it hit a grate like prison bars designed to keep large objects from floating through.

One day, we were all in the water, splashing around and making up games. One of my friends stood bolt upright, his spine as stiff as a pole. He pointed at something he'd seen in the water. His finger trembled. His eyes were wide. "Fish!" he cried. "Big fish!"

We catapulted out of the water and stood on the shoreline, shivering. Staring at the sheet of green, we watched for movement—and saw it. How could we have missed it? The shadow under the water was wide. It moved very slowly, like a drunken bus. I remember thinking, *That's not a fish. It's too big to be a fish. That's a whale.*

I knew about whales. My father had bought many books to interest me in the sciences. He hoped I would be a doctor someday. Perhaps a nuclear physicist. A Chinese Albert Einstein.

A whale, I thought. *Now isn't that odd! What is a whale doing here?*

My friends and I started to jump up and down. We shouted and danced and pointed. Looking back, it's fair to say we were equal parts terrified and excited.

Eventually, we organized teams and waded back into the water. It took a bit of splashing around, lots of shouting and waving. But we finally cornered the biggest carp I had ever seen in my life. We caught this fish with our tiny bare hands, our fingers slipping over the scales, which glistened like mother of pearl. Heliographs burst in pinwheels where sunlight struck the fish's flanks. Colors spun. Rose and purple. Blue. A verdant green. We hauled that carp from the water and threw it down on the grass. It took all of us to do it, a capering, screaming phalanx of children. The fish was as big as we were. Later, we took it to get it weighed. It was close to thirty pounds.

But before we could do that, my father strolled by with his hands clasped behind him, his courier sack bouncing against one hip. His head was held high. He whistled a tune. He stopped in his tracks and looked down at the fish we'd pulled up onto the shore. He blinked at it, surprised. "Well, well!" he said. "What have you there? My, that's a really big fish!"

"We caught it!" we screamed. We were laughing and dancing a ring around the carp. The fish looked up at us, gasping for air, its eyes gone wide and black and staring. Gills like accordions folded, unfolded, searching for water to breathe.

"Isn't it big?" we screamed. "We caught this fish in the water!"

My father made a startled face. "*Did* you now?" he asked. "Well, *well*! Look how lucky you are! And what will you do with such a big fish?"

"Eat it!" we cried. "We are all going to eat it!" Carp being synonymous with delicacy in Hunan.

"Uhm hmm," said my father. "That seems wise." He made a show of thinking it over. "You know, if I'm not mistaken, this fish is so big, there should be enough for all of your families to eat. Share and share alike. That's what good neighbors do for each other. Isn't that right?"

We agreed. So my friends and I banded together, an army of giggling pygmies. We helped my father pick up the fish and bring it to town to be dressed. The monger followed my father's suggestion, cutting the carp into many pieces so everyone took some home to their families. Everyone ate it for supper. What a glorious find! What a glorious day! I had never been so happy.

Later that night, as I fell asleep, I heard my parents fighting. I crept from my bed and up to the door and slid down the hallway, wiping my eyes. Pressing myself to the wall, I listened. That's when I learned the remarkable truth.

My father. The carp. He had planned the whole thing. Evidently, he'd gotten a bonus from work. Unbeknownst to anyone, he'd rushed right out and bought the carp, which must have cost a small fortune. And somehow he'd hauled the fish upstream, alive, and slipped it into the canal. Clever of him. He knew all about that canal. He knew that the flow of the water would bring the fish right to us. The grate at the end would trap it. There was no chance it could escape. We children would think that the carp was a miracle. No one would be the wiser. This was the kind of man he was. He loved to play games. He loved to give gifts. He loved to make people happy.

My mother, however, was furious. In her mind, this stunt with the fish was the final brittle straw in a basket whose bottom was falling through. "Once again, Tang Rentong!" she said. "Once again, generosity comes at your children's expense."

My father began to protest. Bad move. My mother silenced him by ticking off a long list of household items we needed. Things enjoyed in most Chinese homes. Things that could have been bought with a bonus rather than, say, a giant fish.

I stood in the hallway, loving my father and wishing my mother would not be so stern. Of course I saw her point of view, but I heard the groan of a wicker chair and knew that my father had just sat down. I pictured him, enduring her scolding, the way he had so many times before. Head hung. Lips pouting. A child trapped in a grown man's body, wishing that life could be more carefree.

Logical or not, my father possessed a certain gift for making people happy. If the world had a few more people like him, I'm sure we would all be better off.

6

I was born the only son among five sisters. In China, by tradition, this accorded me great status in my family. Sons have prestige over daughters. The reasons arise from history. Back in China's agrarian roots, sons would carry the family name. Sons could inherit the family estate. Sons embodied the hope that your clan could survive the coming hard winter. A barren harvest. A summer of locusts. War. Disease. The outbreak of famine.

To be the only son was an honor but also a great responsibility. My father made that very clear. And the older I grew, the more he pushed me, growing stern, no longer the man who happened along by the shores of a pond, whistling innocent tunes while a carp the approximate size of a rickshaw swam circles below the waterline, fulfilling his little prank.

I found this hard to reconcile. Who was this drill sergeant who goaded me harder and harder to succeed? And what had he done with the puckish man whom everyone in town adored, whose playful spirit I loved? I started to study my father closely, looking for clues the way boys will when they want to know what being a man is all about. However, the more I studied my father, the less I seemed to know him. His contradictions abounded.

For instance, my father was an excellent teacher. His easy humor, his ready smile, and his natural largesse made imparting knowledge second nature. The students who took his classes all counted themselves quite lucky. Teacher Tang was a popular man, his lectures always full. But here was the first contradiction I noted. I often saw teachers persecuted. Farmers and workers would ridicule them, sneering at them for speaking many languages, or the fact that they read books, painted pictures, wrote poems, or played musical instruments. The farmers and workers would often use a special word for teachers. They called them *stinky intellectuals*, a dirty term in word and tone. Men would tighten their fists and growl whenever they spoke it. I had no idea what an intellectual was, so I asked my father, who told me this: "An intellectual? Well, *Xiao* Tang. That is someone who uses his mind. Who thinks about things independently. Who constantly hungers for knowledge."

"But what could be wrong with that?" I asked. Now I was very confused. "You've told me that knowledge is so important. You said that it had no price."

My father sighed and tried to explain. "Those farmers and workers are just quoting Mao. Mao divided citizens into a hierarchy. Workers were Number One. Without workers, Mao said, there would be no steel for making guns and factories. Farmers, he said, were Number Two. Without farmers, there would be no food. Soldiers were Number Three. Without soldiers there would be no army. And so on. You see?"

"But where are the teachers?" I asked. "Where do the intellectuals fit?"

My father gave a little laugh. "Very far down the chain, I'm afraid. To Mao Zedong, intellectuals were the 'stinkiest Number Nines.' He said that people with intellects are prone to counterrevolutionary thoughts. So he put dunce caps on their heads and paraded them through the streets of China to teach them their place in society. Mao said that intellectuals are enemies of the state, no better than landlords, reactionaries, rich farmers, and spies."

"But Father," I said. "Aren't *you* an intellectual?"

"Yes," he answered. "I suppose. But I'm also a Party officer, chairman of a branch committee that covers several educational districts. You see, *Xiao* Tang, you cannot become a principal unless you join the Party. No one would ever allow it."

That was when I started to see the tightrope my father was walking, his eloquent balancing act. He walked the line between two worlds without any net to break his fall, and he never showed any fear. That's when I began to see that there are really two Chinas. One is the land where a little boy's father teaches a lesson by buying a fish and slipping it in a canal. The other is a darker place where thinking can be punished.

I knew that my father was a good standing member of the Party, meaning he did what the Party wanted and said what the Party told him to say. Did he question the wisdom of certain decisions? Of course. He was a thinking man, also a man with principles. But he also had six children to feed. He had a wife. He had a good job. The Party could sweep all those things away, a gust of wind to the man on a tightrope. A little gust is all it would take to push my father over, and us, his family, with him. All of us falling, spinning, hitting hard ground and breaking open. This was the Chinese way, I learned. The way of the CCP.

My father knew the risks of his act. He would never let our family fall. And so he followed the Party line and balanced, keeping his spine so straight, his skull poised high, like the jewel on a crown, elegant looking, but heavy. Like a master performer in any art, he made the impossible look easy. The trick is in the illusion of grace, the one that defies stark danger.

Because of all his hard work, my father became the subject of an article that ran in the Party's provincial newspaper, *Hunan Daily*. The story said how inspiring he was, that his school was a model for excellence. I kept this in mind and redoubled my efforts in order to make him proud.

7

By the time I was thirteen or fourteen, I was always number one in my grade and often served as chief of the class. Quite often, I studied the next year's curriculum on my own, ahead of time. It was either that or get bored. Math and physics and chemistry—the sciences all came easy to me. I remember thinking that my fellow students were joking when they griped about a lesson.

"This problem is awful!" one would say.

"Really? Why do you say that?"

"Don't tell me you *understand* this math, Tang!"

"It's simple," I'd say. "Look here. We know that for a function to be continuous at x equals a, the limit of $f(x)$ as x approaches a must be equal to $f(a)$. Now, the limit must exist, correct? Therefore $f(x)$ must be defined as—"

"Stop! Stop!" the student would say. "You're hurting my head! Please stop!"

I was told that my test scores qualified me to attend a special school across town. Lingling Number Four High School was one of the best in Hunan. It was also an hour away by bus. So my father made arrangements for me to live with his friend Mr. Chen Minghua.

Chen Minghua was an officer of the education committee in Yongzhou city. As such, his apartment was right on the school grounds, his front door barely a dozen yards from the entrance to most of my classrooms. This is how it works in China: most jobs house their employees. Factory workers live in dorms that are honeycombed with apartments, as do government workers, members of the security forces, students, and engineers. Practically everyone.

Quite often, husbands and wives live apart because of their employment. Each spouse keeps a separate apartment. In China, we call this *liang di feng ju*, or "two locations, separate domiciles." It's a very common arrangement, and I was used to it. My parents were both in education. My mother taught Chinese language, my father taught political science. But they worked at different schools in Yongzhou, so my mother and father kept different apartments for years while I grew up.

Chen Minghua had a wife who lived at another location. So Chen shared his tiny one-bedroom apartment with his daughter and his niece. His daughter was three years younger than me, the niece about a year. Neither liked me very much since I didn't pay much attention to them. My nose was always down in my books. The apartment was very small for three people. With four, it was downright uncomfortable.

We lived like baitfish packed in a can. Chen's daughter and niece slept in the bedroom while Chen and I slept in the living room. Chen had moved a big bed in there for himself. My bed for the next four years was a narrow wooden board placed across two stools.

I was thankful for Chen's hospitality, though we didn't really get along. He never paid much attention to any of us, preferring to focus on work instead. Between Chen's brittle disregard and the girls who loathed my very existence, I started to see my time at Lingling as an exercise in patience. Each day became a challenge for me to develop inner fortitude. In China, we often say, *Shi nian shu mu, bai nian shu ren*—"Grow a tree in ten years, men a hundred." Success will come when you stick to a process of growth, no matter how difficult.

So essentially I left home when I was fourteen. It was the early 1980s and very few people in China had phones. To communicate with my family, I had to write letters or take torrid rides through sweaty streets on buses that lurched and burped gas. I noted the glitter and cackle of merchant stalls humming past the windows, the smell of smoke and fry fires, the spice of Hunan in fall and spring.

I didn't go home very often. Classes kept me too busy for that. My father would often drop by, however, pulled across town by committee meetings, Party mixers, and rounds. Each time he saw me, he checked my grades, squinting like an accountant tallying figures. He'd nod and grunt and shrug. "Not bad," he'd say. "But these could be better." It was the closest thing to a compliment he ever paid me.

In the course of living with Mr. Chen, I'd learned to keep my façade impassive, a ritual of manhood I had very nearly perfected. In China emotions are frowned upon. Our society is collective. The whole is the good, the parts are nothing. Extolling the individual indicates arrogance and greed. But secretly, I was pleased. I'd worked very hard to make Father happy, even if he never admitted he was.

"You still want to go to Qinghua, don't you?"

"Yes," I would say. "I do. Very much."

Qinghua University was the very best school in China, the MIT of Beijing. It showed particular excellence in the fields of math and science. My father still believed that I could be the next Albert Einstein. I know this because he told me so.

"One day you could be Einstein, *Xiao* Tang. Wouldn't that be something? A Chinese who could lead the world in the fields of math and science."

And so I set my sights on Qinghua and studied for all I was worth. I knew how the application process worked. Students who wanted to study at college chose five schools they wished to attend. The government then reviewed your scores. Committees placed you wherever they thought your profile was appropriate. Students whose work was very good almost always got their first choice of schools. And my work was exceptional. I made certain of that to please my father, no matter what effort it took.

But for all his talk that knowledge was priceless, my father's attitudes often surprised me. He thought, for instance, that learning a second language was utterly worthless, a kind of hobby at best, at worst a corruption of all things Chinese. This was a very traditional view.

Back then, it was fairly common for students in China to study English. English was seen as the rising tongue of global business and politics. Russian, though much less ubiquitous, served as a link to our communist roots, a throwback to the olden days when Chinese leaders traveled to Moscow to study Marxist theory. But relations between Beijing and the Kremlin had frayed in recent years. As a result, only the finest high schools taught Russian anymore. It was taught at Lingling Number Four.

I thought that learning another language might open many important doors. But my father shook his head. "What good is another language, *Xiao* Tang? Math is the purest language of all. All bright people speak math." Then he spoke an oft-quoted adage: *Xue hao shu li hua, zou bian tian xia du bu pa.* "Learn math and physics and chemistry well, walk through all the world without fear."

"But Father," I would argue, "the world is a very large place, you know. Perhaps being able to speak a language would help to broaden my view."

My father scoffed aloud at this, raising his eyebrows behind his glasses. "And why should your vision be so broad?" he said. "Think about this, *Xiao* Tang. China: the largest country on earth. China: more people than anywhere else. Someday, the world will speak Chinese. That much I can promise you."

He would practically wax poetic when extolling the virtues of Mandarin. "Listen to our tongue, *Xiao* Tang! Can't you hear its beauty? See how gorgeous the characters are when you write them, sweeping and large! Look how they represent a culture older than any on earth. Hear me now, *Xiao* Tang! It's more than enough to speak and write Chinese. That is all you will ever need to be a leader of China someday."

I wasn't sure I believed him. But I was a good and obedient son. I did as I was told.

8

In the summer of 1984, my last year of high school lay ahead and everything was going my way. My grades were high. My test scores showed a solid line of excellence. I was also a student leader, very active in clubs, organizations, and student government. I could look ahead and see the seal of Qinghua in my future. The school flowers: redbud and lilac. In my mind, I strolled the *He Tang Yue Se*, the ancient Moonlit Garden, once part of the palace of Qing's mighty prince, now the university's arboretum.

My dossier had attracted attention from local Party officials. They would chat with me at sporting events, award ceremonies, debate contests, and speeches I made to the student body.

"A shame," said one. "You cannot join the Party until you are eighteen years old. This is a long-standing policy."

"But we will wait," said another, smiling. "Good fruit ripens best on the vine. We follow your exploits with admiration. Keep it up, *Xiao Tang!*"

I was very involved with basketball, the most popular sport in China. It helped that I stand over six feet tall, an anomaly in China. One day in August 1984, I was practicing on the court and felt a discomfort down in my gut, low, on my right-hand side. When practice ended, I told our coach, a teacher named Zhou.

"A cramp?" he asked.

I shook my head.

"Torn muscle?"

"More like a bloating sensation."

"It's probably just a cramp," he said. "Hop on the table. We'll knead it out."

He started to probe with his fingers using traditional massage. But then he stopped. I saw him frown. "When did this start?" he said.

"Just now."

"You noticed nothing before?"

I didn't like the tone of his voice. "What do you mean? Notice what?"

Teacher Zhou looked very concerned. "I think you should go to the hospital. Now."

At the hospital, a doctor repeated my coach's massage. He also repeated my coach's frown. "A tumor," the doctor said.

He stepped outside and came back in with a dozen medical students, all of them dressed in white lab coats.

"See here," said my doctor. "This could be a cancer. A lump as round and smooth as an egg, but hard. Just sitting there. Feel for yourself."

The students came over one by one and touched my abdomen, nodding. *Yes*, they were saying. *Cancer. Yes.*

"So," my doctor turned to them, voice raised high so the crowd could hear, "the course of treatment is surgery. We'll schedule it for the winter."

One of the students raised her hand and asked why we had to wait so long. "Shouldn't we do it now?" she asked. "What if the tumor's malignant?"

My doctor waved a dismissive hand. "If it's malignant, the patient will die and there's nothing we can do. If it's benign, the winter is better. The patient will suffer less chance of infection. Lesson: to get at the tumor, we must cut the abdominal wall. The risk of infection is very great. That's why we wait until winter."

I thought my physician was joking, but then I saw that he wasn't. There I was, alone in a room. Lying back on a table that was hard and cold as a slab of quartz while strangers gawked. The hospital reeked of effluvium, the stench of toxins and abattoir. It was so overcrowded that patients slept on the hallway floors and doctors used the same hypodermics over and over on different patients with different diseases. No one bothered to sterilize them. It's one of the reasons that AIDS soon erupted and swept across the country, killing hundreds of thousands of people. I was certain the Chinese medical system would be the death of me. If you weren't sick when you arrived, you'd be sick by the time you left. Sick or dead. One or the other.

My prognosis was very hard on my parents. My father was devastated, my mother inconsolable. First she went into shock. Then, when she finally came around, she started to cry and couldn't stop. She wailed for weeks.

My teachers said I didn't have to attend classes anymore. Friends brought me my homework. I was encouraged to work from Chen Minghua's apartment, in relative ease and privacy, and presumably with a lack of stress. I did my assignments, but not very well. I found it hard to focus. It's tough to concentrate when you're eighteen years old and told you have two years to live. In China back then, the word *cancer* was synonymous with death.

I wiled away my time shooting hoops in a local park. The goal of becoming a Chinese Einstein had settled like bitter herbs on my tongue, but I marveled at my own energy. While being eaten alive from within, I still knew how to drive the net. I still had a wicked hook shot. My grades, of course, were falling fast, presumably leading the way for my vital signs. I was too upset to feel upset. Not scared. Not angry. Just shocked. The lump in my gut had stolen my future. All of my hopes and dreams. But all was not yet lost.

Back then, the government gave free healthcare to anyone who lived in a city. But if anything serious ever happened (a possible case of cancer, for instance), you had to pay lots and lots of money or nothing would ever get done. My family didn't have lots of money. That's why I was very surprised when, over the winter holiday, my parents and I boarded a train that was bound for Changsha City. They were taking me to a special hospital. Don't ask me where they got the funds. To this day, I don't know.

Changsha is Hunan's capital city, northeast of Yongzhou by 640 *li* (a *li* is Chinese for half a kilometer, or about a third of a mile). Changsha straddles the shores of the river Xiang, a tendril of the great Yangtze, the mightiest river in China.

Picture Changsha, an ancient place dating back to the time when the Qins ruled China, about 220 BCE. Even back then, Changsha was important, a fortified city that served as the hub of culture and progress throughout the south. Over the years, she traded hands in too many wars to list, but her population exploded in the early twentieth century. By the middle 1980s, Changsha boasted six million people across its outlying suburbs. It was a major port, an industrial center, and a tourist trap, thanks to Mao Zedong.

Mao had spent a lot of time in Changsha as a student at Hunan Number One Teacher's Training School. Then he worked at the school as a principal from 1920 to 1922. Like my father, I used to think. Look at the pictures of young Mao Zedong with his full head of hair and his sleepy eyes. Back then, he was already a communist, having attended the Party's first National Congress, held in distant Shanghai. Soon after that, he would be elected as one of five commissars who governed the Party. A star was born, with all the room in heaven to rise—and with it, China as well. Changsha has made a museum of Mao's former offices. His former apartment has been enshrined, as well as the places he used to swim or sit to write lines of poetry. Photos from that bygone era hang on the walls in attractive frames.

But all of this meant nothing to me. Picture me riding the train to Changsha. Slumped in my seat, I stared out the window, not caring about the Party or communism or Mao Zedong or anything. What would be the point? I was young and I was dying. Everything else was smoke on the wind, scattered and drifting away.

9

A specialist at the hospital read through my charts. Then he had me lie on a table and started his exam. Very soon, the look on his face twisted into puzzlement. "Well," he said, his fingers probing. "According to the notes from your previous doctors, your tumor was the size of an egg. But now—see here? I can barely find it. Feel for yourself."

In turns, the specialist took my parents' and my hands and guided them over my abdomen. Yes, I thought, surprised. He's right. My tumor had certainly shrunk. I could still feel it under my fingertips, but it wasn't the size of an egg anymore. More like the size of a peanut.

"Unbelievable," muttered the doctor. Then he called a meeting. A lot more doctors entered the room. White coats, stern faces. A repeat of the scene from half a year earlier. Everyone took turns feeling my abdomen. I lay there, like a pig on display at the butcher's stall, wondering what this meant.

"It used to be very big," said the specialist. "Now it is very small."

The doctors nodded. They all looked baffled. One of them asked what treatment had been used. My specialist shrugged and said nothing. He seemed a little embarrassed. My mother, I noticed, was beaming.

The doctors cautioned us, saying we shouldn't jump to conclusions. "The tumor might come back," they said. But to this day, nearly three decades later, it hasn't, and I can't explain what happened. I've since been checked by American doctors who tell me they find nothing wrong. My only residual symptom is a lifelong suspicion of doctors. I've tried to work on tempering that, but I have to admit it's been a tough haul.

In the end, the only thing that died was my academic career. My grades had fallen off drastically while I waited around to expire. I was no longer a viable candidate for Qinghua. But it turned out my father knew a dean at Hunan Normal. Father took the dean out to dinner and discussed my situation. The next thing I knew, I received a letter admitting me to college. This was no disgrace, by the way. Hunan Normal wasn't Qinghua, but it still ranked high as a top school in China with many distinguished graduates. In late summer 1985, I declared myself a science major and started classes. My parents were ecstatic.

My first year passed uneventfully. Once in a while, the bloated feeling returned to my abdomen, and sometimes I felt twinges of pain. So I'd make an appointment and go to see the campus doctors, who always scratched their chins and consulted their books and never seemed like they knew what to do. Ultimately, I stopped going to see them. No more physicians for me. I had learned to sneer at doctors.

But then something very important happened, an event that would change the course of my life. Call it the crossroads that ushered me down the path that has led to where I am today. Indirectly, this change in direction began with a very important man in China. His name was Hu Yaobang.

part two
Student

1

Hu Yaobang was born in 1915 to peasants who lived near Changsha. He ran away from home at age fourteen to join a new group called the Communist Party.

Imagine what China was like back then. The Xinhai Revolution was over. Upstart generals had recently ended the 250-year Qing dynasty. China would never again fall subject to imperial rule. The generals promised to start a republic but ended up fighting each other. This began the Warlord Era, which lasted for many years.

At a high-level view, this period produced two main political factions. On one side, you had the Guomindang, also known as the GMD, or the Chinese Nationalist Party. On the other side, the Communists, a fledgling organization provisioned both materially and ideologically by the Soviets.

Throughout the early twentieth century, the GMD and the Communists battled the warlords together in an alliance built from necessity. The warlords were like a pack of wild bulls, charging each other, colliding, goring, while China was trampled beneath them. Most of the warlords were neutralized by the end of the 1920s. With no common enemy left to oppose, the GMD and the Communists turned on each other. The last two bulls alive in the pen were battling for command, so blood continued to fall like rain, staining the earth of China.

Hu Yaobang grew up in this era. The late 1920s and early 1930s were terribly violent years. The Communists' Red Army and the army of the Guomindang hammered each other again and again in too many battles to list. But eventually, the GMD won and forced the Communists into retreat, a relocation that historians call the Long March. By the time the Long March was over, the Communists had lost more than nine-tenths of their number to battle, desertion, disease, insanity, and starvation.

During the Long March, not incidentally, a young man started his rise through the Communist ranks. His name was Mao Zedong, a former teacher and school principal turned soldier and revolutionary. Mao's ascension was aided by several close aides and confidantes, among them men like Liu Shaoqi and Zhou Enlai, and a crafty farmer from Szechuan whose name was Deng Xiaoping. Hu Yaobang allied with Deng and became Deng's trusted right hand.

Despite his rise in popularity, Mao's base remained volatile during much of the 1930s. Power among the Communists was ephemeral at best. Each time a new faction took control, it set about killing off rival elements in bloody, remorseless coups. Since he was allied with Deng (and therefore Mao), Hu Yaobang's life was also at risk. With Mao and Deng, Hu staggered west, another doomed, bedraggled soul fleeing into exile.

The Communists remained depleted in numbers and spirit until 1937, when the Japanese attacked China and the Second Sino-Chinese War began. Deng Xiaoping and Hu Yaobang were among the first to realize that neither the Communists nor the GMD could beat Japan alone. However insane it might have seemed, they had to work together. Deng and Hu urged their Communist brothers to throw away their hatred and embrace their lifelong enemies for the overall good of the nation.

Incredibly, this came to pass. The war with Japan eventually merged into the greater conflict we call World War II, but by then the tables had turned. The Communists held all the power, and the GMD fled to Taiwan. Hu Yaobang was known far and wide as Deng Xiaoping's protégé. So, eight years later, Hu followed Deng to Beijing. He was there in October 1949 when Mao Zedong stood at the Gate of Heavenly Peace and declared the nation the People's Republic of China.

The Gate of Heavenly Peace, by the way, is the Chinese name for Tiananmen Square.

From that moment forward, Hu Yaobang was a major part of the new establishment. But in 1966, Mao had Hu and Deng purged from the Party as part of his Great Proletariat Cultural Revolution, which was really a naked grab for power. Mao felt his influence waning, and, not wanting to be overthrown, he labeled many former allies "capitalist roaders" and "enemies of the people." Technically, a "capitalist roader" was someone who wanted to steer China down the avenue of a capitalist economy. And an "enemy of the people"? No one really knew for certain what that meant. But one thing was clear enough: Mao would stoop to any level to keep his regime in order. He would torture and kill whomever he pleased. He would even send his oldest friends away for occasional disagreements.

While living in exile, both Deng and Hu endured the standard Party "political rehabilitation." In other words, a life of poverty, hard labor, and suffering. Both men were eventually reinstated to power but were exiled a second time right before Mao Zedong passed away. When the Great Leader finally suffered a fatal heart attack on September 9, 1976, Deng and Hu took advantage of a nation plunged into uproar and started to seize control.

They openly criticized Mao Zedong and encouraged others to do the same, which wasn't hard to do. Many of Mao's vaunted plans had left the nation in shambles. By encouraging people to vent their outrage, Deng and Hu became popular. They started encouraging capitalists to join the Communist Party. This was hardly an altruistic move. The economy was terribly close to collapse at that point and something had to be done. So Deng and Hu brought about economic reforms that caused a brief period of liberalization between 1977 and 1978. We Chinese called it Beijing Spring to honor a similar process that took place in Czechoslovakia in 1968.

Deng Xiaoping was in his seventies but didn't let age deter him. The regime he began to establish was just as bloody and ruthless and cruel as any led by Mao Zedong. To make sure he was guaranteed support, Deng had his old ally Hu Yaobang inducted into the Politburo, a CCP committee of five to nine members that essentially runs the country to this very day.

To be fair, the China that Deng had inherited was ridden with cancer at every level—social, political, and economic. Under Mao Zedong, China had been a fear-filled nation. Totalitarian rule. You did what the Party said or you died. There was no contact with the outside world. Mao kept the door to China closed. Deng and Hu swung it open.

Though still officially communist, Deng instated socialist policies. Or, as some folks have labeled them, *Leninist with Chinese characteristics.* Deng's reforms had all the drive and grandiose sweep that Mao Zedong had been known for, but Deng's programs were largely sane, tempered by more modern reforms, and usually pragmatic. For instance, Deng officially sanctioned a plan called the Four Modernizations. The Four Mods, as most of us called them, outlined key improvements in areas of nation building: Agriculture, Industry, National Defense, and Science and Technology. If pursued, the Mods were supposed to raise China to world-power status by the end of the twentieth century.

Deng also made it very clear: China must enter the global market. His Open Door Policy resurrected trade and diplomacy with the outside world. He encouraged foreign investment and leveraged connections to the West using gateway locales like Hong Kong, Taiwan, and Macau. But Deng was just getting started. He also constructed factories in four major coastal cities: Shenzhen, Zhuhai, Shantou, and Xiamen. Along with the southern province of Hainan, these cities were earmarked "Special Economic Zones," or SEZs for short. Each SEZ was offered tax privileges, as well as reduced tariffs on companies importing capital goods and raw materials. The SEZs took off like a shot. More were opened in subsequent years.

China began to reap massive rewards. Her economy soared. The standard of living for most Chinese improved very fast, and dramatically. Suddenly people had money to spend on personal interests and hobbies. The poverty and ignorance that had flourished under Mao began to abate as foreign cultures and foreign money seeped into the mainland.

But Deng Xiaoping was not done yet. He upped the ante on world relations, becoming the first Chinese leader to visit the United States. Then he shifted decision-making powers from the level of centralized government to province or state domains. Again, this move wasn't altruistic, merely essential to creating market-based economic development in regions with unique manufacturing power.

The overall result? By 1979, local elections were being held at township and county levels. Congresses were forming. The tiller of China's destiny had been placed in the hands of her people. The waters lay open before us, the horizon bright and shining. It's hard to describe the excitement we felt. For the first time since 1949, Chinese people were being asked to participate in our government.

2

Meanwhile, by 1982, Hu Yaobang had risen to become the party general secretary. It was the CCP's highest position, but everyone knew what was going on. Deng Xiaoping chaired the Party's Central Military Commission, which meant that Deng had control of the army and therefore held the true power.

But Hu Yaobang was popular. Over the years, he'd gained repute as an open-minded reformer. The Chinese people loved him. Yes, Hu was following orders from Deng when trying to clear Mao's tainted legacy. But Hu always took his actions further. He seemed to possess a deep desire to see his country change. His policies always slid toward the right and the promise of democracy, toward a free and open society. In Chinese politics, the right is the way of progressive reform, the left is the way of conservative values. This is exactly the opposite of politics in the West.

Throughout the 1980s, Hu Yaobang rehabilitated thousands of party members who'd been unjustly marginalized, condemned, and imprisoned during Mao's Cultural Revolution. In doing so, he healed many old and festering wounds. He opened new possibilities for political reform. He was our Benjamin Franklin. Our Theodore Roosevelt. A man who examined the past with an eye for charting a course to the future. He had earned our respect in most every matter, especially when it came to Tibet.

In 1912, Tibet had proclaimed itself free from Chinese rule. China did not respond since it was busy with other matters. The GMD and the Communists were slaughtering warlords, after which the two parties made war on each other, followed by the Second Sino-Chinese War, which morphed into World War II, and so on. The new People's Republic clarified its stance on Tibet when Mao Zedong sent an invasion force to seize the region in 1950. Chinese troops outnumbered the tiny Tibetan army nearly five to one. The Chinese killed half the Tibetan soldiers before the Tibetan army surrendered. After this, the Chinese forced Tibet to sign the Seventeen Points Agreement, which Chinese officials insist confirms their sovereignty over the region. The Tibetans have always disagreed; they argue against the veracity of an agreement signed at gunpoint.

Tibet is a small, religious nation that wants to be left alone. But China will not let the Tibetans be. Worse, there is a long and unfortunate list of Chinese human rights violations against Tibet and her people that includes, but sadly is not limited to, the deaths of Tibetan citizens by military action, imposed starvation, execution, unjust imprisonment, and torture.

In 1959, the CCP cracked down on Tibet, killing thousands of rebels and massacring civilians in the capital city of Lhasa. The fourteenth Dalai Lama escaped to India by walking over the Himalayas on foot with an entourage of twenty men. The United Nations condemned China's behavior, as did several noted independent watchdog groups. Around the world, Tibet's very name has become political nitroglycerin. Handle it with care or it could blow up in your face. Not that Tibet is the problem. Tibet is merely the fuse. The real explosive threat is China. No one wants to anger China. But that doesn't mean what China is doing is right.

Actually, I should clarify. The real explosive threat isn't China, it's China's government. Most Chinese want Tibet to be free. Tibet, they say, should stay under Chinese rule but with democratic dispensations. Having another region like Hong Kong or Macau would certainly be preferable to the ghastly situation that has prevailed since 1950.

Hu Yaobang set change in motion by paying Tibet a visit in May of 1980. During that trip, he became convinced that Tibet was not only prepared but entitled to see to its own affairs. He ordered the withdrawal of several thousand Chinese troops and required that any Chinese who remained in the region must learn the Tibetan language. He also encouraged Tibet's identity as a region. But that was just the beginning. Hu increased state funding to the region and mandated that these funds be used for such endeavors as education reform. He seemed to enjoy Tibetan culture! He went on record saying that any plans for Tibet that didn't directly improve her situation should be discarded at once. It was such a bold departure from the previous stance of the CCP! But most Chinese applauded it. As, of course, did the Tibetans.

3

Eventually, Deng Xiaoping backed off from criticizing Mao. Most likely he felt that public opinion was swinging too far to the right. And so the Party's Central Committee produced a report that it released in 1981. The report was called *On the Various Historical Issues since the Founding of the People's Republic of China*. But really it was a naked attempt to plane the offensive burrs and knots too often found in the planks of Chinese history. Deng was creating a more stable platform on which to build China's future.

The report never questioned that Mao Zedong was the nation's founding father. It praised him over and over again and made much of his driving goal: to see China ascend to world-power status. Mao's atrocities were downplayed through wordcraft and innuendo. *On the Various Historical Issues* laid most of the blame for the Cultural Revolution on the so-called Gang of Four, a leftist faction, four Party officials who pressed the nation under their thumbs, squeezing the lifeblood out of it. The Gang of Four's leading member was a woman named Jiang Qing, a former actress and Mao Zedong's wife, who was arguably insane. *On the Various Historical Issues* labeled Jiang as the mastermind behind anything untoward.

In all, Mao escaped the report with his legacy mostly intact. Deng was oft quoted as saying that Mao was "seven parts good and three parts bad." It was a brilliant political move. Stances like this gave Deng the room to pursue reform without decimating Communist culture by calling for a revolution.

But many Chinese felt disappointed when Deng backpedaled on Mao. And Hu Yaobang was still out there, a maverick in the Politburo. It wasn't hard to attach our hopes to his latest and greatest reforms. When we heard about what Hu was doing, the challenges he was tackling, it was easy to convince ourselves that China was well on its way to reform. To democracy and transparency. A true culture of freedom.

Eager to see that day arrive, we students began to hold demonstrations. In autumn of 1986, we called for the Party to open channels and start establishing dialogue. Talk to students and workers, we said. Hear what we have to say. Let us participate in our own future. Was that too much to ask? We certainly didn't think so. Hu Yaobang had inspired us. We followed his example.

In 1986, I was a sophomore at Hunan Normal and active in student government. By tradition, most student leaders were really CCP-sanctioned cadres. Pro-democracy factions were present but never telegraphed their intentions. The system was still too staid for that. Anger hadn't boiled over just yet.

My fellow student leaders and I kept watch on the growing unrest. Hu Yaobang, as always, encouraged us. Ever the right-leaning statesman, he did nothing to quash the rising debate. Tacitly, he seemed to be calling for freedom of speech and freedom of the press. This was a major policy change, and one which we hoped would sweep across China, inaugurating reform.

Emboldened, we took things further. On November 5, 1986, we set the fax wires burning, sending messages to every student organization clear across China and asking for their support. Then we assembled ten thousand students and marched across Changsha. Our demonstration wound through the streets. Calm and collected, we all held signs with characters written large. No one screamed or shouted. We walked with a certain dignity and took our time. The focus was not on getting there, it was more on being seen. Finally, we arrived at the buildings of the provincial government in May 1st Square, a kind of little sister to Tiananmen Square, Beijing.

At that time, a man named Xiong Qingquan was governor of Hunan. Interestingly, Xiong had also once served as Hu Yaobang's secretary. We said we had two pressing issues that required Xiong's attention. Please, we said. Will the governor hear them?

Myself and about a dozen leaders were led inside. We were taken down a corridor to a grand hall where the governor met us, stern-faced, not really smiling, but open. He bowed, business-like. We started to chat. Some tea was served. The conversation lasted two hours. Both parties, I think, were well aware of what an occasion this was, a meeting without any precedent. Before that moment, no government official had shown the slightest inclination toward speaking with student leaders. Cautiously, and with great respect, my colleagues and I presented our issues.

Case number one: a math professor, Wei Liren, had recently been assaulted. Wei had recently taken a job teaching classes at Hunan Normal. He was a very popular teacher. Before that, he had taught next door at Hunan University. Therein lay the source of the trouble.

Officers at Hunan University had been angered by Wei Liren's departure. They'd sent workers to force him to leave his apartment. During the altercation, Wei Liren was nearly killed. Strangled, as it appeared. The marks around his neck were proof, as was the fact that he was hospitalized. He said he knew his attackers. The workers from Hunan University had mocked him while they beat him. They'd called him a turncoat, a coward, and a rotten intellectual.

The attack itself was an outrage, but that was just the beginning. Worse was the fact that neither university would address what had happened, nor would police and government agencies. Nobody lifted a finger. It simply wasn't in vogue to champion intellectuals who'd been assaulted. What would the Party say about that? Someone might be demoted.

The issue of Wei Liren hit me on a very personal level. As far as I could see, we were right back to Mao and his Stinkiest Number Nines. Right back to my father and the teachers in Yongzhou who were chased down alleys for speaking Russian or reading books or playing the violin. Who were persecuted by workers who were little better than thugs that reveled in their own ignorance, unwilling to take control of themselves, consigning control to the Party.

I'd led the campaign to create massive posters we'd hung all over our campus. Some of the posters said "REEXAMINE THE ASSAULT ON WEI LIREN." Others said "WHY IS WEI LIREN BEING PUNISHED FOR TEACHING?" Hanging massive posters was a trick I borrowed from Mao. He'd used them to convey messages during the Cultural Revolution. Now we were using the same technique to champion human rights. If Mao had still been alive, I wonder what he would have said.

Governor Xiong Qingquan spread his hands. "What would you like to see done?" he asked.

"We want to see the law upheld," said one of my fellow student leaders.

"Yes," I said. "We want to see the workers arrested and tried as violent criminals. This is what would happen to suspects in any similar case. Why has it not happened here?"

The governor nodded and thought for a moment. "I will have your answer in seven days," he said. "Now let's hear your second issue."

I'm embarrassed to say this, but our second issue involved protesting the poor food served in the university cafeteria. The food was hardly a breach of human rights and clearly not a topic worthy to bring before the governor. We'd added it more as an afterthought when we realized—quite in shock, I might add—that Xiong Qingquan was willing to speak with us at all.

Xiong seemed amused by our request. "Better food?" He laughed and slapped a hand on his knee. Then he went off on a long dissertation, recalling his own days as a student at Hunan Normal. He'd clearly enjoyed his time in college. "But the food, you know. It wasn't so good. I promise you, I'll look into it."

We thanked Governor Xiong and departed, feeling immensely pleased with ourselves. How could we not? It was our first real experience seeing democracy in action. Personally? I was thrilled. The day had been a complete success. For Wei Liren. For the awful food. For the process of call and response. Our voices had been heard! But the day wasn't over yet. The fax machines started chugging out paper, and phones began to ring off the hook. We began to receive some amazing reports. Clear across China, other schools had heeded our call to arms. There had been other marches, other demonstrations on issues of human rights, and many of them had been successful. That day, we later heard through channels, had riled the Party somewhat. They referred to it as the "11/5 incident" in their official documentation.

Tiny sparks in a sea of dry grass. A flame was catching and starting to build, merging toward conflagration.

4

A few days later, Fang Lizhi publicly declared his support for student protestors. This was a major piece of news. Fang Lizhi was a Party officer, and vice president of the Chinese University of Science and Technology, a famous institution over five hundred miles east in Hefei, capital of Anhui Province. Fang Lizhi was also a close friend and adviser to Hu Yaobang. Many people were saying that Fang Lizhi and other bright men were counseling Hu Yaobang to get with the times and integrate more liberal social and economic policies. And not just for SEZs, but for all of China. So now it was clear that high-level members of the establishment also sought reform.

Hu Yaobang did not react to Fang Lizhi's announcement. Which meant that, tacitly, Hu condoned what Fang was saying. This made Hu even more popular, a hero of the people. The streets of Changsha clamored with whispers. Would Hu's reform succeed? As it turned out, the answer was no. One month after demonstrations ended, Hu stepped down from his position as party secretary general. It was January 1987.

Did I say stepped down? He was actually removed. We all understood what had happened. A bloodless coup. Hu Yaobang had lost his office, but everyone wanted to know: was he still on the Politburo? Most of us thought that he was, but a Chinese international weekly, *Yazhou Zhoukan*, said that Hu may have indeed been ousted from the Communist inner circle. In either case, the message was clear: the Party no longer welcomed Hu Yaobang's slant toward the right. Hu had been guiding China down democracy's demon road, away from Mao's vision, away from the Party's total control. Now that journey had ended.

The country absorbed the news quietly. More whispering in the streets, more back room conversations, the Chinese way of discussion. It was tempting to get demoralized, but the intelligentsia remained upbeat. Some of us thought the Party had dealt itself a terrible blow by ousting Hu from office. We thought that Deng Xiaoping had shown his true colors. Now it was very clear that, regardless of what he said in public, at the end of the day he'd return to his office and carry out Maoist policies. To punctuate his disregard for reform, he purged three famous so-called right-leaning elements from the Party. Fang Lizhi was one of them, as well as two famous writers, Liu Binyan and Wang Ruowang.

But the Chinese people weren't stupid. We had all begun to wonder.

Why was the government fighting so hard to contain us? What did they really fear? What kind of future did China have if her people would not be heard? What was our future if men like Hu Yaobang were deposed instead of being allowed to serve?

Time kept moving. The spring of 1987 arrived, and life resumed its previous pace. I settled back into my routine of classes, meetings, and activities, and never once suspected that Hu Yaobang's sacrifice was merely a prelude to a much greater drama to come.

It was a very turbulent time for me. The more I thought things over, the more I became convinced that I could no longer study math and science. Though I was skilled in these disciplines, they weren't my passion. They weren't what I wanted to do with my life. I decided that I liked helping people. I wanted to mete out justice. It had energized me to fight on behalf of Wei Liren. It made me feel as though I was following in my father's footsteps. Not the stern and serious man who dutifully toted the Party line, but the man who'd intervened in countless arguments in the streets of Yongzhou. The man who enjoyed other people, whom everyone thought of as the ambassador of fairness.

At about that time, it was also my pleasure to read from the work of Lu Xun, considered the founder of modern Chinese literature. Some have called him a champion of common humanity. Lu Xun was Mao Zedong's favorite writer, though Lu never joined the Communist Party. He said he was too liberal for that. As a young man, Lu Xun had studied to be a doctor, but he switched careers to become a writer. As a doctor, he said, I can treat a limited number of people. As a writer, I treat mankind. This notion resonated deeply in me. I began to ask myself: how many lives will I touch as a scientist? Doctor? Mathematician? What would be my impact as a Chinese Albert Einstein? What would I contribute? Theorems and formulae? Studies on esoteric subjects, such as flatworm behavior? Fluid dynamics in heel blister pus? A Punnett square for rare species of leafy spurge? I started to doubt my calling.

Then I thought: how many lives have I already touched by marching on May 1st Square? By talking to Governor Xiong Qingquan? By being a student leader? Certainly, Wei Liren's life had been affected. Governor Xiong had made good on his word; Wu's attackers were punished accordingly. But it hadn't ended there. The precedent of our campaign had rippled clear across China. We had heard the fitful murmurs of a nation waking to change.

The governor had spoken to student leaders! He had listened to our concerns and agreed to intervene! What other feats were possible? This was the way I could help to change China, as an activist and a student of politics. As someone willing to get involved. To lead. Perhaps one day, if things went well, I could help change society. I would finally be the leader that my father always hoped I would be.

I went to the college registrar's office and told them I wanted to switch my major. But changing your major in a communist-run education system is very hard to do. My request was denied, so I had no choice. I called my father back in Yongzhou and told him what I wanted to do. He wasn't very pleased with me, but he made an appointment to come to Changsha to look up his old friend, the dean.

As it turned out, he had to come to Changsha twice. Once to see the dean, and another time to meet the chair of the Education Department for all of Hunan Province. Meeting them was a massive undertaking, like building the Great Wall from soap bubbles. My father looked exhausted after talking with the chair. "Walk with me, *Xiao* Tang," he said.

The chair had assured my father he would intervene on my behalf. In essence, I would be granted my transfer. Once again, I found myself in debt to my father's connections. I knew it, and I was grateful.

That afternoon was brilliant and sunny. We strolled the campus of Hunan Normal, and I watched my father from the corner of one eye, not liking the droop of his spine. He looked older since the last time I'd seen him. Graying hair and sallow skin. He was smaller in stature than I remembered, or maybe I had grown. Such things are hard to assess sometimes. His courier sack was still on his shoulder like some tired vestigial organ, inseparable from his body.

"I was a student leader once," he said, apropos of nothing. He kept his eyes on the ground before us. "I majored in political science."

"Yes, I know."

My father nodded, then fell silent. He didn't speak for another hundred meters or so. Then: "I wanted better for you," he said.

"Better? What could be better?"

My father didn't look at me. He watched the ground before us as if fascinated by grass. "*Xiao* Tang, I want you to think about this. Think about what you are doing."

"I'm following in your footsteps, Father."

"Then you are a fool," he said.

I blinked and stared at him, stunned. He'd never spoken like that to me. Clearly, I had offended him. I started to stammer apologies. He stopped me with a hand. "Listen to me," he said. "When I was your age, I wanted change, too. I wanted it very much. A lot of us did back then. So we ignored the hard realities and we paid a hefty price. There is only one Party in China, *Xiao* Tang. You join it, or you cannot succeed. You do what it says, or you do not progress. This is the life I have led. I joined the Party to change its ways, but the years have turned as years will do, and nothing has changed at all."

It was the first time he'd ever admitted to being unhappy. Over the years, I'd had inklings that he'd hoped for more out of life, that he wasn't really satisfied, but he'd never talked about it to me or anyone so far as I knew.

"The Party tells you that shades of gray are really black and white," he said. "You nod. You tell them you understand and praise them for being wise. It's a difficult life for a thinking man to be a Party official. You sacrifice what you know is right for the gift of staying in favor." He looked at me then. "You're a very bright young man, *Xiao* Tang. Your future can be whatever you want. I'd hoped that I would never have a talk like this with you."

I saw things very clearly then. All that my father had done for me. The constant push to study harder. Chiding me to do better and better, to be Hunan's Albert Einstein. How he'd sacrificed to send me away to the very best school in Yongzhou. Each of these pieces now fit together, a puzzle completing a picture. How had I never noticed how my father had tried to protect me? To steer me away from the life he'd led, toiling for dust in the Party's shadow. He'd slaved so I could have all the opportunities he had been denied, and now I was turning them down. I was the ungrateful son. The shame I suddenly felt was like a physical weight pressing down on my heart. What a terrible form of betrayal I'd managed. Yet still, I couldn't turn back.

"What would you have me do?" I asked. "Work in the sciences, unfulfilled? Take the job that the Party awards me. Live. Marry. Have children. Grow old. What would happen then? One day I would wake up, as you, and see that the years have passed. And nothing would have changed. Again. Because I had not tried to change it."

My father listened. He shook his head. "You are young," he said. "You do not understand."

"Forgive me. Yes, I am young. Perhaps that's *why* I understand."

My father nodded. "Those are precisely the words I used when I was your age, *Xiao* Tang."

We walked another long while in silence.

5

I transferred departments and started my classes but soon was disappointed. Two months into my new course of study, I realized an ugly truth. Learning political science in China was a lot like a four-year sentence to a Marxist brainwashing camp.

My professors didn't have us read great treatises on political philosophy. They didn't challenge us to think. We were graded on how clearly we regurgitated Communist platitudes, how willingly we wanted to serve as gears in a big machine. It was forbidden to question whether or not the machine really worked, to wonder why it had been constructed, or who it was built to serve. Thinkers were not welcome. Parrots earned high marks. Our lessons focused entirely on Marxist/Leninist theories, and how Mao had used these theories to change China for the better. A widely debatable notion at best.

For instance, we were taught how Lenin described the country as a tool that one class uses to fight another. We all had a good laugh at that one, even some of my teachers. By that point, Deng Xiaoping had said the struggle for class was wrong. It was another of his attempts to contradict Mao's policies in order to curry favor with a new generation of Chinese. We all knew Deng didn't care about Lenin. The man was a stone-cold realist. He would do or say whatever was needed to stay in power, as evidenced by his famous quote: "It doesn't matter if a cat is black or white, so long as it catches mice."

Democracy was only discussed in the most cursory of ways, and then only to deride it as the private playground for capitalist overlords. My teachers said that democracy was the tool by which the rich enslaved the masses, rigging the game so the wealthy class could survive. I was taught that American-style democracy featured three branches of government. That each branch was run by rich old white men from acceptable family pedigrees who did not mingle with common folk and enacted laws for their benefit. Their children were hooked on drugs and raped each other and crashed the family car for fun and then got depressed and committed suicide.

Maybe, I thought. But how did this compare to life during the Cultural Revolution?

During the Cultural Revolution, schools were closed and private homes were invaded. Citizens were thrown in jail by the thousands under the slightest pretenses. Perhaps someone said that you were not loyal. Perhaps someone thought they'd overheard you saying the chairman had put on some weight. Remember the drunk in the park who slept on a picture of Mao? He was taken to prison and shot. Ask anyone who lived back then, especially in the cities. People were interrogated and tortured. Many simply disappeared. Here one day and gone the next, no trace of them ever found.

Red Guard members prowled the countryside, hunting for "class enemies." A person could be convicted of not having "boundless loyalty to Mao." Whole families were beaten to death with clubs. Infants and very small children were killed for not showing proper patriotic zeal. Millions were sentenced to work camps. They became the Party's source of cheap labor for creating infrastructure: bridges, dams, railroads, farms, factories, buildings, bomb shelters. I once read how Pol Pot cited Mao as his inspiration to form the Khmer Rouge. Savages worshipping savages. But China had its own Killing Fields.

Chinese society turned on itself, feasting on its own tissue, a cancer that grew and grew. Co-workers spied on co-workers. Families called the police on neighbors, in-laws, and each other. Children were taught that cruelty was good, that cruelty made you stronger. Intelligence was seen as a disease that had to be eradicated. The Party outlawed individuals. It wanted robots who could stand up and shout, "Chairman Mao! A good example!" Death stalked the streets in every town and every city in every province. People could feel the Red Eye upon them. This nightmare lasted ten long years. My father remembered it well.

But now it was my generation's turn. After so much suffering, so much loss, I thought we had earned the right to look back, to evaluate our past. Wasn't that how countries moved forward? Wasn't that how cultures progressed? You have to admit what has happened. Own up to what went wrong. Mourn and then forgive. Only then are you free to begin a new path.

We'd given communism a shot for close to a hundred years. It had failed. The country was in trouble. Inflation was running rampant. The cost of living had blasted sky-high, but workers' wages stayed frozen. Everyone was hurting—unless you worked in the government, of course, or were connected to the Politburo. Then you were living on easy street. Everyone knew this. They felt resentful but had no way to express it. People who spoke their minds got arrested. The government controlled the media, so according to TV and newspapers, the situation was rosy. This only made people feel more disenfranchised, angrier day by day.

Why not try something different? I thought. Why not try an open society? One where human beings are valued, not suppressed? Where government works to make life better, instead of simply seizing control? Ideals like these had driven me to change my major, and these were the topics I longed to discuss with my teachers and my classmates. But I couldn't. The Party controlled the conversation. The Party approved which figures were heroes. Which facts were valid. Which version of history was true. Dissent would not be tolerated.

Two months into my new degree, I realized I was trapped. I knew I was learning nonsense, but I still believed what Lu Xun said: I could help more people through leadership than by being a scientist. So I stopped attending classes and went to the library every day where I checked out forbidden books. I didn't know which ones to start with, so I started at the left-hand side of the shelf and worked my way to the right. Sir Francis Bacon. John Locke. Friedrich Nietzsche. Jean-Jacques Rousseau. Johann Wolfgang von Goethe. One at a time, I read them all.

Someone once asked me, Why would Chinese universities keep Western books on file? Answer: So students can refer to them when criticizing the West.

My list continued. Thomas Paine. Mahatma Gandhi. Sir Thomas Aquinas. Voltaire. Alexis de Tocqueville. Hegel. Cicero. Kant. Hume. Schopenhauer. I checked out these books and devoured them all, keeping an open mind. I wanted to hear what these writers were saying, to compare their thoughts to the ones I'd had. My secret view of the world.

I read from nine in the morning to nine at night. Friends brought the assignments from all my classes. I finished them, but not very well. I remember eking through my class on Scientific Socialism with a 61. A score of 60 was failing. A lot of my grades were little better, but I didn't care. I was working just enough to keep from being expelled. Staying in school was essential since I needed the library. The books were the door and school was the key. I had to keep reading and learning.

My friends became concerned. A few were certain I'd lost my mind, and maybe I had, in a way. My dorm mates sought me out one day. They asked if I was feeling all right. I told them I'd never felt better, which only made things worse. A mental patient is worthy of pity, he doesn't know what he's doing. An oddball, on the other hand, is making a conscious choice. His eccentricities point to danger. He is someone who must be watched.

I would pass through the halls of my dormitory, enter a crowded cafeteria, or walk under arches of whispers and turn my head in just enough time to see other eyes rolling away. To be fair, most of my peers approved, but a small, select few remained aloof. These were the so-called elite, the students who prided themselves on following paths that were blazed by the Party. The group to which, until recently, I had belonged.

One day, I received an invitation to call on my faculty adviser. She was a severe woman with high hard cheeks like hatchet blows in her face, and hair pulled tight like a black second skin that stretched across her scalp. Her posture was impeccable. Her name was Teacher Gao.* She asked me to come to her home. This was very unusual. In China, there are many rules. The most powerful ones are unspoken.

I dragged my feet on the way to Teacher Gao's apartment. I could only imagine what she had heard, what she wanted to say to me. She sat me down and served me tea and said, "So. Let's get right to the point. I don't want you doing too much."

I blinked at her. "Excuse me?"

"You know what I'm talking about."

I tried to play dumb. "I really don't."

Teacher Gao gazed calmly at the steeple she'd built from her fingers. "The librarians tell me what you've been reading, as if the rumors aren't clear enough. Here is what I advise, *Xiao* Tang. Focus on your class work and play the university game. Graduate with high marks and secure an excellent future. After that, you can do what you like."

"I'm not doing anything wrong," I said.

She made a face, as though her tea were especially bitter. "This is what worries me. Let me be clear. We're not talking about right and wrong, we're talking about what's smart and what's not. I'm not telling you what you should and shouldn't read, I'm telling you don't burn bridges. They're awfully hard to rebuild, you know. Some of them can't be rebuilt at all. So get good grades and get a good job. Work your way up through the Party. You're very bright. I know you'll succeed. Once you reach a high-enough level, then you can start to make changes."

Of course, I thought. Look how well the process had worked for people like Hu Yaobang. I shook my head. "I've seen what happens when people join the Party. Change is hardly the first thing they seek. In fact, if you follow the Party line, change rarely happens at all."

---

*Asterisks denote a pseudonym.

Teacher Gao cocked her head at me. "The Party provides for those who serve it. That is how the system works."

"The Party works for those who indulge in corruption and hypocrisy. It doesn't work for the common man. It doesn't work for China. And therefore, it doesn't work at all."

Teacher Gao set down her tea cup. "You have been given many gifts, for which you should be thankful. You are smart and have great character. Why not choose the path of success?"

"First of all," I said, "A person does not choose their gifts. Therefore, they cannot take credit for them. And as far as character is concerned, Sir Francis Bacon once said that character determines fate. Therefore, I will not choose success, I will choose my character instead and let my path play out as it will."

Teacher Gao went stiff. "You are obstinate."

"I mean no disrespect," I said. "To you, or anyone else."

"Obstinate," huffed Teacher Gao. "You walk a dangerous path."

"This meeting has showed me that," I said.

Teacher Gao sighed and looked at her fingers and did not speak for a moment. Then: "Think about this, *Xiao* Tang. Think long and hard, then ask yourself a simple question: do you think your convictions are strong enough to take on all of China? The Party, and our history? The fabric of our culture?"

I'd never thought of it quite like that. I could not give her an answer. Gao seemed to sense my hesitation. She offered a tiny smile. "Remember," she said. "Better men than you have tried, and wound up with nothing. Is this what you want?"

6

When I left Teacher Gao's apartment, my thoughts were spinning in tight little circles like leaves caught up in a cyclone. Was she right? I didn't know. What she said made a cold kind of sense, but more, it echoed a sentiment that was gaining ground in China back then. Some people said, Let reforms be gradual. Let them happen province by province, or city by city if that's what was needed. These people argued that China had already suffered so much. Now she was finally turning around. Why not let her evolve like a glacier's creep, progress measured by inches? What was the point of making a stir? Change would happen, you just had to wait. Patience was better than passion.

I had felt the pull of this very same logic many times before, seductive as the current's tug on the feet of a drowning man. *Embrace me*, said the water. *Let go. Give up. Give in. Slide under. Rewards aplenty lay under the ocean.* Everything Teacher Gao promised. I could have a good job, a good salary, privileges, power, prestige—a life. But what *kind* of life? I found myself wondering. Did I want to end up like my father? A cog in a great machine that was built to serve the few instead of the many? A gear that clicks without knowing why? A spring that somebody else has wound, doomed to snap forever to a rhythm that isn't mine?

The CCP was the problem. A one-party system. No choice. No debate. No freedom. No competition. Human beings deserve destiny. A road with many forks. Take away the power to turn and a road is not a road. It's a jail cell without a roof, narrow and impossibly long, stretching toward the horizon.

I resolved right then to make my stand. I didn't know how and I didn't know when. But I knew that the time would come. As luck would have it, I didn't wait long, nor would I make my stand alone.

Hu Yaobang had a heart attack in the spring of 1989. Reports said he was taken to a hospital, but he never recovered. He passed away on April 15. By that point, he curried no favor. Party officials regarded him as a has-been, an eccentric. In their official statement regarding his passing, the Politburo downplayed his life and demeaned his contributions. Hu Yaobang, they said, was a "retired" official who'd made a lot of career "mistakes," notably in Sino-Japanese relations. There would be no official state funeral.

This was no slight, it was an outrage—an assassination of character. Hu Yaobang's life and legacy, all the reforms he'd worked to achieve, were being tossed on the bonfire. The Party wanted him gone. Forgotten. That was their biggest mistake. They should have thought it through some more and taken the pulse of the people.

Most young Chinese already felt that the Party disdained the citizenry. But to blatantly disrespect a hero? Such arrogance was astounding! Of all the post-Mao leaders, Hu Yaobang had leaned furthest to the right. Many citizens feared that his passing would signal an end to reforms. The lack of a funeral seemed to confirm this. The Party was saying, *Hu Yaobang didn't matter. His policies weren't the Chinese way. They were nothing but smoke dispersed by the wind. The ravings of a lunatic.*

The fax machines in the offices of the student government started to chug and hum. Long tongues of paper fell to the floor. Phone lines jangled and clamored. We pieced together the crazy reports arriving from Beijing. Five hundred students from the China University of Political Science and Law had entered Tiananmen Square on April 17 to mourn for Hu Yaobang. They positioned themselves in front of the Great Hall of the People. Gave speeches to honor Hu's memory. By all accounts, they conducted themselves with grace and simple dignity.

The government responded by sending in police who told the mourners to disperse. Evidently, they were interfering with the Great Hall's normal functions. The conversation was even and sane. No one employed any violence. But the mourners did not go home.

At midnight on April 17, more students began to arrive. They came from Beijing University and Qinghua. This brought the overall total of mourners to something close to five thousand. The impromptu memorial started to change. Now it was more like a demonstration or a rally.

"They're singing songs." My student government secretary had torn a sheet off the fax machine. He was scanning it, frowning, shaking his head in disbelief. His name was Liu Shao.* "They're drawing up a list of demands to take to the Politburo. This message says the tenor is peaceful but insistent. The police have approached the mourners again and asked them to leave, but no one did."

"We're going to need more paper," I said. The fax machine was running low. I went to the supply closet.

More students arrived in the square the next day. Now there were several thousand mourners planted before the Great Hall of the People, and several thousand more who stood in front of the government's residential complex. They were chanting and singing, demanding an audience that would not appear. And so they staged a sit-in that ended two days later when police dispersed the students by force, swinging their batons.

It was another grave mistake. The government wasn't endearing itself to anyone. People began to call the students heroes. More support began to pour in. I remember on April 21, I tore a fax off the tired machine and read it very quickly. I couldn't believe my eyes.

"They're saying that more than a hundred thousand people have assembled in Tiananmen Square!"

Liu Shao, with his wide white eyes. He was a freshman then. How old? Eighteen? Excited. Scared. "What will they do to them now?"

We all knew who *they* were.

"I don't know," I said. "The right thing, I hope."

Which turned out to be true. The Party must have sensed it was losing control, and fast. And so it relented. A funeral would be held after all. Hu Yaobang would be honored the next day, April 22.

Most of the CCP leaders attended the ceremony. Deng Xiaoping was there, along with Zhao Ziyang, the Party's general secretary. But so were a lot of people who had amassed in Tiananmen Square. Their outrage was palpable. Fists shook like the limbs of trees stirred by hurricane winds. Shouts split the air. It was as if all of China were screaming that Hu Yaobang's legacy be reviewed at once.

Another fuse had just been lit, but no one figured it out right away. We wouldn't know the strength of the charge until the flame touched powder. By that point, it would be early June and, in many ways, already too late.

part three
Protestor

1

Tiananmen Square is the world's largest city plaza, over half a mile long, more than a quarter mile wide. Picture a great slate of charcoal-colored flagstones, flat as an ocean becalmed. The square is flanked on the west by the Great Hall of the People, to the east by the National Chinese Museum. Its surface is only broken by two distinctive features. Toward the north, a narrow stone obelisk rises 125 feet in the air. This is the Monument to the People's Heroes. A more recent invention stands toward the south, the Mausoleum of Mao Zedong, which features the chairman's embalmed remains encased in a crystal coffin. Like Lenin, his idol, Mao is permanently on display. Visitors are quickly ushered in and out. The body is crumbling thanks to dated mortuary techniques borrowed from the Vietnamese. At the square's far north, the Tiananmen Gate guards the Forbidden City, which served as China's imperial palace from the time of the Mings to the fall of the Qings, a span of nearly five hundred years. Beijing grew up around the gate. For that matter, so did China.

Now picture red flags raised high on poles and fluttering in the breeze. People walking across the square seem like ants on a field of gray. The towering gate features row upon row of stairs leading up to a great pagoda whose sloping roof is clawed like the foot of a dragon. Tiananmen Square: there's no place like it on earth, and with good reason. Excellence must be rarified if it's going to be respected.

Tiananmen Square has often served as the stage for China's political protests. I'm thinking of one particular incident that took place back in the mid-1970s. A popular leader named Zhou Enlai announced he was ailing from cancer. He could no longer hold down his day-to-day chores as China's premier, a largely a ceremonial post awarded to leaders who toe the line. So Zhou lobbied Mao to release Deng Xiaoping from exile. Deng has learned his lesson, said Zhou. Let him serve me as a kind of *chargé d'affaires*. Let him handle the rigors of state that I can no longer attend to due to illness.

Mao must not have been pleased. Everyone knew that Zhou Enlai was a patron of Deng's. Mao possibly saw this bid to resuscitate Deng as a way of building support for the right, for whom Zhou was known to harbor sympathies. Finally, however, Mao relented. Deng was called back from exile. Mao declared him "rehabilitated" and gave him the office of first vice premier in 1974.

In public, Deng made a big show of championing Mao's policies. Behind the scenes, however, he worked to heal the more grievous wounds that China had suffered because of the chairman. Mao knew what was going on, of course. He practiced his own kind of subterfuge, supporting Deng in public while secretly working to sabotage him, thereby upholding the Cultural Revolution's principles. Once again, China teetered on the brink of political chaos.

Finally, Zhou Enlai passed away on January 8, 1976. The death of this longtime government servant triggered a massive outpouring of public grief. In the waning days of the Cultural Revolution, Zhou had marked himself as a liberal, countermanding the rabid attacks made by the Red Guard on innocent people in every province of China. Zhou had pushed hard to implement the Four Mods, his way of counteracting the damage caused by Maoist policies. Most citizens saw Zhou as ballast against the power of the Gang of Four. This alone made him beloved. What would we do now that he was gone?

The Gang of Four delighted in Zhou's passing. They looked for a way to discredit his memory and found it by attacking his protégé, Deng Xiaoping. Before Zhou's body was even cold, the Gang of Four began a campaign called *Pi Deng Fanji Youqing Fanan Feng*. Loosely translated: To Criticize Deng and Oppose the Rehabilitation of Right-Leaning Political Elements. Deng dug in for what looked to be another long bout of political infighting. And with him was his own protégé, the ever faithful Hu Yaobang.

Mourners appeared in Tiananmen Square within days of Zhou Enlai's passing. They piled white chrysanthemums at the foot of the Monument to the People's Heroes until it looked like a blizzard had suddenly struck, carpeting flagstones with fallen snow. The mourners also brought poems praising Zhou Enlai's goodness scratched onto slips of parchment. They fastened the slips to the monument's base, papering over the stone inscription carved in Mao Zedong's handwriting. "Eternal glory to the heroes of the people!"

Picture the thousands and thousands of poems taped to the sides of the monument, haphazard as the scales on a dying fish, fluttering in the breeze. Many poems lambasted the Gang of Four and the CCP by resorting to allegory, a tacit mode of protest that the Chinese have perfected. Toward the end of the Cultural Revolution, we had learned we could not express our pain and outrage directly. The police would arrest us for being overt, but they couldn't arrest the anonymous authors of poems referring to ancient tyrants found stuck to a great stone obelisk in the middle of a public place.

The Party was not deceived, of course. Allegorical poems aside, the number of mourners did not abate. If anything, it grew. Over January, February, and March of 1976, citizens filled Tiananmen Square. Whether they brought flowers or not, the intensity of their sentiment was clear. By April 1, 1976, Tiananmen Square was full of people mourning the death of Zhou Enlai. More were due to arrive in four days to celebrate *Qingming*, which is a very important day in China. We call it Tomb Sweeping Day, the festival for mourning the dead. The Gang of Four must have feared a revolt. They ordered police to clear the Monument to the People's Heroes.

Security forces arrived in Tiananmen Square on the evening of April 4. They tore down the poems and scooped up the wreaths and tore up the chrysanthemum carpet and piled it all into heaps, which they burned. Then they set up cordons so that no one could get to the monument. Guards were posted along the perimeter and told to keep the area clear, through violence if necessary.

When people arrived the following morning, they couldn't believe what they saw. They stood there, staring, with mouths agape, weeping with shame and grief. The tokens they'd left for the dead were gone, clearly removed by the soldiers. It was an insult to the deceased, a blatant violation of customs alive in China for thousands of years. The festival of *Qingming* demanded that the dead be mourned regardless of their station—whether politician, peasant, enemy, friend, Party leader, or swineherd. The mourners got very angry. The pot of dissent that had simmered for months began to boil over.

Demonstrations broke out on the spot. People began to chant and march. The cobblestones writhed with lines of mourners twisting in makeshift conga lines. The square became like a bucket of snakes, roiling and plunging, a soup of motion. Leaders shouted through bullhorns. The rank and file brandished jerry-rigged signs and jabbed their fists in the air.

Mao Zedong's wife, Jiang Qing, lashed out. She branded the mourners capitalist roaders and said that anyone mourning Zhou Enlai in Tiananmen Square or across the country was a counterrevolutionary and therefore should be purged at once for the betterment of the nation.

As evening fell on April 5, 1976, the Gang of Four sent a crack militia to seize Tiananmen Square. The soldiers beat back thousands of mourners. Clubs rose and fell in the stadium lights. Bones snapped and flesh burst open.

The protestors grabbed their fallen comrades and dragged them back beyond the fray, but still the troops kept coming, swinging, clearing the square like the blade of a scythe, cutting down all who stood in their path.

The demonstrators were routed. Then, in a brilliant feat of cunning, the Gang of Four had the media broadcast the following message: The violence in Tiananmen Square was deeply regrettable, clearly a blow to the people's spirit, and Deng Xiaoping was responsible. Deng Xiaoping, the media said, had ordered this awful attack. Therefore Deng Xiaoping must be seen as an enemy of the people and removed from office at once.

This simple act of subterfuge worked incredibly well. Deng was once again stripped of his titles and ousted from government service. Once again, he was sent to live in a "rehabilitation camp." So was Hu Yaobang. This time, however, the two men wouldn't have long to wait before their release.

Only five months later, Mao Zedong suffered his third and final heart attack. Doctors declared him officially dead on September 9, 1976. And less than one month later, the entire Gang of Four was crushed in a lightning-fast coup d'état that the nation received with hearty approval. We hoped that the worst was over, but it wasn't. Not by a long shot.

A new man took over as chairman of the Chinese Communist Party. His name was Hua Guofeng. Hua made very few changes, a factor that led to his downfall. Though technically ousted from office, Deng had begun a silent campaign to seize control of China. Assisted as always by Hu Yaobang, Deng began to encourage people to rail against Mao's atrocities. He pointed out that Hua Guofeng continued Maoist policies. That was all people needed to hear. The balance of power shifted again, and Hua Guofeng stepped down.

By the late 1970s, Deng Xiaoping had finally gained control of the Chinese Communist Party. And Hu Yaobang was there, as well, as constant as a star in the sky, and just as bright, in many ways. A new age was dawning for China, we thought. An era of reform.

The passing of Zhou Enlai had set off protests that threatened the Party's power. But history can repeat itself. Thirteen years later, a new generation of martyrs would baptize Tiananmen Square with blood. This time, the death of Hu Yaobang would spark the controversy, and this time the violence would climb to heights that no one had ever imagined.

2

In the spring of 1989, I was dating a girl named Sun Dan.* We'd been going steady for more than two years, and I'd started to wonder why.

Time is a very powerful lens. You point it backward and give it a twist, it can pull the blurriest shapes into focus. Sun Dan was certainly pretty, intelligent, and outgoing. We had a lot of fun together. Were we in love? That's hard to say. In the first place, we were young. Affection can be a mirage at that age, shimmering, lovely, but always distant, blurred around the edges. If you walk a little closer, you'll see that nothing is real, only illusions of things substantial. Waves of heat rise off the ground and dissolve when they hit clear air.

Sun Dan's father was a man who'd held several high-level posts in Hunan's provincial government. Her mother was a past president of the Hunan Childhood Education Normal Institute; she had once worked for Mao Zedong himself. In short, the family was well positioned with excellent contacts, and rich. They offered the kind of advancement that career-minded men often dream about. But not me. By the spring of 1989, I'd grown disenchanted with politics, with communism in general, and with China's overall system.

Still, there was something thrilling, even perverse about dating Sun Dan, to be so close to the daughter of a leading Party officer while harboring powerful, growing anticommunist sentiments. And maybe the thrill was a two-way street. Maybe Sun Dan saw dating me as a way of rebelling against her family, her station in life, her prospects. A destiny carved in stone. I've heard it said that good girls sometimes bring home the man their parents warned them about just to rub their faces in it. A kind of test of authority.

Honestly, though, Sun Dan was hardly a counterrevolutionary. She wasn't even political. Sometimes we talked about corruption in the Party, the grotesquely disproportionate privileges CCP officers often received. I called it an abomination when those in charge got treated better than normal citizens. Sun Dan agreed in principle but declined to go any further. She didn't want to rock the boat her family was currently sailing in. She never challenged my politics, but she never supported them either. In the early days of our courtship, I could tolerate this attitude. But as the spring of 1989 progressed, I found it more and more taxing.

"You're too tepid," I told her once. "You know how the system works, you've seen your father deal with it. A one-party system offers no choice, therefore it's a dictatorship. Totalitarianism masquerading as enlightened humanism."

"Here we go again." She would sigh and roll her eyes. "It is what it is, Baiqiao Tang, and that's all it will ever be."

"You can't do that forever," I said.

"Do what?" she asked, but she knew the answer. She'd long ago mastered the skill of equivocation.

Spurred by the Party's reaction to the passing of Hu Yaobang, demonstrators in Changsha damaged some storefronts on April 22. Also, on the same day, some police cars were burned in Shanxi Province. All in all these were mild incidents, but by April 23, the student leadership in Beijing had put out a nationwide call. They were asking every college and university student in China to walk away from their classes. Teachers and faculty, too. They wanted a countrywide boycott. Reports began to pour in. Schools in over four hundred cities had heeded the call and mobilized.

But to everyone's surprise, it wasn't just students, but workers, too, walking away from their jobs. Common people were turning out, and not by the thousands but by the *tens* of thousands. They were filling the streets with marches, chanting, shouting, waving signs.

This is what I'd been waiting for. A tidal wave gathering force. A demonstration unlike any that China had ever seen.

In Changsha, police began to look nervous. They shuffled their feet and cast their eyes down, slumped their shoulders and tucked in their chins, assuming the posture of the vanquished. You could smell their fear and reluctance as a spice in the crisp spring air. You could feel the pressure of an oncoming storm. It was powerful and traveling fast. Everyone was excited! This time when the weather struck, what would the rains wash away? This time, there would be thunder and lightning, winds and water raging.

Sun Dan shook her head. "I can't believe that all of this is for Hu Yaobang."

I looked at her, realizing only then how little we had in common. "It isn't for Hu Yaobang," I said. "Hu Yaobang was the catalyst. This is for us."

It was a bold statement, but in those days my vision had started to crystallize. And it wasn't just me. So many students felt the same way. You could look old friends in the eye and see right away whose side they were on. Or bring up a news report from Beijing or talk about an upcoming rally.

Most people would look you dead in the face and smile and nod and say, How can I help? Only a few would look away, mumbling little excuses.

Sun Dan was one of these. She rarely looked in my eyes anymore and mumbled a lot whenever she spoke. Mumbling had become her new language. A dialect of the deniers.

"You'll have to decide eventually," I said.

That got her attention. "What do you mean?"

"You can't serve both the Party and China. The time for a decision is coming." I should have just said, *You have to decide between your father and me.*

She shot me a derisive look. "You think too much of all this. I don't have to decide anything. This is all blown out of proportion."

"Choosing not to decide," I said, "is still a choice."

Sun Dan shot me another one of her looks but said nothing and turned away. I knew it was over right then and there, and it didn't hurt as much as I'd thought. Like a drawn-out sigh, it offered release. But then: a new inhalation!

The Party did not respond well to our demonstrations. Student leaders asked to meet with officials, but the government refused. Then on April 26, Deng Xiaoping went public with an editorial he'd ordered written in the *People's Daily*, the CCP's official press. In this article, Deng made light of the demonstrations. He also grossly misreported the number of actual participants, a ploy to render the movement insignificant. He dubbed the protestors "opportunists," as if they, in fact, were the enemy. The title of his editorial said: *"Uphold the Flag! Oppose Turmoil Elements!"* No one was fooled. We Chinese had already eaten our fill of blatant propaganda.

But Deng was clever. He cited the isolated events of April 22—the damaged storefronts, the burned police cars—as evidence that the whole nation was starting to riot. He hinted that the military would descend upon any rabble-rousers.

Undaunted, protestors assembled another march. On April 27, some fifty thousand people stood in front of the government buildings in Beijing. They demanded that Deng retract his statements and urged him to count their number correctly. I remember hearing this news and having mixed feelings. On one hand, I was excited. I felt compelled to take my own activism to the next level. On the other hand, I was very sad. By refusing to listen, our leaders were causing the rift in our country to widen. They were forcing us apart in much the same way that Sun Dan and I had been split.

By the final week in April, Sun Dan and I were doing our best to avoid one another. It was all for the better like that. The positions each of us hoped to defend now stood on opposite sides of the fault line fracturing China.

3

The unrest reached a new plateau a few days later. In another parallel to 1976, it happened on a national holiday, May 4, also known as *Wu Si Qingnian Jie*, the anniversary of the New Culture Movement, a protest whose roots sprung from civil unrest in the wake of World War I.

This warrants a quick explanation. In 1919, the Allies had finally beaten the German army. Ambassadors in black suits with starched-collar shirts had convened in Versailles at tables as long as full-grown trees to divide the spoils of war. China had aided the Allies by sending 140,000 workers to France. The so-called Chinese Labour Corps had provided support services to battle-line troops. China had a vested interest in combating Germany. The Germans had settled in Shandong Province, a cornucopia of natural resources such as cotton, wheat, gold, and diamonds, all of which were being exploited by the outlanders.

So China sent ambassadors to Versailles asking that Shandong be returned to China as thanks for China's support. The Allies ignored this request. Then they added insult to injury by giving Shandong to the Japanese.

It's hard to describe the impact this made on the Chinese people. Japan was China's outright enemy. Giving Japan a chunk of the Chinese mainland was like putting a fox in the henhouse, offering eggs, and showing it where the hatchlings were. News of the treaty's provisions set off explosions of anti-Western sentiment. Many Chinese officials had lined their pockets with Western gold by supporting the Treaty of Versailles. The Chinese people knew this, and so they turned on their government. Protests broke out in Beijing, led by students and intellectuals, a caste that has served as China's bellwether for change since the days of Confucius. The Chinese people look to students in times of crisis, searching for cues on how to act, what to think, and how to feel.

The Shandong problem could hardly have come at a worse time. Imagine conditions in China back in 1919. The Qing dynasty had just been overthrown. With bickering warlords on one side and fervent nationalists on the other, China was seeking its identity. Up until then, students and intellectuals had strongly considered democracy as a viable form for China's new government. But all that changed when the Western powers hung us out to dry. The main architects of Versailles were the United States, France, and Great Britain. It was normal then for China to ask: Why should we embrace a system that's treated our nation so poorly?

On May 4, 1919, demonstrators amassed in Beijing. Students from the city's thirteen universities marched through the streets, lighting firecrackers, carrying flags and signs, and beating drums. They chanted, "Don't sign the Treaty of Versailles!" and "Get rid of traitors at home!" People came out of their homes to watch. The students' passion made them weep. Workers started to leave their jobs and take up with the rally. The ranks of the protestors swelled, becoming unwieldy. The mob needed a home. Guess where they chose to convene? Of course! Tiananmen Square.

The protestors went to one official's home and burned it to the ground. The police responded by making arrests. The unrest spread like a contagion until it infected over a hundred cities in twenty provinces. And, like a contagion, the movement mutated. Now the protests weren't just about foreign powers in Shandong Province. People demanded better working conditions for the lower class. Repeals of unfair taxes. Release of political prisoners. Cures for rampant poverty.

Inspired by their nation's outrage, the Chinese officials who'd been dispatched to Versailles refused to sign the treaty. It was a good moral stance, but not enough to stop the impending action. Shandong Province went to Japan. It would not be returned to Chinese rule for another three years. Another story for another time. For now, the operative point is this: after the May 4th Movement, certain intellectuals, among them a young man, Mao Zedong, would seize on anti-Western sentiment. They would use this anger to recommend China's next form of government. Why not try communism? said Mao and others of his ilk. It's working for the Russians, you know. Maybe we should consider it.

I think it's safe to say that, when dawn broke on May 4, 1989, every protestor clear across China felt part of a sacred tradition. We saw ourselves as the next generation of patriots and leaders, a powerful wave that had to break lest the tide stand still, grow stagnant, and die. Would you call us opportunists? Hardly. Damn you, Deng Xiaoping. We were fighting for what we knew was right, the government we deserved.

At 8 a.m. on May 4, students from Hunan Normal had planned to meet and light firecrackers. Then we would march through the streets, merging with marchers from other schools and mixing with them, growing in size, becoming a unified force. The march would then head toward May 1st Square and the buildings of Hunan's provincial government. Back to the place where, three years before, we'd amassed to talk with Governor Xiong. Only this time, we had new demands, none of which involved poor cafeteria service.

The group I'd assembled from Hunan Normal numbered some ten thousand strong. I was scheduled to lead the march. But shortly before 8 a.m., university representatives came to my dorm, accompanied by a security guard.

"Mr. Tang, would you be so kind? The University President has asked to speak to you."

The security guard had a club. His look was sullen and ready. The representatives' tone was clear. This was not a request.

Liu Shao was there. "What should we do?" he asked.

"Carry on as planned," I said.

Liu Shao stared at the guards. His eyes were wide. He looked afraid.

"Liu Shao?" I asked.

He returned his gaze to me, and his eyes swam back into focus. He nodded. "Yes," he said. "Okay."

I walked out the door, past the guards, and away.

4

The president wasn't in. Instead we were ushered down the hall to the vice president's office. The guards knocked. The figure who opened the door was painfully thin, like a skeleton dressed in sophisticate's clothing, impersonating a man in his mid- to late fifties. Seeing me, the cadaverish man bowed low and extended his hand. We shook. He introduced himself as Dai Hai. I nodded. I knew who he was. A university officer who was also a high-level CCP cadre—the government's watchdog at Hunan Normal. This was common knowledge on campus.

Dai Hai waved me in and motioned to a chair by his desk. "Please, Mr. Tang. Sit down."

As if I had a choice. The security guard took a position outside the door.

I sat down. Dai Hai served me tea, a very expensive brand, worth a week's salary for a common factory worker. My father had brought some home one time, a gift from a Party principal's conference. Dai Hai served his tea in bone cups whose sides were thin as paper, nearly transparent. I put the cup to my lips and drank. Such a hot and bitter taste on my tongue! Outside, the air began to tear in a series of drawn-out *riiiiiiiiiiiips!* Firecrackers were going off. *Wu Si Qingnian Jie* had commenced. The march had started without me.

Dai Hai shook his head and said *tsk tsk tsk* and wondered what the unrest was about. "You young people," he said. *Tsk tsk tsk.* "Did you know that I grew up very poor? Oh, yes. As poor as poor could be. Everyone was poor during the Cultural Revolution."

"Except the rich," I said.

Dai Hai continued as if he hadn't heard. "Did you know that I was once sentenced to a work camp in Shandong Province?" He stiffened as though he'd been stabbed in the kidney. "Oh, yes. Yes, indeed. They say that Mao Zedong himself assigned me this terrible punishment. I was there for many years, did you know? And you young people think conditions are bad? Hmmm. Let me tell you, Mr. Tang. Respectfully, of course. People your age don't know what bad is."

I averted my eyes and sipped more tea as Dai Hai rambled on and on, sharing his thoughts of life under Mao.

"When I was your age, the government was ten times worse than today. A thousand times worse! But look at what we have now, Mr. Tang! Peace. Prosperity. Change. Look at what this poor child has gained." He gestured to his office, which was lavishly appointed. "Tell me what's wrong with this, Mr. Tang. Please. I'm curious. Talk to me. Why aren't you young people satisfied?"

I found it hard to stay focused. Dai Hai was making several good points, and landing them soft as kisses. His manner was never combative. Instead, he wielded a deadlier weapon: a childlike curiosity. Sitting there in his office, I envied him for that. And yes, I had to agree. China had come a very long way since the Cultural Revolution.

But his argument also had holes in it. In essence, Dai Hai was saying that we should be happy that life in China had gone from hellish to merely atrocious, a point that I couldn't agree with. I thought we still had more work to do. I mentioned this to Dai Hai.

"Mr. Tang," he sighed, and shook his head. *Tsk tsk tsk.* "More tea?"

If someone had walked in the room that day, they might have thought they were interrupting an uncle advising his favorite nephew. Dai Hai said he was scared for me. I was bright, he said, and I could go far. He urged me to weigh my current actions. How would they impact my future, he asked, and that of my family? I told him I didn't want a future without democracy, without an open exchange of ideas. Markets free from government rigging. A genuine valuation of individual citizens. Talent triumphing over connections. A country working to better itself, committing itself to laws instead of the preservation of status. A country whose people were proud of her.

Dai Hai listened to what I was saying. To this day, I swear I saw conflict flickering deep within his eyes. Part of him approved of my vision. Part of him believed. But he was a CCP cadre, born and bred to tradition. His time for choosing another path had passed him long ago. He reminded me of my father then, and I pitied him.

We stayed in his office for more than an hour. Our conversation stalled several times but always reignited. Then, just when I thought we'd run out of topics, Dai Hai proposed that we go for a walk, which took me by surprise. It was such an unusual request. I started to beg off, but Dai Hai insisted, and, once again, the security guard appeared, providing his silent assurance that all my opinions were moot.

We left the office and went outside. I could see the lines of demonstrators passing by in the distance. The clamor they made was a shuddering din from over a hundred yards away. Chanting. Songs being sung. Drums beating. Dai Hai seemed not to notice. He turned on a heel and strolled away, heading across the campus. He said he wanted to show me the dormitories reserved for foreign visitors.

Most Chinese universities maintain two sets of dorms, one for students and one for foreign visitors. The student dorms are hellholes. Peeling paint and crumbling bricks. Roofs that are barely maintained. In winter, their faulty heat admits a bone-cracking cold. In summer, each room is a life-sized kiln. No air-conditioning, of course. Plumbing that gurgles rusty water. The aesthetics of a disaster zone. The visitors' dorms by comparison are as lush as five-star hotels. Carpeting. Fabric draped on the walls.

Ceiling fans stirring the air. You can smell the sensual newness to them, and of course they're empty for years on end. I looked around in silent awe and wondered why I was there.

"More tea?" said Dai Hai. The guard hustled forward bearing a thermos and cups. He poured us more tea.

"I really have to go," I said. Several times, in fact. But each time, Dai Hai would shake his head.

"No, no," he would say. "Please stay a bit longer. There's so much I wish to discuss, Mr. Tang. Look! What do you think of that mirror? We had it imported from Italy." And then he would change the subject again, talking as though I'd said nothing.

I started to get the feeling that Dai Hai was stalling for time. Dai Hai remarked on the weather, saying how pleasant it was. A perfect spring day with excellent sunlight, soft but not too warm. Perfect for taking photographs. He suggested we go back outside, this time for a walk through the park. Again, I declined and asked to be excused. Dai Hai appeared shocked, even somewhat hurt.

"Mr. Tang!" he said. "If you were to join your friends right now, who knows what kinds of things would happen? The police might arrest you, or the university president might expel you. No, no, Mr. Tang! I really think it's best that you stay. Why don't we sit on this bench." By then, we were already walking outside. "That's it. Such a lovely bench. And lovely weather, you see? Care for something to drink? Hmmm? Let's have some more tea over here."

Again the guard with the thermos appeared and the ritual was repeated. But at noon, a new security guard came hustling across the line. This guard bowed low in front of Dai Hai and stepped in very close. He whispered something in Dai Hai's ear. Dai Hai nodded and turned to me.

"Well, Mr. Tang," said Dai Hai. "This has certainly been enjoyable. Thank you for keeping me company. I hope you will consider all the things we talked about."

Frankly, we hadn't talked much at all. Dai Hai had talked and I had listened, incredibly for four hours. I cocked my ears and strained to hear but there were no more drum beats, no more songs. The demonstration was over, or very nearly so. Now I began to see what had happened. Dai Hai had barred me from attending the rally. In essence, I'd been kidnapped. And why? To neuter Hunan Normal University's pro-democracy movement. But had he succeeded? I didn't know.

Leaving Dai Hai, I ran back to my dorm, picked up my bicycle, hit the streets, and pedaled as fast as I could.

5

The closer I got to May 1st Square, the more I understood why Dai Hai was scared. The streets were alive with people. Students. Workers. Shop keepers. Families. Everyone milling about and shouting. "Human rights! Freedom of the press! Fight corruption! Fight special powers! Treat students and intellectuals better!" But most of all, they were shouting, "We must reassess Hu Yaobang!" That's when I knew we were winning. The demonstration had been a success.

In Chinese culture, we often invoke this word, *reassess*. It means we demand that someone be scrutinized, his actions called into question. Even when someone has passed away, we can demand that his character be reevaluated. Now that I've been exposed to the West, I suppose it's a bit like the Catholic Church considering people who've died. Are they worthy of sainthood? In China, a reassessment isn't about religion, of course, this is a strictly secular practice, a call to review a person's actions in order to transform his reputation, to elevate it within the culture, as well as in the historical record.

People believed that the CCP had sullied Hu Yaobang's name. Now they wanted his memory cleared, his character expunged.

Local police had turned out in force, but they weren't doing much in May 1st Square. What could they do? May 4 is a national holiday that celebrates demonstrations. The Chinese always celebrate it by holding demonstrations. So police were standing around, watching the crowds with glazed expressions. Even if they'd wanted to intervene, they were grossly outnumbered. Ants cannot police a bull. There must have been two hundred thousand people marching in Changsha that day.

But there was another, more important reason police did not crack down: the government had issued no orders. Two weeks since Hu Yaobang's death, the signals coming from the Central Committee were murky at best, sometimes nonexistent. Most Chinese had begun to suspect that the Party was rent by a schism. On one hand, you had the rightists led by the Party's general secretary. In a style reminiscent of Hu Yaobang, Zhao

Ziyang had kept mum on the protests, and he hadn't ordered a crackdown. This seemed to hint that Zhao Ziyang thought the people ought to be heard. But, on the opposite side of the coin, the leftists led by Deng Xiaoping had adopted a very hard line. His editorial in *People's Daily* had called the protests "unrest" and "incidents of revolt." This was tantamount to saying that anyone caught demonstrating was violating the law and would therefore be dealt with swiftly, using any means deemed necessary.

Zhao was the titular head of the Party, but Deng still held the army. Another curious battle of CCP leadership was playing out at the highest levels. Meanwhile, the rest of the country waited, hoping to witness a sign that would show us which course was to be followed.

I found my group in Changsha Veterans' Memorial Park around 12:30. The demonstration was nearly over, but a huge crowd was hanging around like smoke after a bonfire, churning and lying low to the ground. All heads had turned toward a stage on which student leaders were making addresses. Shouts, cheers, and applause would punctuate certain phrases like the rolling din of thunder trailing brilliant flashes of lightning.

I reunited with Liu Shao and another student, Long Jinhua. When I asked them what happened, they beamed. "You planned it very well," said Liu Shao. "We followed your orders and merged our group with the others. Then all of us marched right here to the square. Baiqiao Tang! It was quite a scene!"

"What happened to you?" said Long Jinhua. "What did the president say?"

A crowd quickly gathered around me. Everyone wanted to know what had happened. Once I had been taken away, word had spread throughout the contingent from Hunan Normal, and from there, to the rest of the protest. I told my little group what happened. People were shocked and appalled.

"You must tell everyone," someone said. Someone else was grabbing my arm and pushing me toward the stage.

"Yes!" I heard someone saying. "Tell the crowd! They must know what Dai Hai did!"

Before I knew what was going on, I was staring at a flight of steps that ascended to the platform. There were other speakers in line before me. Their tide pulled back. They urged me forward. It seemed like only a moment later that I was standing up on the stage, looking out on a sea of faces, a crowd of nearly a hundred thousand people, or so I was later told.

Someone shouted, "Baiqiao Tang! This is Baiqiao Tang who speaks! His university kidnapped him!"

Applause and shouts of support. Thousands of hands were thrust high in the air, fluttering fists like little round banners.

There was no podium. No microphone. Just naked space between me and the crowd. I cleared my throat and raised my voice, projecting as best I could. That's never been a problem for me. I've always had a strong voice. "My name is Baiqiao Tang," I said.

The crowd got very quiet. It was eerie, looking at so many people, and none of them saying a word. Everyone was listening now, watching. My countrymen, waiting.

I kept my remarks very brief. No more than three minutes, or so I am told. It seemed like so much longer to me. "My friends," I said. "I'm sorry to join you so late. I'm sorry I could not be with you today. I guess by now you know what occurred. I was detained by a leader of my university."

No one spoke. They knew, all right. They knew.

"Was I threatened?" I asked. "Was I punished? Did they offer to expel me? No. They did something more despicable. I was served several cups of excellent tea and made to feel important. Not to you, but to them. To the Chinese Communist Party."

The crowd began to rumble, a low noise, like the moan of a tide. I held up my hands. The rumble dropped to a shudder that I felt through my feet, as if the very earth itself were offering bass notes deep from its core. "The truth is I was kidnapped," I said. "Held for hours. They didn't put me in jail. They didn't put me in prison. Still, it was the first time in my life I have ever lost my liberty. The tea was quite exceptional, but I prefer the taste of my freedom."

The rumble came back, started rising again. This time, I didn't think I could stop it. "Please," I said. "Whatever you do. Do not stop fighting today. Let today be the first in a lifetime of struggles that last the rest of our lives. Let the struggle continue until we are free. Do we deserve any less?"

The crowd began to shout, "No! No!"

"Does anyone here deserve any less?"

"No!" they shouted. "No!"

"Then what will you do?" I asked. "What must we do next?"

"Fight for freedom!" someone shouted. The rest of the crowd followed suit. "Fight for freedom! Fight for freedom! Long live Baiqiao Tang!"

I turned away from the stage. The roar that hit my back was strong, like the blast of heat from a forge. I climbed down the steps, the fire blazing behind me. Liu Shao was the first to greet me, grabbing my shoulder, his hand like a claw. "Listen to that!" he said. "Do you hear what they are saying?"

I hadn't really processed it. I turned and listened again.

"Long live Baiqiao Tang! Long live Baiqiao Tang!"

That was my very first inkling that my destiny had changed.

6

Later that afternoon, I convened with student leaders from almost every university in Changsha. We met right there in Veterans' Memorial Park and agreed that our work was just beginning, also that we would have greater strength in numbers. And so we voted to bond together and form a brand-new congress. We called ourselves the Students Autonomous Federation, or SAF for short.

The word *autonomous* indicated our separation from CCP control. As I've mentioned, student groups in China were subject to government oversight. The CCP appointed members of the Communist Youth League to key positions in student organizations. These young cadres sent reports back to their handlers, who in turn reported to the Politburo. Calling ourselves autonomous made it clear that we rejected this chain of command. In essence, that we rejected the Party.

"We should explore our own ideas," I said. "Not those which the Party approves."

Everyone nodded their heads, agreeing.

We chose the word *federation* since our group encompassed fifteen schools, including Hunan Normal, Hunan University, Changsha Railway College, Hunan University of Agriculture, Hunan Medical University, Hunan Hydraulic Normal University, and Hunan College of Finance and Economics. But we weren't an official body yet. We'd simply formed an action committee. On that afternoon, May 4, we made certain that delegates were chosen, and a board was quickly approved containing up to eleven members. The smaller institutions did not produce representatives.

"Now we need a chairman," said someone.

"I nominate Baiqiao Tang."

"Wait," I said.

"I second that."

"All in favor?"

Hands rose into the air. I was stunned.

This was all because of Dai Hai, I thought. Dai Hai had kept me away from the rally. Which incited a kind of interest. Which ignited when I gave my speech. Which led to my being placed in charge of the very thing that Dai Hai had opposed: the Changsha students' pro-democracy movement. I wondered how the old man would react when he heard about what had happened.

Not very well, as things turned out. I returned to campus at around four o'clock that afternoon. Immediately, I sensed a chill. Teachers and faculty, people whom I considered mentors and friends, scattered at the sight of me. I had no idea what was going on until one of my favorite professors appeared and clamped a hand on my shoulder, pulling me into an alcove. He whispered at me in furious tones. "Baiqiao Tang!" he hissed. "I heard what happened this afternoon. This little speech you gave! What were you thinking?"

"I'm not sure what you mean," I said, which was the truth.

My professor shook his head and glared. "The CCP will be angry with you. Very, very angry!"

"Why?" I asked. "I was hardly alone. Plenty of students made speeches."

"But how many speakers' names were chanted by the crowd? 'Long live Baiqiao Tang?' Do you know what this means?"

I blushed. "It means they liked my speech?"

"Insolent!" my professor said. "You are young, with the brains of an ox! Take it from someone who lived through the Party's damnable Cultural Revolution! The only person a crowd has ever said 'long live' to was Mao Zedong!"

Now I began to see what had happened. I'd been accorded far more respect than the CCP would allow. And everyone knew that the Party had ways of dealing with threats to authority.

I walked around campus the rest of the day, sympathizing with lepers. My spirits sank as the faces of friends and strangers alike turned away at my approach. Bands of people broke and moved off, leaving me bare patches of earth. No succor and no support. I was twenty-two years old with very strong convictions, but now I confess, I had to admit that I felt like I'd made a mistake. Crossed some kind of perilous gorge of the soul from which no one turns back. Perhaps Teacher Gao had spoken the truth after all.

Over the course of the following week, Dai Hai called me back to his office two or three times. He continued to ply me with tea and admonishments, but how could I change my position? My father even got word of events and came to Changsha for a talk. But even he could not sway me. Now there were people counting on me. But most of all, I was counting on myself.

Meanwhile, the SAF met every day. Instead of more demonstrations, we organized a congress. We thought that a strong organization would be the key to our success. Already we had gotten word that another body like ours was forming in Changsha. The Workers Autonomous Federation would eventually represent employees from many government-founded companies: the Changsha Textile Mill, the Hunan Electrical Battery Plant, the Changsha Non-Ferrous Metals Design Academy, the Changsha Automobile Factory, the Dongyuan Engine Parts Factory, and so on. We knew the WAF's key leaders and looked forward to working with them.

"Do you see what is happening here?" said Liu Shao. He was very excited.

"The workers," I said, and I nodded.

If the workers were getting involved, it meant that the movement was gaining ground. The government could afford to sneer at students and intellectuals. What could we really threaten to do? Stop reading textbooks? Stop writing papers and articles? But the workers were another matter. If the workers rose up, the economy would slow, then grind to a halt altogether. Worse, a workers' strike would pierce the heart of the communist ethic. Workers were Mao Zedong's Number Ones. If they weren't satisfied, who the hell was?

"Why are we sitting around?" asked Yue Weiping. He was a student from Hunan Hydraulic Normal University, noble looking and proud. "We should be out in the streets right now! We should be shaking things up!"

Liu Wei shook his head. He was sober and calm, a student from Changsha Railway College. "I disagree," he said. "The pot that boils slow heats fastest. Why exhaust our energy now? We may very well need it later."

"I think Liu Wei is right," I said. "We should bide our time and watch Beijing. Wait for a clear call to action. If this movement is going to be a success, we have to work together. So far, we've taken our signal from the leaders in Tiananmen Square. Students are boycotting classes. Now the workers have joined us, too. The pot is getting hot, indeed." I looked at Liu Wei, who nodded once but stayed quiet, as was his wont.

"This is fast becoming a factional war between Zhao Ziyang and Deng Xiaoping. Once it reaches a clear conclusion—"

Yue Weiping cut me off with a moan. "But *everyone's* doing that, biding their time. The whole damn *country's* doing that!"

It was true, I had to admit. China stood like a frozen waterfall, locked in a state of tension as we waited for one leader only to assert control of the Party.

"Democracy is the answer," said Yue Weiping. He thumped his hand on the top of the desk.

Liu Shao agreed. "Democracy has its share of problems, but none like China is dealing with now."

Liu Wei was still thinking hard. "If Zhao Ziyang prevails," he said, "we might get the reforms we deserve. If Deng Xiaoping refuses to buckle, we'll have a fight on our hands. Baiqiao Tang is right. Today, we must save our energy."

"But it's May 11!" cried Yue Weiping. "We haven't heard a peep from Beijing. I say we should take the next step forward. We can't allow our momentum to slow!"

"It's not going to slow," said Liu Wei. "Demonstrations have taken place almost daily since Hu Yaobang's death."

But Yue Weiping shook his head. "I don't like it. We need to know more of what's going on. We need to be closer to this."

"What are you saying?" said Liu Shao.

"We should send a delegate. Try to establish direct lines of contact to Tiananmen Square. They need to know that we're here and we're waiting. They need to know we'll lend our support the moment the time is right!"

"I agree," I said. Now all heads turned to me. Everyone looked surprised. "It's not a bad idea. Let's send someone to Beijing. They can tell the student leaders there that we in Changsha support them. The larger our web of contacts is, the more the movement can work as a unit."

Yue Weiping was nodding. "Fine," he said. "Then who should go?"

Liu Wei said, "I nominate Baiqiao Tang." I started to protest. He shook his head. "You are the SAF's chairman. Therefore you should represent us to our comrades in Beijing. Will you do it?"

I swallowed. They were bestowing an honor. Who was I to reject it?

"We fight for democracy," I said. "Therefore, we should comport ourselves as a democratic body. I accept your nomination. But let the federation vote. Only then can decisions be made."

Liu Wei smiled. "Your answer proves what I suspected: that you are the proper choice." He turned to the rest. "If anyone has another nominee to propose, please do so now."

No one offered additional names. Liu Wei nodded. "Then let us vote. Who supports the motion that our chairman, Baiqiao Tang, should go to Beijing and represent the Changsha Students Autonomous Federation to our comrades in Tiananmen Square?"

The vote was unanimous. I was going.

7

I had been to Beijing before in the summer of the previous year on a student government junket. During that trip, I met a number of student leaders from Beijing Normal University. I was certain they'd put me up if I asked and provide me with access to high-level leaders. But I tried calling them again and again on the phone; I couldn't reach a soul. One look at the TV told you why. Beijing was in an uproar. Tiananmen Square was packed. My friends were most likely there.

We convened the SAF leaders to weigh the odds. We decided that I should proceed to Beijing without a concrete itinerary. In other words, I wasn't sure whom I would meet with, how, or when, or where I would stay. I was flying by the seat of my pants and hoping they wouldn't rip. I scheduled myself to leave on May 13.

But shortly before that happened, we heard a report on TV. The student leaders in Beijing had decided on an official reaction to Deng Xiaoping's editorial. They were mounting a hunger strike.

In many ways, this was an apt response. There is power in self-deprivation. Mahatma Gandhi understood it. So did Dr. Martin Luther King. Both great leaders knew that peace can never come from a gun. It takes an inner revolution. Peace through sacrifice. By practicing self-deprivation, you show your opponent the strength of your convictions. You are saying you'd rather harm yourself than anyone else when effecting change.

A hunger strike was the perfect rebuttal to Deng Xiaoping's accusations. His editorial had insinuated that demonstrators were dangerous. But how? Our rallies had continued for weeks; the number of people participating in them had grown to epic proportions. And yet, apart from those two unfortunate incidents, there had been no violence at all. We hoped our actions would dare Deng Xiaoping to reconsider his stance. We wanted to show him that we meant no harm to the Party or to the nation. We only wanted to open talks. We were willing to follow the law, provided the law could be reasonable.

The SAF was very excited. We decided Changsha would participate in the hunger strike as well, to show our solidarity.

"And it's perfectly timed," said Liu Wei.

I nodded. He was right. The hunger strike would coincide with a visit by Mikhail Gorbachev. At that time, Gorbachev was general secretary of the Communist Party of the Soviet Union. His visit to Beijing would mark the first visit to China by a Russian head of state since the 1960s. Five thousand members of the international press were scheduled to be in Beijing. The journalists' cameras would capture the students' protest on film, or so we hoped.

But now I was torn. The SAF was aboil with motion. The hunger strike was due to commence on May 13, the day I was scheduled to leave. Where is my proper place? I wondered. Where can I be the most help? In Changsha, leading the SAF? Or in Beijing, dropping by unannounced, hoping to strengthen our ties with the core of leadership there?

I asked Liu Wei. "Should I still depart?"

"You must," he said, quite firmly. "Don't worry about us, Baiqiao Tang, you've left us excellent plans. The SAF will see this through. You must go to Beijing and show our support. Show them how much we are with them."

I agreed, and continued preparing to go.

On May 13, Beijing once again acted like a stone dropped into a pool. Ripples undulated out from the hunger strike in Tiananmen Square, washing across the country. I can't say how many students turned out to participate nationwide. Millions, would be my guess. I know that, in Changsha alone, two thousand students starved themselves while hundreds of thousands of people demonstrated in other ways. They came to the city from outlying regions and assembled in two locations predetermined by the SAF. Some took up posts in May 1st Square, outside the government buildings. Others went to the train station so we could not be ignored. Anyone entering or leaving Changsha would have to stop and look.

The students depriving themselves of food were our martyrs, our heroes. The SAF called attention to their sacrifice by mounting another march through the city, this one bigger than ever before. On May 4, the populace had merely been angry. Now they were inflamed. Since I had already boarded my train, I had to rely on Liu Wei's descriptions told to me later on.

He said that people were chanting and holding up signs and beating on drums, but still without any violence. This was an unstated rule, he said, to which everyone cheerfully adhered. By this point, several prominent university faculty members had joined the cause. One in particular was Professor Peng Yuzhang. Professor Peng was an elderly man, a longtime teacher at Hunan University. Close to retirement age, he was bespectacled and wise, with a wry, kind face. He had always supported democracy, even before he officially joined the WAF. In fact, he'd often advised me on the best course the SAF should take. This wonderful old man liked to participate in sit-ins. He even took part in the hunger strike.

"For the people!" he would cry. "For democracy! For China!" His spirit was ebullient, far younger than his failing body. The protestors, plucky from their recent success, giddy with hopes for the days to come, would mimic the Party-approved response to proper Communist doctrine.

"Professor Peng!" the crowd would shout. "A very good example!"

The hunger strike was scheduled to last one week. That first day in Changsha, police did nothing to stop the crowds. Liu Wei said that one look at the security guards' faces told the whole tale. They'd lost control and they knew it. But more than that: they sympathized. Their wages had been frozen, too. They lived in deplorable apartments with no money to purchase new clothes or shoes, no future to look forward to. In many cases, police were no longer reporting for duty. And where were the bureaucrats? Departed like evening shadows that flee from the hot light of day. Liu Wei said the Changsha march arrived at May 1st Square to find the government offices empty. The CCP was losing its grip. The nation was wriggling free.

"We've done it!" cried Shui Lianan.* He was a standing committee member from Hunan University, and also my very good friend. The leaders of the SAF were standing in the empty government offices in May 1st Square, claiming them for the movement.

Sober Liu Wei made a steeple with his fingers. "Now comes the hard part," he said.

Shui Lianan calmed himself and nodded. "Now we have to hold on."

They went back outside to watch the hunger strike commence.

A dissident named Geng Zhi* made a speech on the steps in front of the government buildings. The strikers had lined up before him, a wall of flesh that was soon to be reduced. The speech ended—applause, applause—then the strikers began their fast. They would not eat for the next seven days. They would sleep outside, exposed to the sky, refusing to leave their posts. Many would swoon and fall after only three or four days. Ambulances would screech on in, the attendants disembarking, gathering bodies like cordwood and stacking them into the backs of the vehicles, driving them to hospitals where physicians could attend them. But none of the strikers broke their pledge. They all continued their fast. The meaning of their actions was clear: these patriots would harm themselves before they raised a fist against China.

By that point, I had boarded the Number Two special express train bound for Beijing. My world just then was the throaty hiss of brakes, the wheeze and squeal of *click-clacking* metal as the train rattled on and on up the tracks. A hard seat and an aching back for more than a thousand miles, about twenty hours all told.

And what, I wondered over and over, would happen when I arrived?

8

Beijing is the jewel of Hebei Province. The city was formerly known as Peking, but how many names has she borne? Zhongdu. Daidu. Beiping. Dadu. Marco Polo called her Cambuluc, a fact that Beijingers prefer to forget. How long has she stood? No one can say. Fossils found in the silent caves of Dragon Bone Hill point to human occupation some twenty thousand years ago. Emperors rose and emperors fell. Beijing has outstood them all. She was burned to the ground by the Mongols. Rebuilt by Kublai Khan. Captured by the Mings, who built the Temple of Heaven in her center. Years later, a gate was added to guard the temple's entrance. The plaza before it: *Tian'anmen Guangchang*. Heaven's Gate, or Tiananmen Square. A symbol of all that is China.

Beijing is the very hub of the nation. Skyscrapers jab toward the sky in the heart of the business district. At night, they resemble gleaming daggers scraping at heaven's breast. But next to these modern monstrosities are the palaces, temples, tombs, and fountains. Sculptures of stone with faces worn smooth. The architectural treasures bequeathed by an age forgotten by man, still standing under the iron sky.

The city sprawls carelessly under such tokens. Far-flung districts serve as home to twenty million people. Crowded streets rattle with the *cheeng cheeng* of bike bells, as well as the chatter of Cantonese, Mandarin, and dozens of dialects, ripping and clashing like teeth on gears unevenly hung. Silk clothes sway on hangers from racks outside the clothier shops. The smell of smoke and spices wafts from restaurants, tea houses, side street bodegas. Ancient pavements of crackled cobblestone entwine with twentieth-century blacktop. Pigeons strut and bob their heads, pecking trash from the ground. You can spend a single day in Beijing and feel like you've lived through a whole other life.

I arrived in the city just before midnight, the evening of May 14. The hunger strike was under way. I had already heard updates broadcast over the loudspeaker system of my train car. This was not a normal occurrence. Public service announcements had always been pro-CCP. Hearing the train's announcer detailing a nationwide hunger strike highlighted two important themes. First, it told me the railways, and therefore most of the workers, had sided with students and intellectuals, and therefore the lenient, rightist stance adopted by Zhao Ziyang. Second: that despite the CCP's stance, the country was already sliding toward change.

The train station in Beijing is like a city within a city. I found my way out and hailed a cab and headed for Beijing Normal. My plan was to meet an old friend, Tang Linghua, who was no relation to me. I'd known Tang when he was an undergraduate at Hunan Normal. Now he was at Beijing Normal for graduate studies, and a very active participant in the pro-democracy movement. Tang had hosted me on my trip to Beijing in 1988. I knew how to get to his dormitory. I told the driver to head that way.

The city we passed was like a carnival. Marchers and chanters mobbed the streets. Signs flickered like strobes under the halogen street lamps.

"CHINESE PEOPLE DESERVE TO PARTICIPATE IN THEIR GOVERNMENT!"

"CHINA NOW OR CHINA LATER? WHICH DO YOU THINK IT SHOULD BE?"

And all the bodies! I'd never seen so many. Row after row. Wall after wall. Throngs so thick you could walk half the city by stepping on people's shoulders.

Surely, we will win, I thought. How can we do anything but?

Tang Linghua was not at home, but his roommates let me in. They told me he'd gone to Tiananmen Square and hadn't been back for days. Before then, he'd rush in for a few minutes, mostly to collect supplies, then dash back out to rejoin the mob, which, at that point, ruled the city. Yes, I could stay in his room, they said, remembering me from the summer. They introduced me to mid-level student leaders, all of them breathless, exuberant, back from the square, feeling certain the battle was being won. They were thrilled to hear of our strike in Changsha, another brilliant point of light in a constellation spreading out, forming the shape of China.

And so began my ad hoc adventure. Evenings were spent huddled in meetings with leaders from Beijing University, Beijing Normal, the Beijing University of Technology, and the China Institute of Industrial Relations. Days were spent marching the city streets, watching citizens leave their shops and offices, their factories, their apartments. Cheering us on. Some of them weeping. Some of them offering food. We were the new People's Army, soldiers who had no need for guns. Troops representing a nation's conscience, urged on by our countrymen.

Our columns would snake and twist and wind through the maze of downtown Beijing. Though Tiananmen Square was only five miles away, our route took three or four hours. In the square, we would join the milling crowds in a carnival of protest. The demonstrations had snowballed by then, the same way they had in Changsha. Students were joined by thousands of workers of varying professions whose banners read like a listing from the local department of commerce. The Beijing Steelworkers. Beijing Journalists. Beijing Bankers. Beijing Automakers. Though everyone shouted for different demands, they were largely the same at their core. Freedom of speech. A free, investigative press. End corruption and undue political influence. Better pay for everyone. Better working conditions. More voice in government affairs.

The square was choked with people shouting, chanting, and singing. They held up signs and played guitars and pounded on makeshift drum sets made from plastic buckets used in construction. You could look across that great expanse and see the Monument to the People's Heroes rising like a lighthouse over a sea of black-haired heads. Our column, like a river flowing, merged with this churning sea. You could smell the salt of sweating bodies. Clear sky overhead. Our voices like the roar of waves and cackled like the cries of gulls. The mass of us rocked in a to-and-fro motion, like water never-ending.

My group and I would spend a few hours, then start the long walk back to campus where we would debate for the rest of the night the proper way to advance our cause and how best to use the following day.

I lost a lot of weight that week from all the walking. This, coupled with the fact that I had no appetite. Still, disappointment filled my guts. The movement in Beijing was large, there was no denying that. The whole city was in an uproar. But I felt that it was doomed to fail and hated myself for thinking that.

How could I be so pessimistic? Simple reasons. One: I never got a chance to meet with Tang Linghua during my seven days in Beijing. He'd sequestered himself in Tiananmen Square, along with about three thousand other high-level student leaders participating in the hunger strike. These student leaders had set up their own security teams that barred anyone from disturbing them, including family, friends, loved ones, and supporters. Not even messengers were allowed from without. I thought this move ridiculous, a brand-new form of elitism. These three thousand Beijing student leaders had formed their very own cadre. No one else was allowed into their ranks, nor did these leaders acknowledge the protests raging clear across China. Their message, to me, seemed clear. *This is our fight. The glory is ours! Watch us take on the CCP! Cheer us on and celebrate!*

Bitter congratulations were due. Hurray for you, Beijing! You've replaced governmental insularity with your own. By secluding yourself, you cannot unite the nation that stands behind you.

I was not the only student leader visiting Beijing. I ran into many more from almost every province, and all had the same basic gripe. *We have thousands of people ready to help. Together we can turn this tide. Tell us how we can lend a hand!* But no liaison came forth. Without this bond, without this solidarity in function as well as spirit, I felt the movement would surely collapse. Logic said that it must.

Another problem I saw in Beijing: leaders were being overthrown daily, usurped by up-and-comers who clawed their way through the ranks, hoping to seize a moment of glory, desperate for recognition and power. It happened almost hourly in the group I was with from Beijing Normal. We heard it was also taking place with the leadership starving themselves in the square. No unity. Only chaos. This infighting led to a massive dilution of power and direction. The CCP, I felt sorry to say, would not have to work very hard to topple our movement. Our leaders seemed more than willing to topple it for them.

I remember a march I took one day toward the end of my trip. We were walking through the streets. The cacophony still raged, but I noticed demands had changed. Students now opposed each other. Different factions shouted, *Desist! We must return to class!* Others said, *No! If we leave Tiananmen Square, we die! The CCP will kill us for what we have done.* Another group cried, *Stop the hunger strike! You'll only hurt yourselves.* Others said, *No! The hunger strike must persist at all costs!*

That's when I knew that Beijing had fallen. The government had lost control, but sadly, so had we. This latter revelation frightened me most of all.

9

While all of this was going on, Zhao Ziyang flew back to the country from Pyongyang. He'd been to North Korea on an official visit with Kim Il Sung. Seizing upon Zhao's absence, Deng and other CCP hardliners had labeled the protests a full-scale "counterrevolution," a term they'd chosen with purpose. Legally, a counterrevolution could be quelled by military force. Deng Xiaoping was setting up an endgame he could win.

Upon his arrival, Zhao examined the situation and wasted no time throwing himself into the debate. He argued that the protests were inevitable, given the CCP's policies. He urged the Politburo not to see this as an "uprising." If anything, this was an opportunity for progress and self-examination. China, Zhao said, should take this moment to steer toward greater reforms, a more democratic society.

Zhao set to work putting student leaders in touch with Party officials. He urged the media to cover the protests without censorship. He even prepared legislation aimed at legalizing the same. The people rallied hard behind him, but alas, it was not to be. The CCP cast Zhao as an upstart. They said he was trying to break from the Party and readied themselves to depose him.

The situation came to a head on the night of May 16. Zhao Ziyang met with Gorbachev. This was a momentous event in our history: Russia and China, together again, shaking hands after so many feuds. But Gorbachev's trip must have frightened him. On practically every street in Beijing, the Russian leader found his motorcade blocked by protestors, marching and shouting. Picture Gorbachev, sitting in the back of his limousine, looking out the tinted, bullet-proof windows, watching all the faces pass on this horrifying safari. He must have compared this situation to the one he was facing in Russia. At the moment, Soviet Communism had its own flood of woes. Could they erupt into something like this?

Then something shocking occurred. During his meeting with Gorbachev, Zhao Ziyang made it known that he was a puppet, nothing more. Deng Xiaoping, he said, was pulling the Party's strings and making all the decisions from the army's seat of command. The rest of the Politburo did Deng's bidding, dogs intent on satisfying the leader of the pack. Think of Chinese history as an old American film. Like Dorothy in *The Wizard of Oz*, Zhao had gone to the Emerald City and pulled back the curtain to show everyone the little man in the alcove. He wasn't some booming, magnified voice; he was old and feeble with withered lips and funny gadgets and buttons, the heart of this great and secret show.

Most Chinese had known it all along, but Zhao had cheerfully told this tale to a visiting head of state, and one with whom relations were strained. It was tantamount to blasphemy. Political suicide. The Party seized it as concrete proof that Zhao should henceforth be branded an enemy of the state.

Deng waited two full days until Gorbachev left Beijing. Then, on the evening of May 18, he summoned Zhao Ziyang to his home for an emergency meeting of the Politburo Standing Committee. No doubt advised to do so by Deng, the committee voted for martial law. Zhao cast the lone vote against. It was a token gesture, no more. By then, his fate was already sealed. He knew it, but he wasn't going quietly.

Several hours later, accompanied by supporters, Zhao appeared in Tiananmen Square with a bullhorn in his hand. He walked through the crowd like an angel wearing a Nehru collar. His white hair was close-cropped and flat to his skull as though he hadn't slept in days. His glasses were far too wide for his face, the lenses like twin picture windows peering into a soul in mourning. The ranks of Zhaos's inner circle formed a phalanx to either side of him. Another group brought up the rear, like an honor guard. Beside Zhao stood a man named Wen Jiabao, who served then as the director of the Central Party Office.

Zhao's speech was captured on film and broadcast by CCTV. His flickering image rose like a ghost from tens of millions of screens across China. "Students," he said. In Tiananmen Square, his amplified voice echoed far and wide. "We came too late. We are sorry. You talk about us. Criticize us. All of it is necessary." By "us" he meant the Politburo.

Zhao urged those students who were participating in the hunger strike to cease at once. Their efforts, he said, would damage their bodies, crippling them, perhaps for life. A hunger strike was in vain, he said. It would not change the Party's mind. That was a much longer process, he said, but one that he hoped had begun. "You are still young," Zhao said. "There are still many days ahead. You must live. Be healthy. Look ahead to a day when China accomplishes the Four Modernizations."

In this, Zhao appeared to be treading a long and narrow line. He was sympathizing with students while still upholding Deng's political initiatives. But any ambiguity as to where his sentiments lay were dispelled as he continued. "You are not like us," he said. "We are already old. It doesn't matter to us anymore."

Zhao noted that everyone in the square was acting for the good of the nation. However, the situation was out of control. He warned that serious consequences would surely result. Looking back, it seems so clear that Zhao Ziyang was trying to warn us. He already knew that the CCP had empowered themselves to use deadly force. Zhao concluded his speech by saying the government would maintain talks if the protestors left peacefully.

Zhao urged one and all to have patience. He closed by praising the courage the protestors had shown under such great adversity.

It was a very moving speech. But then, of course, it had to be. After that evening, Zhao Ziyang would never speak in public again. He was stripped of his offices and placed under house arrest. Deng replaced him as general secretary with a man named Jiang Zemin, the Party Chief of Shanghai. Jiang was an interesting choice for the job. He was famous for quelling unrest in Shanghai by shutting down a newspaper that had published articles criticizing China's economic future.

But I wasn't in Beijing by then. I left for the train station at 10 p.m. on the evening of May 19. I'd seen enough and had enough. I was going back to Changsha.

I remember standing on the platform waiting for my train to arrive. To pass the time, I wrote in my journal, expressing my disappointment. Zhao Ziyang was right, I thought. The hunger strike was accomplishing nothing. What was the point in starving ourselves? The CCP wouldn't listen to that. They wanted us to martyr ourselves. That way they could declare martial law.

In Tiananmen Square, I'd heard protestors shouting, Bring on the army! Die for the cause! Foolish, I thought. So foolish. Had martyrdom worked for Qu Yuan? No, it certainly hadn't. His kind of elegant sacrifice had proven itself ineffective even in ancient times. It would be ineffective now.

Here is a sample of what I wrote in my journal:

> The student leadership in Beijing has become a disorganized mob of in-fighters. New figures rise to prominence every time you blink and fall from grace just as quickly. What will this do for China?
>
> No one has drawn up a constitution. No one has any great plans. It's more like an orgy of ideas and egos. Everyone wants his pet reform and China indeed has many problems. But now we must bind the movement together. There must be something to give it cohesion and thrust or else it will never go anywhere.

I will go back to Changsha, I thought. I will try to do better. Perhaps I can lead the SAF to claim the next square on this chessboard.

In that moment, I had to admit that Teacher Gao had been right. I would never change China. But perhaps I could change my city. That, I thought, would be a good start.

The next day, my worst fears came to pass. On May 20, a man named Li Peng, the nation's premier, declared official martial law. He was acting on orders from Deng, no doubt. The tail that wags the dog. The People's Liberation Army was sent to seize Beijing. It was the first time in forty years they'd been asked to do so, an awful anniversary. Deng Xiaoping was closing the loop. With the army in control of the country, citizens could be shot on sight for trivial violations. And yet the protests continued to rage in Tiananmen Square. They continued to rage across China.

Later I heard an amazing thing: how the protestors blocked the army, not at just one street, but several. Mechanized convoys ground to a halt as citizens walked up to wide-eyed soldiers and shook their hands and smiled and laughed, offering food and water. Thank you for coming, the citizens said, but we really don't need you here. This situation is peaceful. Everything's under control. In fact, why don't you join us?

The soldiers were mostly country rubes conscripted into the ranks.

You could hardly blame them for that. Being a soldier was better by far than farming a patch of played-out dirt in some barren western province. How many of them had ever witnessed a city the size and breadth of Beijing? Few. Possibly none.

The protestors overwhelmed them, showing them simple kindness. Mao Zedong had famously said, "The people love the army and the army loves the people." And so, by wielding smiles and treats, Beijingers kept armored transports stalled for over three days. By which time, many local police had simply abandoned their posts. Sympathetic to the cause, they refused to stand against their own people.

It seemed like another win for us, but I was apprehensive. Each victory we achieved forced the Party to react. How they would do it was anyone's guess. But the CCP had never been known for gentleness or restraint.

10

Returning from Beijing, I was met by the very sober Liu Wei at the Changsha railway station. I'd hoped we could go directly to meet the other SAF leaders. I wanted to reconnect with my team and bring the committee up to speed on what I'd seen in Tiananmen Square. But Liu Wei carried bad news. "A schism has formed," he said. "Half the democracy protestors are here at the train station, as you see."

"And the others?" I asked.

"At May 1st Square. A student leader named Ren Jun* has seized control of that faction."

So, I thought. It is here, as well, this utter lack of unity. Our counter-revolution was birthing its own counterrevolution. "Take me to May 1st Square," I said. "Let's try to straighten this out."

We went to the government buildings, mounted the steps, and went inside. I already knew the plush red-carpeted halls and crystal chandeliers. Some twenty students were milling about in front of the governor's office. Some of them put up a fuss when we told them we wished to enter. Then one of them recognized Liu Wei and immediately dropped his eyes. Muttering, he told the others to let us pass. The crowd parted, desultory, confused. Liu Wei and I stepped through.

We found a leering young man sitting behind the governor's desk, arms crossed, his feet up. The heels of his shoes were indenting half moons in the flesh of the governor's ink blotter. The young man's demeanor called to my mind the arrogance of the Red Guard, those sharks that had prowled the aquarium of the Cultural Revolution—cocky killers with polished brass buttons and boots that shined like camera lenses, capturing pictures of cringing victims. Power is the ultimate narcotic, divorcing the mind from all things human, including a sense of proportion and compassion.

"You are Ren Jun?" I asked.

The young man leered at me. "Yes, I am! Who are you?"

Liu Wei's cheeks turned purple. It was the first and only time I had ever seen him angry, an occasion not to be missed. "Ren Jun!" he said. "This is Baiqiao Tang! Chairman of the SAF, who is just now back from Beijing!"

The leer on Ren's face faded at once, melting like snow in the gaze of the sun. "Oh!" he said. He dropped his eyes. He also dropped his feet off the desk. Sheepish, he stood up. "Of course. Well. Hello, Baiqiao Tang. Ah. How was your trip to Beijing?"

I struggled to wrestle my fury. I had just traveled well over six thousand *li* on behalf of our cause. My mission to connect with the Beijing student leaders had largely failed. Instead, I had found a city ruled by chaos and parasites, one of which was apparently here, in the midst of our work back home. "My trip to Beijing was fruitless," I said. "Or very nearly so."

Ren Jun nodded importantly. "Well," he said. "We've had our own share of problems here in Changsha. The movement has suffered a rift." He glared at Liu Wei when he said this.

"So I have heard," I said. "Doubtless, we can repair it."

It was clear to me that Ren Jun and I were men of two different elements. He was fire and I was water. These elements, though opposing, can sometimes mix with good result. Now would have to be one such occasion. I vowed to let my calm extinguish Ren Jun's heat. I saw right away that he would not fight. His time to play king was over.

But something else was bothering me. Was there a motive behind Ren's behavior? I knew a bit about him from what Liu Wei had told me. Ren was a student at Central-South Industrial, one of the government-appointed student leaders. In other words, he had worked for the Party. Was he working for them still?

It was difficult to judge, and I'd promised myself that I wouldn't. The SAF had plenty of members who'd once served as government cadres.

We'd taken them all at their word when they joined us and asked to be called autonomous. But now I wasn't so sure. How many were truly loyal to us, and how many were spying on us for the Party?

Later, I voiced this concern to a circle of people I trusted. All agreed that Ren Jun's status as student leader had sprung from inauspicious roots. However, while I was away in Beijing, Ren Jun had denounced the Party in public. His speech had been well received. In fact, everyone I talked to considered Ren Jun an asset to our movement and our purpose. A hot-head? Yes. Ambitious? Yes. But a man we were better off keeping as an ally, rather than an enemy.

Ren Jun eventually joined the SAF as General Director of Sit-Ins. His friend, Lu Qing,* joined our ranks as well. Eventually, Ren and I learned to respect each other. We even grew to be friends of a sort. And though we had no idea of it then, we were slated to share a destiny, but that wouldn't come until later.

11

Notes on the days that followed, as excerpted from my journal:

> May 24. Success! News arrives from all sources at once, such unbelievable news! The citizens of Beijing have convinced the People's Army to leave! Troops have retreated beyond city limits. There are practically no police left, nearly all have abandoned their posts. Reporters are saying that news henceforth will be broadcast freely, uncensored from here on out. Can it be that I was wrong? Is our hour truly at hand?

It was clearly an optimistic moment, and one that would later haunt me. Another journal entry:

> May 28. Here in Changsha, the SAF has decided to pull back from May 1st Square. I believe that staying in stolen offices only provokes the CCP. We have already made our point. Better to show them how gracefully our cause can hold the upper hand.

In Changsha, at least, it seemed very clear that the demonstrators had won. The government had sent no emissaries to parlay with us, no army to rout us, no police. The media reveled in newfound freedom. A reporter from CCTV was sent to engage me in an interview that was broadcast clear across China. During the segment, he took pains to note that our withdrawal from the government offices looked as though the SAF was quitting, a point that I refuted.

"Make no mistake," I said. "The Students Autonomous Federation is very much alive. We are not disbanding, we are merely standing down." Evidently, we were the first organization across the country to do so. When asked why we were doing this, I said, "We want to allow the government time to assess our actions. We hope they will notice that we have not resorted to violence. We are sincere citizens looking for peaceful change."

But then, some shocking news arrived. An official from Zhao Ziyang's Office of Political Reform leaked something that Deng Xiaoping had said in a recent meeting to the press. Evidently, this meeting had centered on ways to suppress the movement. And Deng's advice had been "We must kill two hundred thousand to obtain twenty years of peace." Other official sources confirmed that Deng had made the comment. One man in particular was arrested and charged with "revealing state secrets and counterrevolutionary propagandizing." He was sentenced to seven years' isolation to be served at Qincheng maximum security prison. The SAF discussed this in counsel.

"You see where this is going?" said Ren Jun. "The bastards have said all along they'd use force!"

"I disagree," said Liu Wei. "Given the state of the country right now, they would never dare such a thing."

I admitted Deng's comment sounded far-fetched. Surely he wasn't advocating mass murder to quell a peaceful movement. But then, why had that government official been arrested for reporting what he'd heard?

Over the next few days, we shifted our focus and published magazine articles, newspaper pieces, flyers, all kinds of literature. Members of the SAF passed out pamphlets on street corners, boulevards, and parks. We held regular meetings and set plans for growth and acquired a loudspeaker system to better broadcast our message at gatherings. We created new positions and elected talented people to fill them. We worked on strengthening ties with other student leaders throughout Hunan, as well as clear across China. And, although it seemed unthinkable, we set up a tier of replacement leaders in case SAF officers were arrested.

This was a fruitful time. We knew we were making a difference. My journal entry for May 30 reads:

> Things are going quite well in Changsha but I worry about Beijing. The CCP has lost face. I hope the protestors understand that to force this issue any further would be ungracious.

Looking back through the lens of years, knowing the end before it began—what would you give to change the past? How much is a country's salvation worth?

This is my final journal entry before everything fell apart:

> June 2. Heard a radio broadcast while in the student government offices. Another hunger strike in Tiananmen Square, this one led by a popular singer, Hou Dejian—the one who writes songs about dragons. And three intellectuals with him. The report said demonstrators in the Square have renewed their vigor. I do not like the sound of this.

Close to midnight the very next day, June 3, 1989. I was exhausted after a full day of meetings. It takes so much work to create a new life. Such a great commitment.

Then I heard a knock on my door. I opened it and saw Liu Shao standing in the corridor of my dorm, his face as pale as ashes. Tears stood in his haunted eyes. "Baiqiao Tang," he said. He was choking, barely able to speak. "The army. In Beijing. Opened fire."

part four

Fugitive

1

Here is what we eventually heard: Deng Xiaoping had called in several thousand more troops, this time from different brigades. These were no country rubes, these were shock troops, trained to shoot on sight if that's what they were told to do. They approached Beijing from the city's corners and moved toward the center, angling toward Tiananmen Square. But word spread fast. The people set up makeshift barricades on major roads. They hoped to repeat their performance, placing flowers in the barrels of rifles, offering soldiers tea and dumplings, asking about their families. They would talk about life in other provinces, thank the soldiers for coming, but say no thanks, the PLA wasn't needed here.

On the western edge of the city, in a district called Muxidi, an armed contingent passed the apartments of several high-ranking officials. Protestors saw the army coming and rushed out to meet them with open arms, smiling, calling out hellos, and waving for them to stop. The army opened fire.

Imagine the rattle of Kalashnikovs, and soft lead bullets the length of a thumb tearing through unarmed flesh. The soldiers fired right into the crowds, dropping them at point-blank range. Armaments made for battlefields were used on innocent crowds. Ricochets killed wives in their kitchens as they bent over stoves, preparing the next day's meal. Tanks roared and pressed forward, rolling over bodies, leaving the asphalt stained with red, the pulp of an abattoir. The troops and the tanks pressed on toward the square. The horror had just begun.

The rest of the SAF leaders and I stayed by the radio all through the night, taking breaks only to consult the TV, to answer the fax machine or the phone. We couldn't believe the dark history unfolding. Ironically, by that point, the demonstrations in Tiananmen Square had tapered off. The ambiance there, from all reports, was more like a street fair than a political rally. Young lovers would stroll along, hand in hand, wanting to see what was going on. Families brought their children, the fathers letting their youngest kids ride piggyback on their shoulders. "See how important this is?" they were saying. "This is a lesson, my daughter, my son. This is your country. Get involved. Take a stand and state your case. Stand up for yourself and your people." It was a gorgeous summer evening. Saturday night in Beijing.

The radio said the troops had reached Tiananmen Square and dismounted. The citizens had heard the rumors of violence but probably didn't believe they were true. Why should they? It was unthinkable. *The people love the army and the army loves the people.* Reports said some of them walked right up to the soldiers to ask what was going on. The soldiers leveled their rifles and fired.

Since our government offered no coverage, we listened to the BBC and the Voice of America. Reports said the wounded lay everywhere. People would dart in and grab them and start to drag them away. The soldiers would shoot the rescuers. Tracer bullets sliced through the night. Ambulances pulled up, red lights flashing. Paramedics would pour out and get shot down in their tracks. Days later, eyewitnesses reported seeing soldiers piling bodies into hillocks of flesh and burning them in mass funeral pyres, pushing back people who came too close to see what was going on.

My fellow student leaders and I were breathless, weeping like frightened children, hanging on every word. I have never felt so impotent, so incredibly confused. Was this some kind of terrible joke? Not at all. Come morning, things got worse. Now students were leaping in front of tanks on the Boulevard of Eternal Peace. The big machines rolled over them in the purple light of dawn. The Chinese Red Cross released a report saying well over three thousand people lay dead. They released another a few hours later, saying they'd gotten it wrong. The announcers spoke in clipped, tense tones, like men being held at gunpoint. They apologized for their error, then replaced their earlier numbers with CCP official statistics. "A few civilians were wounded, that's all. Actually, more soldiers were hurt than rioters. . . ."

It was nonsense, but who could argue? Foreign reporters were herded like cattle and hustled out of the country, their notebooks, recorders, and pens confiscated. In hotel lobbies across the city, the cords of phones they were dictating into got cut by secret police wielding scissors.

Impossibly, protestors stayed in the square. Hovering on the outskirts, they waited to see what would happen next, jeering at soldiers who, acting on orders, would level their rifles and fire again. Again. And again. The horror crept into the late afternoon, when the sky went gray and a light rain fell, tears from heaven soaking the city. The soldiers finally ceased and withdrew, though some stayed behind to uphold martial law.

Hundreds, possibly thousands lay dead. Innocents shot in cold blood by the army pledged to protect them. The hopes of China had been extinguished.

"What do we do?" said Liu Wei.

No one in the council answered.

"The options are basic," said Ren Jun at last. "Continue our actions. Or cease."

"And if we continue?" asked Liu Shao. "What then? How many will we lose?"

He was voicing the fears we all had imagined. Government troops arriving in Changsha. Pouring out of armored transports. Forming phalanxes. Declaring war on the populace—a full military crackdown. How many would die in our city? In Shanghai? Wuhan? Xi An? Cheng Du? Guangzhou? Changchun? How many more martyrs? How many more souls? How much is a country's agony worth?

"Continue," I said. "We continue. After all we have lost, how can we do anything but?"

Everyone nodded agreement.

So the SAF led demonstrations on June 4, June 5, June 6, and June 7, a lamentable dirge of days. But people flooded the streets of China as news of the massacre traveled fast. Hundreds of thousands of people turned out: students, farmers, workers, and children. Men and women. The aged. A new revolution had just begun.

Each day in Changsha, the SAF and the WAF were joined by hundreds of thousands of citizens. Everyone grieved for our sister city, but still no violence was ever reported, no retribution was sought. We'd had enough of that under Mao. We swore not to regress to his ways, or to Deng's. China's lovely hands, we thought, were already stained too dark with blood. Among people of good character, some instincts always prevail. One of them is the outright refusal to compound darkness with darkness.

Each day, those police who had not yet abandoned their posts turned out to watch us. They stood in their uniforms, stiff as statues with downcast eyes, their poses conflicted. You could see that they were ashamed to be called security officers in a state where life was valued so cheaply. None of them offered a whisper to stop us, as if they possibly could. A handful to hold back half a million? Not likely.

I watched one guardsman take off his cap and place it on the pavement beside him. He took off his tie and folded it up and slid it into his pocket. Then he stepped off the curb and joined our march as it wound through the streets of Changsha. It was another successful revolution. We took them one at a time.

The last demonstration I organized was called the Oath-Taking Rally in Memory of the Beijing Martyrs. It was held at the Changsha railway station on June 8, in the afternoon. It turned out to be the last big rally that anyone held across China to protest what had happened. I cohosted the event with a visiting head of the Beijing Students Autonomous Federation, a man named Zhang Xin.* Zhang was touring throughout southern China, rallying student and worker support, inspiring them to continue their stance against the CCP.

The Hong Kong media reported that one hundred and forty thousand people were in attendance that day, including many Westerners—mostly students, teachers, and tourists. But no media. By then, all foreign journalists had been deported or neutered. Those who worked for the newswires were terrified and rightly so at being arrested, or worse.

Here are some excerpts from the last speech I made before my capture. I spoke directly to all those ghosts, the spirits of martyrs who haunted Beijing:

Was it the spirit of Qu Yuan from more than two thousand years ago that took you away? Spirits of Beijing, where do you rest? Qu Yuan, his heart afire with loyal ardor, leapt into the pitiless Miluo River. Today, two thousand years later, you, our loyal brothers and sisters, fell under the guns of the so-called "people's own soldiers." You fell under the tanks of "the most cherished ones."

June 4, 1989! Every common man and woman who seeks freedom, democracy, and peace will remember the day forever. China's national day of everlasting shame . . .

In Tiananmen Square, three thousand lives were wiped out in a single night. You were the sons and daughters of loving parents. You were the students of proud teachers. You were brothers. Sisters. Friends. Sometimes even enemies. But how many dreams you still had to dream! How many poems yet to discover! You would have been fathers and mothers. You had more roads to travel.

You shall always live in our hearts. You shall live forever in history. Fearless and proud, you died standing up. Look now: those who escaped with their lives already have come forward. Look! Out from the bloody rain and the fetid wind. Look! They are your brothers. Fathers. Teachers. Friends. They have stood up, too. And they will not forget you. None of us will forget.

As long as the truth is in our hearts, we will not fear that our blood will be shed. You have shown us what sacrifice is. We hereby make a solemn vow to never turn away from our goal.

Thanks to the SAF's microphone, my voice rose like thunder and echoed across the Changsha railway plaza. It crouched like a storm about to burst over a sea of black-haired heads. At the end of my speech, I called for the hanging of Premier Li Peng, and declared that Deng Xiaoping should be sacrificed on the people's altar in the name of justice. The Party must have been listening. A few days after I made this pronouncement, I found out that I was a wanted man.

2

By June 12, there was a message in every newspaper, on every TV channel, crackling over the radios. "If you are a student leader, a member of the so-called Students Autonomous Federation, go at once to your local police station. Register yourself. You will be asked to report on what involvement, if any, you had in the June 4th Counterrevolutionary Riot."

That's what they were calling it already, a riot, not a massacre.

"This also goes for members of the so-called Workers Autonomous Federation. You must comply with this request for the benefit of your nation. Go at once. You have nothing to fear."

Doubtful, I thought. The purge had started.

For safety's sake, I abandoned my dorm and stayed with a friend named Lu You.* Lu served as a director of a certain well-known institute for durable goods that was famous throughout Hunan Province. His apartment was near Helong Sports Stadium about a mile from the Xiang River in Changsha's southern district. Liu Shao came to find me there, the angel of dread confirmation. "Some people have been taken," he said.

"Who?" I asked.

Liu Shao began to rattle off names. Some were from the SAF's roster, but many more came from the WAF. The workers who'd been arrested were professors, entrepreneurs, labor leaders, and well-known intellectuals. Some, on the media's orders, had gone to register with the police, who took them into custody. More were detained on the city streets by security guards and cadres. Some had been abducted. We heard reports of vans pulling up and doors rolling back. Arms would reach out and snatch bodies off corners, at intersections, in front of shops and eateries. The vans would zoom off in a weal of tires, leaving a reeking blue cloud of exhaust that dissipated, then vanished.

This was the crackdown we all had feared, rising up like a beast in the daylight, rapacious, with a bottomless gullet, devouring all that it hunted. At night, the horror was even worse. People were stolen right out of their beds, disappearing like figments. Dawn would break, showing all traces gone, as though they had never existed. Their work lay forgotten, even their names lost substance atom by atom until there was nothing left. And still the Party's message repeated, inane as a broken record. "Student leaders: turn yourselves in. Government officials would like to speak to you. Fill out a full report on what part, if any, you played in this tragedy. Help us set the record straight."

"What do we do?" said Liu Shao.

"I don't know," I said, and I meant it. Confusion felt like a cowl pulled over my eyes, caulking my ears. Which way to turn? I had no idea. The messages kept coming. If anything, they were now more insistent.

Another day went by. Then two. I stopped going outside, believing that people were staring at me in the streets. Why not? How many people knew I'd been involved? Who would buckle first to the pressure? Old friends? Family members? Which of those in my inner circle would take a bribe and make the first phone call? Should I run? Should I hide? Where on earth would I go? No place seemed safe anymore.

Liu Shao appeared again at Lu You's doorstep. This time, he was accompanied by Lu Qing and several others. Lu You let them in, and we held a hushed palaver over cups of tea.

"Liu Wei left for Hong Kong this morning." Liu Shao stared at the tips of his shoes and forced his next words out. "I'm starting to think that's the right thing to do."

"He might not make it," Lu Qing said. "Hong Kong is the obvious play. They'll catch him at the border."

There followed a spirited, pointless debate on the merits and faults of fleeing the country.

"Stop it," I said. "One thing at a time. For now, we must look to our safety. Anyone still staying in the dorms or on school grounds should leave there at once and hide. Tell them not to show themselves until we know our next move."

Everyone nodded, agreeing. They left Lu's apartment and went underground, along with so many others. The evening of June 12 saw dissidents melting away like ghosts. We had all scratched telephone numbers into notebooks with coded entries, forming an ad hoc secrecy protocol. The phone lines, we knew, could be tapped. The CCP had done it before. The entire Cultural Revolution had been the Party's party line.

I stayed with Lu You for the next two days, feeling it was safe. Lu had been very active in his community. He'd marched for democracy, but then so had half a million others. He wasn't a leader of students or workers. He wasn't easily linked to me. He tried to help me however he could. He was a very smart man, and wise, but even he was unsure what to do. "There are many possibilities," he mused. "So many possibilities."

Yes, I thought. Of course there are. But I needed better counsel than that, and fast, if I was to have any chance.

The messages kept arriving, coming from every direction at once. Printed on posters plastered on walls. Faces speaking from TV screens. Newspaper headlines. Radio voices floating on breezes wherever you walked. Wherever you turned, the same admonitions: "Student leaders! The government wants to talk to you. Go to your local police department. Register yourself. You have nothing to fear. Cooperate. You have nothing to fear. . . ."

The more insistent they became, the more I realized how doomed I was. I decided I would flee.

The railroad was the easiest and fastest way out of Changsha. I told Lu You what I wanted to do. "The train?" he asked. He shook his head. "That's not a smart move. Put yourself in the Party's shoes. If you were looking for people who've gone underground, who might be trying to run, what's the first place you'd start watching?"

He was right, of course. The train station could be a trap. But then I had an idea. I took a bus and found a pay phone and called up a contact I'd made from the marches, a man who'd become my very good friend, Pan Mingdong, vice chair of the WAF.

Picture a giant in oil-stained coveralls whose smile is the size of China's east coast, whose hands are each as big as Australia, whose chest is broad as the engine barrel on the locomotives he fixed. Pan was as strong as a locomotive, too. His eyes were huge and dark and bovine. His teeth stabbed out in hectic lines as though from the mouth of a great white shark. Pan's was a very scary face, and one you would never forget, especially when he smiled, which happened a lot. He was as kind as he was ugly, somewhere in his early forties, the older brother I never had, and no stranger at all to being at odds with the Chinese Communist Party.

Pan's father had been one of the earliest members of the Communist Party. He'd been one of Mao's contemporaries, but the two men had clashed over some vital issue, and Mao, who'd never been big on rivals, branded Pan's father a counterrevolutionary and ordered him executed. Many years after killing him, the Party relented their stance and cleared Pan's father's name, declaring him posthumously rehabilitated. The Party even hosted a little reception for friends and family in Pan's hometown. Pan's father, they said, was no villain at all. He was a very good example, though occasionally deluded.

"Bastards," Pan would hiss to me. He never held his emotions back, even when we first met. "Occasionally deluded? Ha! My father knew right from wrong!"

Pan's uncle was also a famous CCP leader. His name was Pan Hanlian, and he was once the vice mayor of Shanghai, as well as a head of the Party's intelligence unit prior to 1949. In other words, Pan's whole family had deep roots in the Party. But, like good trees everywhere, they were often cut down to make room for progress. And so it was with Pan Mingdong. The Party branded him a traitor and hunted him during the Cultural Revolution.

The way they apprehended him is a very famous story. Pan had always loved a good brawl, a dangerous thing for a man his size, not to mention his training. Pan had served as a boxing coach under Hunan's provincial commission for Physical Education. In other words, he was a *gung fu* master and more than willing to put on displays of his talent and his strength.

When CCP operatives came after Pan back in the late 1960s, he led them on a merry chase to the top of the Tianxige Wall, an ancient section of stonework in an even more ancient part of Changsha. Three or four stories up in the air, the soldiers converged on Pan, who punched the first one so hard, the man fell and hit the ground below. Pan was arrested and tortured in prison. The guards hit his face so many times, they splayed his teeth out in all directions, creating his shark-like smile.

I called Pan up on a pay phone and told him what I was thinking of doing. "Am I crazy?" I said. "Am I out of my mind?" Hoping that he would refute me.

Pan just laughed. His great booming voice was an earthquake rumbling over the phone. "*Xiao* Tang!" he said. "If you're crazy, so am I! Where are you now?"

I told him, wincing at having to state my location over the line. "Wait where you are," said Pan. "I'm coming right now to get you."

He showed up a little while later, driving his *muotuoche*; in Mandarin, "motorbike." His bike just sat there *put-put-putting*. Pan gestured me over. I hurried. "Get on," he said. "I'm glad that you called. We must be careful, *Xiao* Tang. I called ahead and spoke to some colleagues. The news is not very good. The stations are full of government agents. The Party has armed them with photos and lists of dissidents' names. If anyone checks our papers, we're finished."

"We?" I said.

Pan nodded. "I'm coming with you. Both our names are on that list."

"But this is insane!" I said, feeling ill. My stomach had dropped to my toes. "You just said that they'll check our papers. There's no hope we can leave Hunan."

"Not true," said Pan Mindong. He grinned. "Difficult, yes. But impossible? No."

"Then how?" I asked.

He revved the engine. "I have a plan. We'll drive along the busiest streets but stay off the main roads the closer we get to the station. I know a back avenue we can use. No one will be watching it. It's only used by railroad employees, many of whom are members of the WAF. They'll get us around the damned police and onto a train without anyone checking our papers."

His tone was so confident. I started to think we might have a chance. "But where will we go?" I asked.

"Guangzhou," he said. "For certain, we go to Guangzhou. I have friends there who will help us. Are you getting on or not?"

3

How do I remember that trip? Pan's hands on the wheel, his eyes on the road as we wove in and out of traffic. The crass snarl of his *muotuoche*. The wind blowing full in our face. No one paid much attention to us. We were just another dragonfly riding among the swarm, another cacophonous *muotuoche* burping our smoke at the air of Changsha.

Pan had been right, of course. There were no troops guarding the back avenue. We got to the station without any issue. Pan parked his *muo-*

tuoche, got off, and knelt down as though he were checking the engine. He bade me kneel beside him. "Take out your notebook," he said.

I did, and Pan made me write down the names and numbers and addresses of his contacts.

"Guard them," he said. He didn't say why. There was no need. We both understood. With that, we got up and started walking.

Pan led us to a group of railway workers who were hanging around smoking cigarettes out front of the station. They looked at Pan and one of them nodded. Pan nodded back. No one said a word. Two of the workers pared off from the rest and started to walk away. Pan and I fell in behind them.

I have no idea what Changsha railway station is like now. Back then, it was the biggest train station in the country, a huge courtyard, very simple. Travelers bought their tickets inside a building, which our worker guides ignored. They took us directly into the square where passengers lingered, taking seats, or buying cigarette packs from booths while their train got ready to leave.

The two railway workers led us straight to the heart of the square, which was thick with a throng of people. Abruptly, the two men turned to us. "Good luck," said one. The other pressed tickets into our hands, then both walked away at an even pace. Neither man looked back. You'd have had to be watching them closely to know that anything had transpired.

Our train was about to board passengers. I looked at the big steel worm in its trough and wondered, Can I do it? Can I really leave Hunan and flee south like a common criminal? Misgivings began to occur to me. I needed to check one more thing.

"Wait here," I said.

Pan shot me a look. "Where are you going?"

"To make a call."

Pan's eyes went wide in disbelief. He shook his head and snorted, but he motioned me toward a pay phone. "Over there," he grunted. "But damn it, make it quick!"

I wandered over, picked up the phone, and called the local police.

I had a relative who worked for the government—I won't say what bureau. Calling him was a risky move. This relative was very high up in the organization he worked for. I thought the chances were pretty good the Party had tasked him with hunting me. But I also knew he was loyal to family. I figured he would know what to do, so I called his office extension.

"Hello?" he said, and stated his name. I told him who I was.

"Help me," I said. "You know what I'm asking. Give me some advice."

There was a pause on the other end of the line. I could practically hear my relative thinking. Then he said, "Your government wants to question you. It is your duty to turn yourself in."

The change in his voice was jarring. He was suddenly so formal. That's when I knew what was going on. Someone was listening in. My relative had to protect his job.

"I didn't do anything wrong," I said, as much for my own benefit as for anyone who was eavesdropping.

There was another pause on the line, and then: "Listen," my relative said. Again, in his stilted tone. "There is nowhere in this country that the government cannot reach you." I didn't get it the first time around. He had to say it again. "Government agents are everywhere, *Xiao* Tang. Do not try to run. They will find you anywhere you may be hiding *in this country.*"

The way he inflected those last three words. That's when I understood. He was telling me to run, to get to Hong Kong or Macau, get out of China however I could. Staying behind would be very bad, and probably not just for me. There were others whose safety might be at stake. My mother. My father. My sisters.

"The world is simply not a place for poets anymore," I said.

Silence on the other end. It made me sad, but also proud. My relative had risked his safety for me, to say nothing of his career, his reputation. All for that one little hint. The next time he spoke was purely for the benefit of the eavesdroppers. "Tell me where you are, *Xiao* Tang. I will try to help you."

I hung up the phone.

We boarded the train. Pan made us sit in the very last car. The rail guards were too lazy, he said, to walk up and down the full length of the train as they went about their rounds.

"Usually," Pan said, smiling. He was keeping an eye on everything but doing so very discreetly. "Anyway, we shouldn't have trouble. They'll assume that whoever boarded this train has already gone through security. I doubt we'll be disturbed. Relax, and keep your head on your shoulders."

We had an incident anyway, though not the kind we expected.

In those days a train from Changsha to Guangzhou took twelve hours. It was a long journey made longer by the constant worry I felt. The past few weeks had drained me, but I didn't know how exhausted I was until Pan's voice hissed in my ear. "*Xiao* Tang! *Xiao* Tang! Awake!" he said. "There's trouble!" His big hand was thumping my leg.

I came to fast and rubbed my eyes and saw right away what had riled him. Commotion toward the front of our carriage. A band of thugs had burst into the car, jeering and carrying on. Their mob moved about from seat to seat, demanding money from passengers, watches, any items of value. They made a sweep of the car's front end, moving closer to us, and closer.

Packs of roving toughs were a common thing in China back then. From what I hear, they're still common today. No one dares to confront the robbers; their numbers are too overwhelming.

I hadn't the faintest idea what to do. Pan Mingdong, to my shock, was smiling, though not like he thought this was funny. His big knuckles clenched and made popping sounds as the robbers marched up to our queue of seats, demanding people surrender their treasures. A pretty young woman who was sitting beside us shivered and dug out her last two yuan and handed them to a robber. The thug took the money and looked at it, sneered, and leaned in close to her face.

"Little beauty," he said "That's not enough for a pack of cigarettes. What else have you got to give?" He reached out and stroked her flawless cheek. The woman, terrified, started to weep.

I didn't think it possible that a man so large could move so fast. I blinked my eyes, and Pan Mingdong was out of his seat and in the aisle, towering over the whole clique of robbers. "That's enough," he said, still smiling, I was amazed to see. "You want something from her? Come get it from me."

The lead thug took a few steps back, a good move, all and all. Behind him, his cohorts jeered, screeching a chorus of catcalls. They wanted to see a fight. So the thug who was facing Pan Mindong reached under his coat and pulled out a knife. The rest of the thugs did the same. An assortment of blades and clubs slid out. Pan kept smiling and bent his knees.

"I guess it's all of you, then," he said.

The thug's knife fluttered side to side like the wings of a manic steel butterfly. He and Pan began to move, locked in a deadly tango. Then the robber rushed at Pan, who seized him and threw him, using his *gung fu*, slamming him onto the floor. Another thug followed and Pan did the same. Then, from the front of the car, we heard: "Stop!" And everyone turned around.

A policeman appeared at the end of the car, one hand on the butt of his pistol, whose holster flap had been unsnapped. The look on his face was clear: *I've seen enough. Make me draw and fire. Please.*

We stood like statues gracing a garden. One sculpture of me, one sculpture of Pan, one for each of the thugs before us, and everyone in the car. Each statue stared at the guard, and the guard stared back. Nervous and angry, he focused his look on Pan Mingdong. "What are you making trouble for?"

"Me?" said Pan. He snorted at the accusation.

The guard shot a look at the thug facing Pan. He saw the drawn knife and shook his head. "Go on," said the guard. "Get out of here." The tone of his voice was familiar.

The thug didn't like it, but he complied. The knife disappeared back into his coat. He turned back to Pan and shot him a sneer, then he and rest of the thugs filed out, past the policeman and out of the carriage. The guard did not move at all. He made no threat to arrest them, no challenge of any kind. He let them leave while his eyes locked on Pan. Pan returned the stare.

"This has nothing to do with you," said the guard.

Pan said nothing. He watched. The guard shot a final, challenging look to everyone else in the car. The passengers bowed their heads as one, refusing to meet his eyes. The guard made a pivot, satisfied, and marched from the car, moving after the thugs. The door rolled back into place with a clatter, a smack, and a bang, while beneath us, the train continued to shudder, making soft noise as it rocked back and forth. *Chukka chukka chukka chuk.* We plodded south toward Guangzhou.

An old man stood up and turned to Pan, his face a mask of amazement. His withered hands palsied open and closed, cracking out dry applause. A woman in her thirties stood up and did the same. Then a man who looked like a traveling salesman. Then another old man with one eye. Very soon, the whole carriage was clapping. Pan Mingdong blushed the color of wine and nodded and took his seat. The pretty young woman was staring at him. Pan's blush deepened. He cleared his throat, unable to meet her eyes.

"They're in cahoots," I said, meaning the thugs and the guard. Pan shrugged. This was also common in China. Police and thugs. Thugs and police. One wore a nice-looking uniform, but both lived by a similar code, brothers in arms in a war where survival amounted to victory.

Pan suddenly looked exhausted. "And they call *us* hooligans," he said. With that, he turned his head and looked out the window and said no more. The countryside kept rushing past.

I tried to go back to sleep after that but found it next to impossible. I dozed off and on, but one thought stuck in my mind like a sign with characters tall and wide as buildings. *Now I am a fugitive. No place is safe anymore.*

4

Guangzhou is the Chinese Mecca of commerce. Once called Canton, it sits beside the Pearl River and forms the gateway to the South China Sea. It is the capital city of Guangdong Province and, along with its neighbors, Hong Kong and Macau, has served as one of China's most vital ports since the early seventeenth century.

Imagine what China was like back then. Our southern shores had become a bazaar for trade with *gweilo*, the Canton word for "ghosts": pale-skinned barbarians whose faces sported too much hair. Their shops and stalls mashed into each other in alleyways, boulevards, twisting streets. In short order, Guangzhou became a foreign hub for Western enterprise. Dutch, Spanish, and British merchants mingled with colleagues from Portugal, Sweden, Armenia, Prussia, Italy, and Arabia. They traded in spices, silk, and gold. They bought and sold furniture lacquered to sheens that sparkled like moonlight on water. The harbors were choked with clippers and junks, and later by steamships belching their plumes like water dragons swimming in schools, coughing smoke at the sky.

Fast-forward three hundred years or so to 1989. Even then you could stroll through the streets of Guangzhou and hear foreign languages rising and plunging, a cacophony of tongues among the cries of mongers, artists, and vendors. Calling out prices. Cutting a deal. Bemoaning a lack of profit. Rubbing their gritty sandpaper hands the moment the door slammed shut on a buyer. The clink of coins in a cashbox.

Guangzhou was still a part of the People's Republic of China and was therefore controlled by the CCP. But its bustling trade made anything possible. Officials had learned from the Brits in Hong Kong and the Portuguese in Macau. They knew that money creates strange lovers, refining tastes, and creating liberal policies. Embarrassing questions got overlooked in favor of rising sales. Shylock from the Shakespeare play would be put to shame by Guangzhou. Money was the raison d'être for all. Nothing else was considered important. Nothing else even came close.

At the time of the June 4 incident, the governor of Guangdong was openly sympathetic to students. Therefore Pan Mingdong had been right: Guangzhou was the safest place in China for people like us. The hunted.

At Guangzhou station, Pan turned to me and took my hand in his massive fist and pumped it up and down. The motion rocked my body as though I was caught in the grip of a spasm, rattling teeth in the cup of my mouth. "This is where we part," he said.

The train ride had exhausted me. I was bleary-eyed. I needed food, a bath, and a proper bed. I was not prepared for abandonment. "What are you saying? Wait. Where do you think you're going?"

"Back to Changsha," Pan said. "While you were mumbling away in your sleep, I came up with a plan. I'm going back to launch a campaign called Bald Head for Protesting the CCP's Killing of Innocents." In China, a shaved head traditionally represents anger and discontent.

"Isn't that dangerous?" I asked, thinking that now might not be the time to antagonize the Party. But Pan Mingdong just snorted.

"We're safer if we separate. Now listen. The information I gave you. You still have it?" I nodded. All the phone numbers, names, and addresses were scrawled inside my notebook. "Use it," said Pan. "These friends of mine will help however they can."

With that, he clapped me hard on the back and lumbered off. The crowd was thick. It roiled like smoke, so thick that it swallowed even Pan's bulk.

I went at once to a public phone and called the first number on Pan's long list. A woman answered in Cantonese, a tongue I do not speak. I flailed about with the few words I knew. She switched to Mandarin, as fluidly as passing a tool between one hand and the other. She did not give her name, nor did she ask for mine.

"Zhongshan University. You know where the campus is?" she said.

"I can find it."

"Good. Go there directly, and fast. Wait on the library steps. It won't take long. Someone will find you and meet you."

"Wait," I said. "You don't know what I look like."

"Yes, we do," she said, and hung up.

I did as she told me and found the campus. She was right. It didn't take long. I had barely sat down on the library steps when someone said, "Come with me." In Mandarin, not Cantonese.

I looked up and saw the person who'd spoken, a young man leaving the library. He didn't slow down as he walked past. I got up and followed at once.

His name was Hei Ma,* he was very bright, a student of psychology. He looked like a student, too. Gaunt, with a scholar's aesthetic face. Spectacles. Slender hands. A young man more used to books than people, or so he appeared.

Hei Ma took me back to his dorm and got me a place to stay. He introduced me around, using a pseudonym instead of my actual name. Hei Ma told people I had been a leader of the pro-democracy movement in Hunan. That's when I learned that most people in Guangzhou were outraged by what had happened. Beijing was more than fifteen hundred miles away, but the massacre might as well have happened here. The students were boiling under their skin, though outwardly very quiet. They were Chinese citizens, after all. They knew the price of being outspoken.

Guangdong Province was liberal, even lax, but the CCP was still at large. If anything, said Hei Ma, the Party maintained a greater presence in Special Economic Zones. CCP spies were constantly watching to head off the capitalist taint of nearby Hong Kong and Macau, the slow creep of bourgeois ideals galumphing onto the mainland. The student leaders I met in Guangzhou were playing an intricate, dangerous game. They took extra precautions in all their dealings, as I was soon to learn.

But first things first. I had no money. All I had was my little red notebook. So I went to a pay phone and called up one of my Hong Kong contacts. Using a very simple code, I told him what had happened. He promised that he would send money, which was a very dangerous move. When I asked him how, my contact said he'd arrange the drop with Hei Ma.

Sure enough, a few days later, Hei Ma said, apropos of nothing, "You know what I do when I'm low on funds? I go for a walk in Yuexiu Park. It clears the head. Excuse me." With that, he walked out the door.

I found this behavior strange, of course, but not as strange as when Hei Ma returned an hour later and led me into an empty room and shut the door behind us. "Here," he said, and he tossed something to me. I caught it with both my hands. It was a paper sack with something solid inside. I reached in the bag and pulled out a brick of Hong Kong currency strapped together with rubber bands. I stared at the money, then back at Hei Ma.

"What is this?" I asked.

"What does it look like? Go on and count it."

I did. Imagine my shock to find I held $100,000 in Hong Kong dollars, a small fortune in 1989. I couldn't believe it. "Where did you get this?"

Hei Ma shrugged. "Specifically? A pay phone in front of the main entrance to Yuexiu Park."

I stared at him. "Someone left $100,000 in a pay phone in Yuexiu Park?"

Hei Ma laughed. "We do it all the time. The courier knows to wedge the package into a nook behind the phone. You'd have to know that the nook was there in order to find what was in it."

"This is too much," I said.

Hei Ma's look grew grave. "Not really. The people who donated those funds don't think our struggle is over. They know what freedom costs, and this is their gift to us. We have to use it wisely. A lot of good must come from that money."

"Take some," I said. I split the brick and handed him half. "For safe-keeping. I'll go to back to Changsha and pass out the other half to pro-democracy leaders."

Hei Ma shook his head. "You cannot return to Changsha. We're planning to get you to Hong Kong. You have to get out of the country."

There it was again, this notion that I should flee. It didn't make any sense at the moment. I felt very safe in Guangzhou. "Maybe I shouldn't," I said. "I think my place is here, in China."

Hei Ma tilted his head and gave me a funny look. He squinted at me from behind his glasses as though I'd said something crazy.

"I mean," I said. "They're probably not even looking for me."

Hei Ma spoke very slowly, measuring every word. His eyes were bright and very direct, boring through mine with intensity. "I think," he said, "you will seriously have to consider Hong Kong."

Looking back on that moment, I can see how deluded I was, how ignorant of the danger. I hadn't prepared myself for the truth. Despite what my relative told me over the phone in the Changsha railway plaza, I never thought I would have to leave China. Guangzhou, I thought, would be far enough for a fugitive to run. How could I go to Hong Kong? What about school? My family? My life? Too many questions beckoned at once. I pushed them out of my mind, made an art of procrastination. Telling myself it would all be worked out, that time would illuminate all.

This was easy to do in Guangzhou; it was such a fascinating place. Police were posted everywhere I went, but that was normal for any big city, and none of them seemed concerned about anything but their usual duties. I saw no one being arrested or detained or questioned about June 4. Everyone simply minded their business and went about life in the SEZ.

I decided my relative had been wrong, that Hei Ma was wrong as well. I shouldn't have run away from Changsha. I'd panicked, and blown everything I'd seen out of proportion. So desperate was I to believe this that I began to fabricate the truth, ignoring the facts at hand. For instance, one day I went to a pay phone and called up Liu Shao. His breathless voice sounded scratchy over five hundred miles of telephone line.

"Baiqiao Tang! Wherever you are?" he said. "Do not come back to Hunan!"

"Why?" I asked. "What's going on?"

I crimped the phone cord in my hand and looked out the pay phone windows, watching the people slide past on the street. The sun was shining. The sky was blue. The city had the erotic thrum of a modern center of trade. Guangzhou was such a vital city. I thought I might move there after I graduated college. Why not? I could continue my reading. Keep working on behalf of—

"Baiqiao Tang! Are you listening?"

"What? Sorry, what did you say?"

"They're looking for you. Your face is on the TV. In the papers."

A colossal exaggeration, I thought. Liu Shao needed exercise, and possibly a good night's sleep. We'd all been through a lot in the past few months. "I'm just a student," I said. "They can't think I'm some sort of threat. What is my crime? I made some speeches? Held some meetings? There's nothing wrong with that."

I was speaking out of character then, like someone who hadn't been born in China, clutched to her spindly dark bosom and weaned.

I should have noticed it right there and then—my deepening pit of delusions. It would have saved me a whole lot of trouble. It would have changed the course of my life.

5

I stayed in Guangzhou for nearly two weeks, a very difficult time. I was addled by all the Cantonese, a language I'd never been strong in. I got by picking out words here and there, and learning pidgin phrases. Gestures helped and I smiled a lot. Man Who Cannot Speak Local Tongue Must Show He Is Willing to Grovel. I felt like half my energies were spent ingratiating myself, thanking Mandarin speakers who intervened on my behalf, offering translations, advice, the proper way to make change. No wonder I didn't heed Liu Shao. His warnings were like Cantonese to me, words that I heard but did not understand.

The people I met through Hei Ma were kind and very generous. They spent time with me when I wanted companionship, left me alone when I didn't. They answered my questions and showed me around. In all, the perfect hosts. But I started feeling restless. I wanted to go home. I wanted to see my family. I wanted to rejoin the SAF, hold counsel, and plan our next move.

Hei Ma noticed my agitation and tried to offer distractions. He gave me a tour of the Guangzhou student underground, a subject that held special interest for me. I saw this as an excellent chance to compare the secret techniques of Hunan democracy fighters to those of our Guangdong brethren.

"Constant vigilance must be maintained lest the CCP infiltrate our ranks," said Hei Ma.

I nodded. "One must not steal a bell while his ears are covered." This ancient Chinese expression mocks the person who thinks he can pull off an escapade without attracting notice.

"The phones," said Hei Ma. "The mail. Every means of transport. Our first rule always assumes that the cadres control everything. They are watching and they are listening."

Which was true, I thought. The Cultural Revolution had proved this time and again. Even the most innocuous message could dictate the movement's damnation. A twenty-second phone call could lead to a prison sentence. An intercepted note or letter meant that someone could be tortured, his mind cracked open as though made of eggshell—knowledge of contacts, leaders, the network, all sucked from his brains like pigeon yolk. And that was a best-case scenario.

More often, dissident leaders vanished, leaving scant traces they'd ever existed. An open inkwell. A story unfinished, halted mid-sentence. Curtains that hadn't been drawn against night. A bird in a cage that hadn't been fed, whose water and paper needed changing. Desperate and beady-eyed, starving to death, it clutched its roost pole and prayed for attention, someone to free it or help it survive.

"We use phone booths a lot as drop points," said Hei Ma. "But you already know that. The exact locations and times for pickups are guarded with utmost secrecy. No pattern is ever established, so there's no way for cadres to intervene, but they try. The Party's operatives use cameras equipped with very powerful lenses."

"How do you know this?" I asked.

"Our contacts extend to within the Party. They've told us certain procedures. When CCP agents suspect a person, they follow them day and night. Certain members of our group have been photographed extensively. The pictures are kept on file. They come in handy when the cadres try to piece together indictments."

"But what about you?" I asked. "Are they watching you?" Feeling a sudden heat that prickled the flesh between my shoulder blades.

Hei Ma snorted and took off his glasses. He pulled a handkerchief out of his pocket and started to polish the lenses.

"Of course," he said. "As a student leader, you take such things for granted. But the Party thinks I'm oblivious, so why dispel their illusions? They're easier to manipulate if they think I've no idea that they're there. It's a lot more fun like that, as well. I make a *habit* of visiting phone booths. I call my mother, my sisters, my friends. Sometimes I order from restaurants. I can make twenty calls a day so my tails are always busy. By the time I finally pick up a package, my shadows have grown inured."

"In Hunan we use the same technique. Sesame Seed versus Watermelon. Hide a big thing among small things."

Hei Ma nodded. "You understand." He put his glasses back on. "There are also procedures for handling funds. We never pass money directly. Like everything else we do, the rabbit has three openings to his warren."

I nodded again. This was another old saying. It meant that a person or group must prepare many alternatives to find success at one thing.

"For instance," said Hei Ma. "The money I picked up the other day? I spoke to your man in Hong Kong. He said he'd send word through the usual channels to tell me when my package arrived. I have a regular contact whom I've never met in person. I don't even know her name. At any rate, she called and told me where and when the money was hidden. She got the information from *her* contact—someone *she* has never met. And so on. I'll wager that message went through six or seven links before it reached me. The money was probably passed that way as well."

I nodded. This made sense to me. There were many ancient ways to move funds, ways that required no banks, no deposits, and no withdrawals: accounting by way of complicity, loan validation through fervor. Many years later, in the wake of 9/11, I heard of a system called *hawala*, which is used by Muslim extremists to make money cross borders in total secrecy. Evidently, we Chinese are not the only culture to use this technique.

"And no one's ever been caught?" I asked.

Hei Ma adjusted his spectacles. "It's happened," he said. He looked away. Then he went on to explain how actual names were never used in dispatches or conversation. How messages were always expressed in code. The Guangzhou students used simple counter-surveillance techniques, nothing too sophisticated. In fact, the simplest code, said Hei Ma, involved the Chinese dictionary.

Years later, when I arrived in America, I was shocked to learn how many dictionaries exist for the English language. In China, students used only one, the *Xinhua Zidian*, a pocket-sized reference guide first published in 1953. Any message that came through our network would make no sense to untutored ears. You had to decode each transmission using a copy of the *Xinhua Zidian*.

First, you wrote the message out on a sheet of paper. Then you took your dictionary and looked up the first word, which was a ruse. The word you really wanted was the one directly beneath that in the dictionary. So decoders would go through the *Xinhua Zidian*. Look up a character for the first word. Jot down the character right beneath it. Go to the next word. Do the same. Over and over and over again. It was a tedious process, but simple. And of course when you finished decoding and had your instructions, you destroyed the piece of paper on which you'd jotted your work.

We thought this system was very good. Dogs bark. Cats meow. Birds fly. The natural things in life pass unnoticed. What could the Party possibly say about students checking characters in a dictionary? But there was another advantage to using the *Xinhua Zidian*: there would never be an occasion where our codebook fell into enemy hands. They probably already had one. At that time three hundred million copies of the *Xinhua Zidian* had been sold in China and abroad. Out in the open, as everyone knows, is the very best place to hide things.

"We have news," said Hei Ma one day. "Your friend Liu Wei made it safely to Hong Kong."

"How do you know this?" I said.

Hei Ma shrugged. "The network is vast." He left it at that, but his face grew dark. His eyes darted back and forth. "We still think you should go."

I wouldn't hear of it. I still thought flight was ludicrous, a terrible over-reaction. Which is why, two weeks after leaving Changsha, I hopped a train and left Guangzhou without saying good-bye to Hei Ma or to any new friends I'd made. I now know this was the wrong thing to do, but I thought my reasons were sound at the time. In the first place, I didn't want them to worry; they'd already done so much for me. But I also thought that slipping away was best in case anyone thought to betray me.

Was this contradictory thinking? Yes, of course it was. But looking back, I see that my state of mind was very precarious. I felt like it was my duty to return to the SAF. What kind of leader, I wondered, would flee when the cause needed him most? What kind of example was I setting by running away? I did not belong in Guangzhou. My place was in Changsha.

Hei Ma had already changed my share of the donated Hong Kong funds into Chinese yuan. So now I had this stack of yuan as thick as a piece of masonry. I wanted to put this money to work in Changsha right away, to pass it among leaders of the pro-democracy movement.

It was crazy thinking, I see that now. I should have listened. I should have fled. Left the country like so many others. Instead, I boarded a train to Changsha. I'll never forget the day. It was June 30, 1989.

6

My train passed into Hunan Province and stopped at Chengzhou City. Passengers got on and off. The announcement said we would be delayed a few minutes. I seized the moment to disembark, hoping to stretch my legs.

I walked down a hallway off the platform, rubbing my eyes, feeling tired. Then I stopped and stared. My face was staring back at me. It was a surreal moment. I shook it off and realized I was looking at a poster of my own image, with copies of some official-looking document hanging under it. I leaned in close and read the text, a warrant for my arrest.

Shocked, afraid, I spun around and darted my eyes all about. Yes, there were more posters everywhere, slapped all over the hallway walls, on platform columns, the gates. How could I not have noticed this? Passengers looking to enter the station were being stopped at security checkpoints and scrutinized by police. And here I was, over six feet tall, much taller than anyone else around me. I stuck out like an accusation. Hei Ma and his friends had been right. I could not go back to Changsha.

Quickly, I went back onto the train and slumped down into my seat. I turned my head toward the wall and threw an arm up over my head. A picture of the Weary Traveler. Don't disturb him, he's trying to sleep. Mercifully, the train began to *chug-chug-chug* away from the station. It quickly resumed its fast shot north while my thoughts churned even faster.

How, I thought? How will I do this? How can I turn around? My head was on fire with dangerous schemes, mile after desperate mile.

Eventually, we reached Hengyang, the second-to-last stop before Changsha. The train slowed down, then hissed to a halt. Security forces got on the train. I saw their crisp shirts and red epaulets. They entered at the front of my car and started to work their way back, checking each passenger's documents. Their heads were down; their eyes were intense, burning under their hat brims.

I got up out of my seat and moved to the door at the back of the train. Could it be that simple? Maybe it was. Anyway, I had no choice. My hair was tousled, spiked at strange angles. The collar of my shirt poked up. I took on the role of a man who's just been roused from a fitful sleep, who was haunted by terrible dreams. But then he wakes up. He looks and sees that his journey is still not over. His face falls flat in the hopeless dismay of the Traveler Far from Home. It was a common sight in train stations. I prayed it would be my salvation.

I staggered onto the platform, blinking at sunlight, drunk with fatigue. A security guard stood straight ahead. I reeled right toward him, rubbing my stubble-rough cheeks with a palm. Man Who Is Badly in Need of a Shave Realizes He Is Confused. The guard saw me coming and looked up.

"Damn it," I said. "Wrong train!"

"Sir?"

"I got on the wrong damn train. Fell asleep. My boss is going to kill me!"

The guard's professional frown melted into a schadenfreude grin. "Where do you need to go?"

"South," I said. Pointing. Vague. "One stop back. Lingling."

The guard snickered. "What, are you drunk?"

I nodded, head down, rubbing my face. "I had a little. Damn train takes so long."

The guard shook his head, his meaning clear: the world is chock-full of idiots. "Over there." He nodded. "Platform 2. Get on the train. The conductor will probably charge you for going back."

"There goes my pay for the week," I said.

Which earned a snort. "Drink water next time."

I nodded and waved my thanks and stumbled away, making sure to keep up the act until I reached Platform 2. Once I got on the train, I moved to the back and made a big show of settling in and falling asleep. But I knew I wasn't safe yet, not by a long shot. A few minutes later, the train started moving. And a few minutes after that, someone tapped my shoulder. Now, I thought. This is it. The most important part.

"Where you going? Sir? Sir?"

I poked my head up and blinked, a bit blind, like a mole coming out of its hole. My hair was a shock. My eyes were puffy. I sniffed the air. Drunk Man Is Suddenly Roused. "Huh?" I said.

"Your ticket, sir?"

"Ticket? No. Don't—damn. I forgot."

The conductor sighed. "Where are you going?"

"Guangzhou. Damn boss wants me to go to Guangzhou."

"You can buy your ticket here."

I nodded and fumbled for bills, rubbing my eyes, which conveniently covered my face somewhat. "He wants me to go all the way to Guangzhou. You believe it? Check on an account. Same as I did last week, I said. He doesn't care. He just says go."

The conductor nodded. He didn't care either. He quickly made change from the money I gave him and tore off a ticket and handed it over. Then he moved away.

I slumped back down in my seat, clutching the ticket, my heart thumping fast. I thanked whatever fates were watching. Now I was free and heading south, going back to Guangzhou. But first I took a detour.

At the next stop, I got off and hurried across the station to another train bound for Yongzhou. I wanted to visit my mother. Since flight from the country was now looking more and more necessary, I thought this would probably be my last chance to see her.

The journey took two or three hours. When I got to my mother's apartment, my youngest sister answered the door. Yan Hong was still in high school then. Her face went bright when she saw me, then it fell flat with fear. "What are you doing here?" she demanded. "Baiqiao, it isn't safe!"

"I wanted to visit Mother," I said.

She shook her head. "She isn't here. Come in. Come in right away!"

I only stayed for an hour. Yan Hong used the phone and called some relatives who lived nearby. They came over, not knowing why they were summoned. Imagine their shock at seeing me. One of them was my cousin Tang Yinchang, who is three years older than me. "What are your plans, *Xiao* Tang?" he asked.

"I have to go back to Guanzhou," I said. "I see now there is no other way."

He nodded. "Then I will go with you, to make sure you get there safe."

Before we left, I used a pay phone and placed a call to Lu You. Quickly, I told him what had happened and told him I needed his help once again. He said he would leave Changsha at once. "I'll meet you at the Guangdong train station," he said and gave me a time for the rendezvous. "I have a new plan. But be careful, Baiqiao Tang!"

Then I took Yan Hong aside and gave her most of my yuan, minus a few thousand I thought I might need for traveling. "Keep this," I told her. "Hide it. Make sure that no one knows that you have it. I may come to pick it up later. Or I might send word and tell you what to do with it. Will you do that for me?"

She nodded, wide-eyed, and took the money and said she would put it someplace safe. "Now go," she said. "Baiqiao, you have to leave!"

So I did, with Tang Yinchang.

When we arrived in Guangzhou, Lu You was there to meet us. He shook hands with my cousin, who turned and clapped me on the back. "Don't tell me where you're going," he said. "It's best if I don't know."

"Take care of my family, Tang Yinchang." But of course I knew that he would. Tired as he was, he got back on a train heading north. I wondered if I would ever see him again.

"Come," said Lu You. "I've called around and heard a few things. The

Party is searching for you here, as well. We've got to get you out of Guangzhou."

"But where will I go?" I asked.

"Jiangmen," said Lu. "I know a place."

Jiangmen is another city in Guangdong Province, a hundred miles farther south than Guangzhou following the Pearl River. Lu and I took a bus to visit Lu's cousin, who lived in a district called Xinhui, very close to free Macau. Lu's cousin was a man named Chen Xiashi. He and his wife were lychee nut farmers. Chen and his wife lived in a house surrounded by lychee tree groves. They came out to meet us, smiling but uneasy. Lu spoke to them in Cantonese. They spoke no Mandarin. I was back to communicating in pidgin grunts and waves, my vocabulary of smiles and exaggerated facial gestures. Chen and his wife seemed to take it in stride, nodding and pointing and shaking their heads. They smiled at me, trying their Mandarin. It was just as bad as my Cantonese.

"Democracy good, yes?" said Chen.

How could I disagree? Lu said good-bye and boarded a bus that was headed back to Guangzhou. I was left with Chen and his wife. They took me inside the house and led me upstairs to a loft where I hid for the next ten days, terrified I would be found.

7

I slept on a simple straw pallet, staring at knotholes etched in the planks. The knotholes, like eyes, stared back at me. A dragonfly entered the loft through a window, providing entertainment for hours. Buzzing around, it looked for exits. I sat on my pallet. Watching. Hungry. Waiting for footsteps to thump up the stairs, the signal that Chen or his wife was coming, bearing another plate of food. Every meal they cooked was simple and rustic and delicious. Chicken or beef, it didn't matter—every dish was prepared with some variation on lychee nuts. Raw lychee. Broiled lychee. Steamed lychee. Chopped, sliced, and diced. Lychee sauces, floral and sweet. I ate so many lychee nuts, I started getting nosebleeds.

Chen and his wife must have sensed that I was starting to come unglued. Once, at midnight, they sent a relative into the village to see if any police were about, anyone they didn't recognize. The relative returned and reported the coast was clear. So the Chens took me into the heart of town, which was sleepy and dark, and mostly closed up for the night.

Chen knew the owner of a particular restaurant and asked if he would serve us. Please don't let anyone else come in, Chen said. I got this all from their gestures. The restaurant owner shot me a look, then nodded and waved us inside. We took a table way in the back, away from the windows facing the square. That meal was one of the best I've ever eaten, before or since. I ordered half the menu, focusing on items that didn't feature lychee nuts.

All was quiet. All was easy. I started to relax. At one point, I got up and went to a pay phone. Using my little red notebook, I called up a contact in Hong Kong and told him what had happened. He asked where I was. I told him what city and left it at that, not wanting to say too much.

"We can get you out of there," he said. "Take you to Macau where you will be safe. Give me your address."

I hesitated, then rattled it over the phone.

"July 12," my contact said. "We'll pick you up at 8 a.m. Be ready to go."

"I will," I said, and hung up the phone.

On July 11, I was getting ready for bed at eleven o'clock in the evening. Tomorrow was the big day. My contacts would come and take me to freedom. But then I heard a knock at the Chens' back door, and froze. I heard Chen the Farmer shuffle across the wooden planks of the floor downstairs. I imagined his wife, like a ghost, behind him, hovering as she always did. I held my breath and didn't move and strained to hear what was going on.

I heard Chen pull the back door open and heard a man walk in. There was hushed, hurried talk. The new man sounded middle-aged; he was guttural and gruff. What was he saying in Cantonese? I hadn't the faintest clue. Then, abruptly he left. I heard the door bang shut behind him, followed by footsteps that rushed up the stairs. A moment later, Chen burst in, flailing his arms and hissing at me in his awful Mandarin.

"We go! We go now!"

I was up at once and yammering questions. Chen answered them as best he could while pushing me down the steps and into the house's main room. What he was telling me didn't become clear until later on. The man who had come to the door was a local high-level cadre, a Big Man in Xinhui who also happened to be Chen's uncle. The uncle had stopped by to warn his nephew. The Party knew of my presence in town, and had for many days.

Lu and I hadn't figured on this. Small towns have no room for disguises. No one can hide in them. No one keeps secrets. People in small towns like to talk, to get in each others' business. Someone had tipped off Party officials. A favor. A bribe. Whatever the reasons. The uncle said that security forces had gathered at the local constable's office, waiting for the dead of night, a common CCP tactic. They like to take criminals when they're asleep, feeling it's safer that way. They would come for me very soon.

As I say, I learned all this later. Right then, all I heard was Chen Xiashi saying, "We go! We go now!" Which was more than enough for me. He shoved me out the back door and into the pitch-black night. We scrambled through groves of lychee trees. The leaves reached out at us, snatching our hair, grabbing our shoulders with skeletal fingers. The dead black night lay cold overhead. No moon to guide us. Not even stars.

We had run for a kilometer or so when I stopped in my tracks and panicked. "My notebook," I said. I clapped my hands to my pockets, though I already knew it wasn't there. I'd set the notebook beside my bed while getting ready to go to sleep. It was back in Chen's loft, forgotten in the turmoil, waiting to be found.

Chen kept tugging my arm to keep running. I resisted, saying the word for notebook over and over in Mandarin, but he didn't seem to understand. A hurried game of pantomime followed. Chen eventually got the idea, but he shook his head and grabbed me again and tried to pull me along. His meaning was clear. *Leave it*, he was saying. I shrugged off his hand and shook my head. "It's got everyone's phone numbers in it," I said. "Names and addresses, all in code, but I have to get it back."

The thought of the Party seizing my notebook and cracking our flimsy student codes was too much for me to bear. All those people in jeopardy because of something foolish I'd done.

Chen and I argued with gestures for over a minute. Finally, he threw up his hands and muttered curses in Cantonese and paced the ground, kicking soil and roots, punishing them for my sin. Then he spun on me, pointed and scowled. *You stay put*, he was saying. I nodded, and with that, he turned and ran back the way we'd come. The black night swallowed him whole.

How long did I stand there waiting? To this day, I don't know. Logic tells me it was forty minutes. It felt more akin to forever. I was so scared and tired. In spite of myself, I began to nod off. Then someone was bustling toward me. I heard the footfalls striking the ground and hid behind a lychee tree, preparing myself for—what? To flee? To strike? To shout? The footfalls suddenly stopped.

I knew that someone was standing close by, but I couldn't see who it was. The night was too dark. Hating the sound of my voice in the blackness, I hissed Chen's name, and he hurried over, filthy, out of breath.

"*Bou jai*," he said, and pressed something into my hand. My little red notebook! I could feel it. Then Chen grabbed my shoulder and hauled me along, away from the village and into the night.

For the next several hours, we trudged along. The groves gave way to fields, the fields to woods that were dark as dungeons. Dogs would bark in the distance, ghostly howls that spoke of sharp teeth. I pictured packs with their tails up, rural guardians defending their masters' farms.

We walked, this quiet farmer and I. The night fell in all around us, and we fell too. Tripped by roots, we collapsed to our knees, cursed, got back up, and kept moving. Sometimes we waded through rice paddies, sloshing through water up to our waists. Torn by burrs and stabbed by needles. Eaten by insects but feeling no pain. Too nervous for that. Tripping again. Falling. Get up, get up! Keep moving into the blackness.

We'd hear a car hissing by on a distant road and hide ourselves under bramble. Once, we hid in the sheds of a duck farm and came out smelling of droppings. I felt myself losing hope by the minute. A couple of times I even imagined how nice it would be if the cadres came, arrested us, and took me away. Just get it over with, I thought. At least I could get some sleep. It seems like it can't be true looking back. But later, I'd reckon the distance we traveled as something close to twelve miles.

Near dawn, we flagged down a bus and got on and moved at once to the back. The passengers stared at us. What a sight we must have made in our shredded clothing, our shredded skin, all of it fouled by duck droppings.

Chen and I didn't care one bit. We settled into our seats and dozed as the bus continued northeast.

8

In Jiangmen City, Chen led us to the house of his cousin and knocked on the door. I remember the cousin answering, seeing his wife behind him in the doorway, the look on her face an open question. What was going on? Then hearing Chen rattle in Cantonese. The cousin looking past him, staring at me, then uttering loud protests. Chen calmed him with some new explanation, which took a little time. Eventually, he persuaded his cousin to let us in.

I remember muttering thank-you's over and over again. Dropping my eyes to show respect, I barely looked at our hosts. I asked to use the phone and called my contact in Hong Kong.

"You have to call your people," I said. "Tell them not to go to the address I gave you, the farmer's house."

I told my contact what had happened. He thanked me for informing him. "Are you safe?" he said.

"For the moment."

"Good. Do you know how to get to the Jiangmen Bridge?"

I told him I thought I could find it.

"Go there tomorrow at 8 a.m. That's where we'll pick you up."

I thanked him and hung up the phone and collapsed in a chair and watched TV. A Hong Kong channel was on. I remember thinking it was surreal, how, within a matter of hours, after all that I'd been through, I would cross the Pearl River and enter Macau, and then I would be free.

I drifted off to sleep and slept for the rest of the day and into the night. Another loud knock at the door woke me up. My sleep, like a raven, fluttered away, indignant, cawing obscenities. Whoever was at the door had big fists and certainly knew how to use them.

I remember feeling disorientated. Where am I? How did I get here? I was sorting out the puzzle pieces, trying to put them together when— *boom, boom, boom!* The door flew open and bodies flowed in, a surge of public security guards. They were all heavily armed and shouting my name. Later, I'd learn it was 2 a.m. on July 13. My freedom, such as it was, was over.

"Baiqiao Tang! You are under arrest!" Hands were snatching me, throwing me down. I hit the floor hard and got back up. Then something heavy and blunt struck my gut. The toe of a boot, which was followed by pain.

I remember shouting feeble words. Pretenses at my innocence. "Why are you arresting me? I haven't done anything wrong!"

Fists clamped around my throat. Blows rained down on my back. I was beaten by cudgels, electric batons, the weapon used most by Chinese police. I curled up into a fetal position and tried to protect my head. No good. The blows kept coming. Flesh began to sizzle and smoke as the shocks struck the back of my neck, my shoulders, and my spine.

How long did it go on? I can't say. What does it really matter now? The next thing I remember, I was hauled to my feet and jerked from the house. I looked around, amazed. The street outside was swarming with a mob of armed police. Security guards and troops from the local garrison stood in front of riot vehicles. Blood-red lights whirled around and around throwing demons across the backdrop of night. Men scurried back and forth in the shadows, an army deploying for combat.

All this for me? I couldn't believe it. The whole thing seemed so ridiculous—funny and sad and terrifying at once, more like a movie than reality.

"On your knees," said one of the soldiers. Another CCP tactic. They make you kneel as a form of surrender, to show that you have been beaten. I pretended I hadn't heard the command and stayed on my feet.

"Kneel!" roared one of the guards. But I didn't. They came at me then, ramming the butts of their rifles into my thighs. I doubled over. My legs buckled. But I would not kneel for them. I looked up and saw that a crowd had gathered. Not soldiers; these were common folks, all of them watching me, mouths agape, their eyes gone wide in astonishment.

Do you see? I thought. Do you see?

Then I heard: "Put him inside the car."

There was another jerk. My body was picked up and tossed like a sack of grain, dragged forward on legs that no longer worked. More blows fell about my head and shoulders. After that, I remember nothing.

part five

Counterrevolutionary

1

I was taken to Jiangmen's Number One Jail and left there for several days. I was badly in need of a doctor's attention, but no one came to look in on me. I could neither sit nor lie down. My body refused to obey my commands—it felt like it had been fashioned from metal and thrown in the sea for thousands of years so the joints and ligaments rusted solid, frozen and inflexible. The beating I'd been given must have damaged some of my organs. There was blood in my urine and stool. I began to run a high fever. One of the guards took my temperature. It came back 104 degrees Fahrenheit.

I begged the passing cadres. "Please let me see a doctor!"

They shook their heads and said that I was a criminal awaiting trial and therefore not entitled to incur any medical bills. No doctors, medicines, bandages, comforts. I'd been lucky to have my temperature taken. What could I do? I clenched my teeth and curled in a ball and shivered myself awake. Asleep. Awake. Asleep. In either state: on fire with pain.

There were other men in my cell, but they left me alone. No one wanted to get involved. Word had gotten around that I was a counterrevolutionary.

Cadres would come in and grab me and drag me down the hall. They had to physically pick me up since I couldn't walk anymore. During these trips, I would sometimes see Chen Xiashi and his wife, or Chen's cousin and his wife. All four had been arrested as well. Our eyes would meet, flickering questions at one another, messages of sorrow and fear. Then we were dragged apart once more.

During those first few days, I told my interrogators nothing. Then an escort of guards arrived. I still couldn't walk, so they picked me up and carried me out to a car and drove me north to Guangzhou where we entered *Huang Hua Jian Yu*, also known as Guangdong Provincial Jail Number One.

It was an ancient place, built during the Qing dynasty, one of the three most notorious prisons in China, along with Beijing's Qingcheng and Shanghai's Tilangqiao. Many famous people have been incarcerated there over the years. You could call it the Chinese version of Alcatraz.

I was there only one week. They were holding me until police arrived from Changsha. The wardens placed me in special confines reserved for political prisoners and international suspects. They said they had to keep people like me away from the general population. Again, I was given no medical treatment. But this time, at least, I made a friend, a man named Fu Jintao.*

Fu had been a provincial foreign trade official, one of the highest-placed CCP cadres active in Guangdong Province. Police had arrested him after June 4 for helping Zhao Ziyang's followers escape to Hong Kong. This was easy for Fu to facilitate since he managed an import/export company. Each day, the government granted him permits enabling back-and-forth travel to Hong Kong, for business purposes only. Fu used the permits to help about forty or fifty of Zhao's most trusted advisers to flee, including a man named Shi Jinghai,* a high-level official who'd worked with Zhao at the Institute for Political Reform. Somehow the CCP found out about these escapes. Fu was quickly arrested, though never sentenced or charged.

This happens a lot in China. The government simply takes you away and puts you in prison and holds you there without any trial. Your official status is *detainee*. It's like the purgatory of law. It's hard to defend yourself against charges that haven't been levied or stated.

Fu Jintao was about fifty years old and an embarrassment to the Party. His father was very well-placed in Guangdong provincial government. "Politics can be a strange game," said Fu. He shook his head. "Very strange."

During my week at *Huang Hua Jian Yu*, I joined Fu Jintao and the rest of the inmates to create various handicrafts, mostly strings of tiny lights that blinked on and off when you plugged them in. But also little hand-carved ornaments that dangled from loops of fabric and twine. I had never seen such goods before. I asked Fu Jintao about them.

"These are for sale overseas," Fu said.

"How do you know?"

"Because." He shrugged. "I used to broker such deals for the Party. Before I was arrested."

Nowadays, I see these pieces for sale throughout the United States. Perhaps you've hung these same products on your Christmas tree each holiday season. It's always interesting for me to see people laughing around them and singing. I know that few, if any, know they were made with *yanlei*, the Mandarin word for tears.

As I was about to learn, the forced labor of Chinese prisoners serves as a source of profit for the state. It's no wonder, really, that China has lured so many overseas businesses into partnership with its slave-labor system. The list includes many Western companies. Well-known American brands. They can't resist such low, low prices. The massive return on investment.

A list of these products made by prison slave labor includes artificial Christmas trees. Christmas tree lights. Jewelry. Tools. Trinkets. Foodstuffs. Toys of almost every variety. And clothing, of course. Running shoes. Cosmetics. Electronics. Handbags. Musical instruments. Cell phones and computers. The steady manufacture of these items and many more continues despite how US law strictly prohibits the import of goods produced in foreign prisons.

You might ask, "So what? Is that really such a bad thing? Prisoners have a debt to society. Why not let them pay it off and do something good for a change?"

This might be an interesting argument, provided the people in Chinese prisons were there for actual crimes. Don't get me wrong, quite a few of them are, but so many more are not. Many, like Fu Jintao and myself, were in prison because of their politics, or were forced to work in political reeducation camps under hazardous conditions for crimes they didn't commit. They are subjected to malnutrition, sleep deprivation, physical tortures, mental abuse, no showers, scabies, lice, and no regard whatsoever for hygiene. The list of diseases that go untreated includes hepatitis, tuberculosis, heart and thyroid conditions, kidney stones, cancers, and on and on.

Detainees who suffer from these conditions are forced to work the same punishing schedule as that of healthy prisoners. Some drop dead while working their stations. Their bodies are hauled away posthaste. The day's work must continue. Productivity must be maintained. Orders must be filled. This is business, after all.

At the end of my week in *Huang Hua Jian Yu*, a four-man team arrived from Changsha. I said good-bye to Fu Jintao, who told me very quietly he would help me however he could if either of us was ever released.

Regarding the train ride north to Hunan, two incidents impressed me. The first was the way my captors took off my shackles when we were in public. They would say, "Well, well. You don't need these for now," then undo my fetters and stow them.

"Don't yell or run away or do anything foolish like that," one said. "Or we'll shoot you." He grinned.

It made me wonder why they were taking a chance in the first place. Why not simply leave me in chains? Then I realized they didn't want me to stick out in a crowd. My shackles would call attention to me. But I was so young and clearly a student. Right then public sentiment was firmly on the side of the students, as well as anyone else whom the Party was rounding up. It says a lot, I think, that my captors were afraid to show they had the upper hand in public for fear of reprisal.

The second incident I recall was our arrival at Changsha railway station. You might have thought some kind of freak show was on display at a carnival, but no. It was only me. A crowd of pot-bellied VIPs and leering government cadres had lined up, grinning and smoking their cigarettes, waving to friends and family. Posing in the glare of flashbulbs, they were eager to get their names in the paper, making it seem like they were the ones who had brought me back to Changsha.

And everyone wanted in on the action. Absolutely everyone. Some Hong Kong businessmen riding my train saw me being put back into fetters before we arrived at the station. The looks on their faces! They were aghast at how close they'd come to missing a perfect photo opportunity! Raising their cameras, they snapped away, the whir of their shutters like rushing water, even as guards and cadres pushed them aside and told them to stop. They didn't want any evidence of a student leader in fetters.

At Changsha railway station, a Mercedes Benz raced up to the edge of the platform and screeched to a stop in front of the steps. Guards rushed down, opened the door, dragged me over, and pushed me into the vehicle. They wedged me between them in the backseat, then pulled the doors shut. *Klunk. Klunk!* A second later, the car pulled away. One of the guards turned to me and bragged. "We're using the best car in Changsha to take you to jail!"

The driver steered for an underground passage that took us below the city streets. Evidently, Mao Zedong had the tunnel installed as a safety precaution. He used it whenever he left Beijing to visit Changsha, his hometown. We entered the tunnel's gaping black mouth and left the sunlit world behind. Soon, I arrived at Changsha Number One Jail.

2

The prisoners already knew my name and the details of my case. This was sort of a dubious honor since many were hardcore criminals, murderers, rapists, and other violent felons—my coterie of admirers. The jail commandant had briefed the cells on my background before I arrived. This is a common practice in Chinese prisons and jails, geared toward establishing biases.

I can still recall my first impression of Changsha Number One Jail. The place reminded me of the Roman Colosseum. Everyone was shouting and fighting, locked in mortal combat over food and cigarettes. I had trouble closing my eyes. There was spectacle everywhere. The other jails I'd been held in had been placid compared to this. Changsha Number One Jail was a jungle of concrete and iron bars stocked with deadly animals: a primitive, violent place. Though anxious, I knew that I was about to commence prolonged research in the curious subculture of the Chinese penal system.

My first and perhaps most important lesson was this: prison commandants often rely on specially appointed aides, prisoners known as *laotou yuba*, or cell bosses. These inmates hope to curry favor with wardens by carrying out their demands. They spy. They protect. They snitch. They enforce. You'll find at least one in every cell. I later learned that the prison commandant asked my *laotou yuba* to listen for any "counterrevolutionary statements" I might make, and to report such statements to him at once. He also urged them to be on the lookout for any attempts I might make to escape or to commit suicide. I hadn't the faintest interest in either, but the commandant was very smart. By making this speech to the prisoners, he had witnesses who could later state he had voiced concern for my well-being, a good thing if I ever turned up dead, shot while "trying to escape," or the victim of apparent suicide.

My interrogation began at once. The sessions, under Chinese law, were to be carried out humanely. But the law and prisons are separate in China. Especially true, as I was to find, wherever the events of June 4 were concerned. First I was questioned by three section chiefs, high-level cadres—an honor of sorts, or so I was clearly meant to believe. The truth was: here were three Party members who'd wiggled free from the killing jaws of the Cultural Revolution by showing their willingness to perpetrate atrocious acts in the name of communism.

I refused to admit any wrongdoing. My support for a free and democratic China hurt no one, I insisted. These men all chuckled and shook their heads. They labeled me a "diehard element," then proceeded to implement every trick and loathsome technique they'd perfected over their long careers. All designed to break my will.

For instance, I was subjected to rotating shifts of constant questioning. One cadre would subject me to a barrage of interrogation—several hours of shouting, cajoling, slaps on the back of the head. The cadre would use insinuations and outright threats. He would taunt me with food and water, both of which I was often denied. When the cadre was through, another would saunter in to relieve the first of his duties. The battery was repeated, with an eye toward making me say something new, to teeter on an admission or buckle on a stance I'd assumed. Several more hours of this would draw out. The second cadre would call in a third. And on and on and on.

Combined, these sessions sometimes lasted sixteen hours a day. The aim, of course, was to break my resistance, wear me down to the point where the cadres could pump me for any knowledge I had of people or places vital to the movement, or at very least discredit me as a leader of anti-CCP ideals. They would also try to make me admit to things I hadn't done.

For instance, they spent a long time insisting I'd contacted one particular leader via coded telegram, a Beijing student named Wang Dan. The cadres said they had twofold proof to back up this assertion. One: that I had been in Beijing during the hunger strike in late May. Two: that sworn testimony had been offered by other prisoners, allying me with Wang Dan.

It was such a trivial matter. Doubly so, since I had no idea what they were talking about. Yet they grilled me on this one point for several days. "Who is this Wang Dan?" I asked. "And why is she so important?"

The cadres thought I was being clever. "*She?!?*" they roared. "So! You'd have us believe that you think that Wang Dan is a girl?"

"Isn't she?" I said, feeling very confused. In China, the given name *Dan* is traditionally reserved for women. I'd never met a man who went by that name. I thought they might be referring to Chai Ling, a student of psychology who was a well-known protest organizer in the Beijing hierarchy.

But the cadres kept up their battering. I refused to budge from my stance, which was the truth. I'd never met this person Wang Dan and had no idea who he was. Later, I learned that Wang Dan had been an important student leader at Tiananmen Square. The CCP wanted him very badly. He was Number One on their Most Wanted list.

The cadres also tried to link me to certain officials they wished to discredit. Routinely, they called up the names of foreigners, cabinet members, and key figures in the Hong Kong Alliance Supporting the Patriotic Democratic Movement in China. One name that came up a lot was that of Zhou Naishan, the former mayor of Changsha City, who'd openly supported the movement. Again and again, I told the truth: I didn't know half the people they'd mentioned. It didn't matter. They hammered away.

"What about Liang Heng?" they said.

"Who is Liang Heng?" I asked. "I don't know anyone named Liang Heng."

"Really! Liang Heng is a former student at Hunan Normal—as if you didn't know! He fled China and went to America almost ten years ago. And yet you claim you don't know this man?"

"Ten years ago, I was twelve years old. So, yes. I claim not to know him."

I don't mean to make this process sound clownish or funny. It wasn't, I can assure you. It was a terrifying ordeal, the worst I'd ever endured in my life. The more I resisted, the more they resorted to making up stories about whom I'd been associated with and all the nefarious activities we'd planned. The crimes that we had committed.

During the first four months of my interrogation, the cadres compiled five volumes of case files. Each file was well over four hundred pages and full of nothing but rubbish. My interrogators wrote down everything I said word for word, even the curse words I used when they would accuse me of doing things I hadn't done. Days later, they would enter the interrogation room and hand me a transcript as thick as a ream, a record of my expletives frozen in time. Soberly, they would ask me to read the document cover to cover, then sign affidavits swearing that these were in fact my words. The whole thing was so farcical, I signed. Why not?

They led me back to my cell after each session. By definition, Chinese jails are grossly overcrowded. Picture twenty to thirty men packed in a single cell about forty feet square. Most of the cells have a sleeping platform that senior prisoners hog at night, packing themselves together like a bunch of smelts in a can. Some prisoners slept under the platform. More learned to stand up against the wall and nod off while still on their feet. But most of us lay on the floor, on our sides. There was no room to sleep on your back. You pressed up against the next man, shivering in the cold, sweating in the heat. If you got up to use the toilet, you had to stay there the rest of the night. It was impossible to cross that room again and squeeze back into the spot you had left. Many simply did not sleep at all.

The food we were served was deplorable, grossly insufficient to sustain any degree of health. We were given the cheapest foodstuffs available. Pumpkin. Winter melon. Seaweed. These vegetables were always served with clumps of rancid white rice. Once a week we were given smears of boiled pork fat for protein. I have never touched pumpkin since leaving prison. I don't intend to ever again.

Later, I learned a startling fact. The subsistence allocation for each prisoner in a Chinese jail amounted to 24.50 yuan per month. That was less than the cost of a train ticket to ride between neighboring cities. Rather unsurprisingly, I often became quite ill for lack of proper nutrition.

3

Not long after my questioning started, one of my cell mates introduced himself to me as Shi Jian.* He was a serious, well-educated man in his forties who said he'd worked as an adviser to the Changsha Worker's Autonomous Federation. Shi told me he knew who I was from my work during the movement. He also said he was being released very soon. He offered to help me however he could. I needed a friend very badly back then, so I gave this man my trust.

"Can you take a letter to someone?" I asked.

He looked around to make sure we weren't being overheard and nodded. "Of course," he said. "Who?"

"His name is Hei Ma."

Quickly, I scratched out a note that said: DON'T WORRY. I DIDN'T TELL THEM ANYTHING. I handed this note to Shi Jian, who folded it and put it away without looking at it. We made certain he knew how to contact Hei Ma, after which I felt very relieved—until I discovered the truth.

Shi Jian was working for the government. The cadres and the security guards used moles like him to befriend men like me and pump us for information. By the time I figured it out, Shi Jian had been "transferred" to another cell. Later I learned that government agents had apprehended Hei Ma and detained him for a week in prison, during which, out of self-preservation, he told them about his share of the $100,000 HKD, which government agents confiscated. I also later heard that Shi Jian's life sentence had been abruptly commuted and that he had been released from jail, no doubt for helping the police.

I suppose I should thank Shi Jian in a way. He taught me a valuable lesson. In prison, beware of those who are kind to you. The only people you should trust are the ones who beat you and humiliate you. They, at least, have clear intentions.

Unfortunately, the inquiries didn't stop with Hei Ma. Somehow, the police found out about the money I'd left with my youngest sister. They went to my mother's apartment and confronted my family. Yan Hong denied any knowledge of the money, so the police dragged her to a desolate area and began to interrogate her.

My sister was alone, a teenager, and terrified. One of the policemen pulled his sidearm out of its holster, a big Type 54 semiautomatic, the Chinese copy of a Russian Tokarev. He threatened my sister with the gun, then put it beside her ear and fired it. Yan Hong gave up the money after that. And something inside her changed. She'd been such a wonderful girl, bubbly and extroverted. She was never really the same after that. What few words she spoke were issued quickly and always in a low voice.

The cadres would also instigate prisoners to attack me physically. Some of my cell mates stood with me at first, but even their patronage started to wane when they realized they would be beaten, too, for the crime of lending support. Soon, I was out of champions.

One occasion sticks out in my memory. Seven or eight of the toughest inmates turned on me at once. Two of them were murderers, famed throughout Changsha. They beat me so badly, I couldn't move for more than a week to come. I complained about these assaults. My jailers shrugged and nodded and moved me to a different cell where it soon became clear that my new cell mates had been told to keep right on beating me.

During all this, I was constantly denied medical treatment. The wardens said they could do nothing for me since—as I'd been told in Jiangmen—I hadn't yet been arrested formally. I was still a detainee and therefore not entitled to the rights of a full-fledged prisoner. As a detainee, said the wardens, my interrogations and incarceration were considered part of "performing one's civic duty."

They were government stooges one and all, willing to do whatever was asked of them, and small wonder. The bar for prison employees is very low in China. Quite often the most brutish and uneducated people end up working in the penal system. As far as I could see, the wardens and guards tortured people for two main reasons. First: to vent frustration over their own pathetic lot in life. Second: to create an atmosphere of fear and intimidation, which thereby allowed them to maintain better control over the prisoner population.

During the period I was incarcerated, prison officials favored the widespread use of electric batons. These weapons first appeared in the hands of Chinese law enforcement during the mid-1980s. By 1989, they were standard issue for all police, who plied them however they wished. The central authorities had drafted regulations governing the use of electric batons, but, like most Chinese laws, these regulations were nothing more than characters written in books. No one actually followed them.

Many times, I would watch the guards order a man to kneel. "Straighten your back!" the guards would bark. "Face the wall! Hands up high! Palms on the wall!"

The prisoner did as he was told, as if he had a choice.

The guard would then flip the switch to power on his baton and touch it against the metal cell door. Sparks would fly. There'd be a sinister crackling sound. The prisoner would be terrified, a natural reaction. The guard would then enter the cell and poke the back of the prisoner's neck, shocking him, burning him, making him scream, making him turn away. But the moment he moved, he had broken the order to remain frozen. So the guard would beat him severely, then ply the electric baton about the prisoner's mouth or his ears. Which, of course, made the prisoner flinch away, and so the cycled repeated itself.

Usually, this kept going until the prisoner passed out, whether from fear or pain or shock, the result was always the same. If the prisoner showed special fortitude, the guard would simply hold his baton against the prisoner's skin to inflict a burn that crackled and smoked, producing a smell that was sweet, like sugar in fire. Melting flesh twisted like sweat-soaked silk, marking the man forever. If necessary, another body part was selected, and the burning was repeated. In prison jargon, this process was called *dianliao*, or "electro-curing therapy."

Another technique the guards used was *gui bian* or "down-on-knees whipping." Evidently, this practice was peculiar to Changsha jails. During my time in Chinese prisons, I met a lot of men who'd been incarcerated in other facilities. None of them had seen *gui bian* practiced anywhere else but Changsha.

Gui bian involved role play. The guard played the part of the parent. The prisoner took the role of the child. The guard would say, "Pull down your trousers! Kneel, and face the wall!"

The prisoner took the same posture he'd assumed for the rite of *dian-liao*, only this time with his buttocks bared. The official then plied a bamboo switch that measured two feet long. He would slice it into the prisoner's flesh, causing great pain and humiliation, but all in the name of good theater. This was the torture part of the act. The guard who played the part of the punishing parent would say, "Ho ho! Are you well-behaved?" Plying his switch with a *whack whack whack!*

The prisoner would cry out, "Yes, sir! I am!"

"Oh, yes?" said the guard. *Whack whack whack!* "If you're so well-behaved, then why am I whipping you, hmmm?" *Whack whack!*

"Yes, sir!" the prisoner would cry. "Perhaps it's true! I'm badly behaved!"

"Aha!" the guard would say. *Whack whack whack!* "Badly behaved, is that what you say? Well, well! In that case, I'll whip you some more!"

I watched the toughest men I had known beg for mercy when treated like this. Men who had terrorized whole city districts. Thugs with heads like iron ingots, their knuckles as knobby as ancient trees, their guts layered in muscle and fat, with arms as thick as prize-winning hams. One and all, they fell and wept like babies. They promised the guards they would henceforth obey their every word, their every command, their every filthy syllable. But it wasn't over yet. God, no. Like all good theater pieces, a finale had to be reached. When the prisoner finally broke, when his sobs were enough to make other men weep, one of the *laotou yuba* would rise and offer the prisoner sage advice.

"Say, 'Thank you kindly, Mr. Cadre.'"

Which the prisoner would repeat, gasping as though this surrender were air itself, sweet in his lungs. At which point the cadre would often bow, a Shakespearean actor finishing *Lear*. He would exit the cell. Was the punishment finished? No. Not yet. The prisoner was left to endure a second, more powerful agony: the dawning realization that he could no longer sit or lie down. His beaten flesh would not allow him comfort in any position at all. Sometimes his buttocks bore permanent scars—a further humiliation, but also indelible testimony. The broken man had been marked for life, tagged as a recidivist, a fact the guards would exploit at will whenever they wished to dine on stale meat.

Another form of punishment was *liao quan jiao*, or martial arts practice. Technically, it was illegal for guards to punch or kick a prisoner. But during my time in the jails of Changsha, there were several young guards who loved nothing more than to bludgeon their captives senseless. Many were local yokels hired as temporary personnel. They had no training in law enforcement, not that this matters in China.

Guards who practiced *liao quan jiao* were dubbed with the moniker *sha*, or "killer." For instance, I recall one guard whose name was Luo Jian. We called him Luo *Sha*, or Killer Luo. Luo *Sha* would beat a prisoner for no good reason at all. Staring through the bars, he would point out a man at random and call him to come to the door. The prisoner would approach and stand before him, trembling, with sweat rolling down his face. Killer Luo would make small talk, asking about the man's family. Then he'd spin and strike without warning at all, dropping the man to his knees.

I once saw Killer Luo tell a prisoner to kneel down and face the wall. The moment the man had assumed the position, Luo *Sha* spun around and landed a flying drop kick straight to the small of the prisoner's spine. To this day, I confess my surprise. It's a miracle that the prisoner wasn't paralyzed. As it was, he couldn't move for two weeks. All things considered, a small price to pay.

Not that Luo *Sha* would have cared. He always remained nonchalant. His first strike done, he might walk around, talking with other prison guards, discussing the weather, gossip, news. Then he'd amble back to the man he had kicked, always in his own time. He'd repeat the kick again and again until he felt that he needed a break, or the prisoner collapsed, whichever came first. After which, Killer Luo would leave, his practice for that day finished. Curiously, he only struck with his feet. To this day, I can't say for certain why, but some of us thought that Luo *Sha* feared he would bruise his knuckles if he ever used them in "combat."

Not all the guards were so rabid, though. There was one I remember, a man called Number Two Officer Yang. Yang was also dubbed *sha*, but he was much more gentlemanly when practicing *liao quan jiao*. Yang would always pick a fight before he beat up a prisoner. It was such an odd thing for a guard to do, my cell mates and I had to wonder. Why was Killer Yang so tender? We thought it must have to do with his station. After all, Killer Yang was only a Number Two Officer, the low man on the totem pole. Perhaps if he ever rose through the ranks, his tenderness would evaporate. Perhaps then he would start to strike without warning, adopting the habits of Luo *Sha*, his superior.

4

Another form of cruelty was a ritual known as "*saochai* descending from mountaintops." *Saochai* is a term that means "those who sweep up the firewood." We prisoners used that special term to describe the PAP, or People's Armed Police, cadres employed by the prison to man the perimeter guard towers.

When the *saochai* descended from mountaintops, the PAP officers left their towers and entered our cells in "lightning raids." Ostensibly they were searching for contraband, though clearly this was a ruse since checking the cells for contraband was a task assigned to the regular guards. No, the real purpose of these raids was to allow the PAP to engage in "contact sessions" with inmates. In other words, it was their opportunity to beat us up and terrorize us to cement a lingering atmosphere of military control.

The PAP would storm the cell blocks brandishing special leather belts that were heavy-duty, military-issue. They would roll aside the door to a cell and plunge in, lashing about at random. Their stated reason for the violence? To drive back "insurrectionists," which was ridiculous, of course. No prisoner would dare attack a *saochai*, but the *saochai* didn't care. They needed the exercise. They spent so much time in their towers, cramped and bored, in need of release. And so they waded into the cells and smashed about at random, their leather straps wound tight round their fists, the belt buckles rising, hovering in midair where they winked in the wan cell light before they came crashing down. The metal whining, vibrating with concussion.

The *saochai* were powerfully built with thick necks, thick waists, and thick arms. Like bulls, they were as ignorant as they were strong, sadists who felt fulfillment when inflicting pain on others, and therefore made for perfect employees of the Chinese penal system.

Chinese prison officers were authorized to use chains and fetters on prisoners. Officially, only two types of restraints were permitted: handcuffs and ankle fetters. But officials often used illegal *tushoukao*, or "country cuffs," thick and heavy irons that looked medieval. No matter the size of your wrist, "country cuffs" were always clamped down tight to restrict circulation. Blood would swell in your fingers and hands, causing such pain that we often called *tushoukao* by another name, "tiger cuffs." Wearing them made you feel as though your hands were being chewed off by a tiger.

Sometimes the guards used *shouzhikao*, or "finger cuffs," which were also illegal and clearly inhumane. Picture two pieces of rough metal wire shaped into rings and welded together, side by side. The prisoner was ordered to put his thumbs through holes, which the cadres then pinched shut with pliers. Finger cuffs were intensely painful. Anything snared in them started to bloat. Permanent damage could result if you wore a set of *shouzhikao* for too long.

Sometimes the cadres used *zhiliao*, or "rod fetters." These differed from standard cuffs since they were joined by a fixed iron bar, not chains. The bar was a foot and a half in length, connected to cuffs for the ankles and wrists that kept the hands and feet apart, and made mobility painful. Anyone wearing *zhiliao* could only move by heaving and plunging himself along in a horribly crippled manner.

Sometimes, when the guards felt very vindictive, they used the *lianliaokao*, or "full shackle set"—wrist and ankle fetters that were attached to either a chain or a rod. These were commonly placed on prisoners awaiting execution. The most torturous *lianliaokao* involved a one-meter steel bar, set in the ground as a post. The prisoner's ankle cuffs were attached to the bottom end of the bar, his wrist cuffs to the top. So fixed, the prisoner could not sit down, nor could he stand up straight. He stood all day in a sort of half crouch, and slept like that, as well. It was an especially cruel position. I once saw a prisoner wear the *lianliaokao* for a whole month. His legs and buttocks swelled with blood. Sores appeared on his skin, and his flesh began to bloat and fester, rotting like old sausage casing.

But the cruelest, most barbaric tool I ever saw employed was the *menbanliao*, the dreaded "shackle board." Picture a large wooden door laid flat on four low legs with a set of handcuffs secured to each corner. The prisoner was laid across the board and shackled there, spread eagle. A hole was cut in the door, toward the middle, through which the prisoner would defecate.

During my time in Changsha jails, I met several pro-democracy fighters who'd been arrested shortly after June 4, detained for months but never charged. Many wound up on the *menbanliao*—left there for weeks in some cases. I also shared cells with common criminals who were made to endure this punishment. Memorably, twenty-six men were executed in Changsha on June 9, 1990, and all had been fixed to the *menbanliao* for days just prior to being killed.

We certainly feared the prison officials, but we often feared our fellow inmates more. Though strictly forbidden by law, the subculture known as the "cell boss system" was thriving wherever I went. When the cell door shut and the guards had gone, the *laotou yuba* reigned. Their word was law, their whims were fate. They would frequently spit on the floor, then order some inmate to lick the spot clean. Few men refused these orders. The ones who did were punished in strange and unspeakable ways, and always in front of everyone else since intimidation further expanded the cell boss's power.

Arriving new prisoners underwent the ritual of *bai lao men*, or "paying respects to the cell god." The new prisoner, nervous and scared, would be ordered to kneel by the *guihua tong*, or "cassia blossom vase." In prison slang: the toilet bucket. The prisoner would do this while holding several rice straws in each fist in parody of a Buddhist offering incense at the altar. The rice straws would come from the filthy quilts we used as our bedding.

The *laotou yuba* would bellow his orders, telling the new man to prostrate himself in front of the toilet bucket. Once for his mother. Once for the cadres. Finally, once for the cell boss. Then the *laotou yuba* would order the man to insert his straws in the toilet and blow bubbles into the fetid broth. The rising fumes could make a man gag, at which point the *laotou yuba* would say, "Well, now. What do you think? Does the cassia blossom taste sweet?"

The prisoner would have to respond, "Yes" or "Delicious" or something like that. If he did, *bai lao men* would come to an end. If he didn't, the tortures began again and continued until the new man was rendered properly subservient.

The prisoner might be subjected to *chi jiyu*, or "eating the golden carp." The cell boss, assisted by lackeys, would kick the prisoner hard in the face, several times, as needed. The sole of his shoe was shaped like a carp. Hence the name of the punishment.

Or the prisoner might be forced to endure *chi hongshao rou*, or "eating red-cooked meat." The *laotou yuba* would punch the man repeatedly in the jaw. The *laotou yuba's* fist, after all, resembled a giant slab of raw meat. The prisoner's jaws would slam together, opening, closing, as if he were eating.

But many cell boss tortures were crafted to injure the victim's mind instead of his body. Like *bao guihua tong*, for instance, "embracing the cassia blossom vase." This was another humiliation that centered around the toilet. *Bao guihua tong* took place at night, after the guards had inspected the cells, counted the inmates, and left. The man to be punished was ordered to kneel and wrap his arms around the toilet bucket and stay there the rest of the night. In the Changsha jails where I was kept, hardly a single evening would pass without someone embracing the cassia vase.

And of course there was always *xue shushu*, the dreaded "learning to count." This punishment was especially good at sowing discontent among men who displayed some alliance or friendship. The *laotou yuba* would take two friends and stand them together, facing each other. One would be ordered to start counting backward, starting from 100.

"100, 99, 98, 97 . . ."

If the prisoner made a mistake, his friend had to slap him across the face, very hard. Then the friend would start counting backward. If he made a mistake, he would get the slap. And on and on.

This is harder to do than it sounds. Try it when people are watching you. At the start of the process, neither man is willing to slap the other. Or they don't slap very hard. Their reticence would never last very long. Once *xue shushu* had gone a few rounds, anger and frustration would take over, clouding judgment. The slaps fell heavier and harder. By the end of the ritual, whatever alliance or friendship had stood was shattered beyond repair.

I could go on and on describing these cruel and petty games. Perhaps it's best if I don't. Perhaps I should end by describing the worst form of torture I ever saw used, a sort of final solution known as *dianliaokao*, or the "electric shackle treatment." Picture a prisoner shackled hand and foot to the *menbanliao*. Now imagine a switch being thrown. Current is passed through the shackles. As with the electric baton, the shock was always kept low so the prisoner wouldn't die—usually, anyway. But the pain was so great that he'd wish he had, would plead for it, in fact. We always knew when *dianliaokao* was being inflicted. The lights of the cell block would flicker and dim. And, of course, you would hear the screams.

Most cells I was in were windowless rooms choked with body odor and cigarette smoke. Cigarettes were currency. We traded for them. Everyone smoked. It wasn't a vice, it was something to do, a way to pass time, as well as a way to kill odors. We smoked to stay alive, though once in a while a man gave up hope and tried to mutilate himself.

The first incident I saw of this involved a fragment of razor blade. Don't ask me how the prisoner got it. Sometimes the guards could be bribed to smuggle contraband into the complex. Or sometimes a visitor hid such an item inside a gift of food. Either way, the man in question jammed this fragment deep into his abdomen and dragged it across, in essence disemboweling himself.

Someone noticed what he had done, and everyone started to shout. We rushed over. The man was on his back like a netted fish that someone had dragged to the shoreline. His eyes were wide open, staring at nothing. His mouth formed a pucker, sucking for air. His abdomen had split like a great pair of lips. Blue loops of intestine spilled out. The stench was moist and rotten like a bag of garbage in summertime, like the stench of a wharf in the blaze of August.

Our shouting brought the guards, who rushed in and ordered everyone back. We stood against the far wall as they entered the cell and took the wounded man out. We never saw him again, but that was the plan, of course. Self-mutilation was a way of getting out of prison. The inmate had suffered a wound so great, he had to be taken outside the complex, to a hospital and a surgeon. His doctors would mandate a long convalescence, one that he could not serve in prison. Which meant he was free, if he lived. Many, I know, did not. Self-mutilation is common throughout the Chinese penal system, though usually more so in hard labor camps where inmates look forward to nothing.

Once in a while, we would hear a great clamor, and guards would enter the cell block. If they were regular prison cadres, we knew we were in the clear. If, however, the guards were soldiers dressed in army uniforms, we knew that someone was going to die. In China, it's a penal tradition to execute prisoners without any warning.

We already knew who was going to die. Prisoners who'd been sentenced to death wore wrist and ankle shackles. They already knew their fate; they just didn't know when the guards would come. That was up to the government. Until then, they had to sit around, immobilized, waiting to die. To eat or use the toilet, they required assistance from other prisoners, otherwise they would be left alone to starve or soil themselves, which is why most prayed to die quickly. In China, appealing a sentence of death is technically possible, but in all my years I've never heard of a single appeal being accepted.

The guards would put only one man condemned to death in each cell. I watched a few of them try to take their own lives by bashing their heads against the stone walls. I guess that was preferable to waiting. The cadres knew the condemned would try this, so they issued ultimatums: if the man condemned to die succeeded in taking his own life before the government got to kill him, everyone in the cell would be punished. And so we created an informal roster, dividing our numbers in two-hour shifts that worked around the clock. We would watch these men, feed them, care for them as best we could. We'd try to give them hope enough to stay alive so they could be murdered.

When the execution squad arrived, they would enter each cell and, without any words, seize the condemned and drag them into the hallway. Sometimes the soldiers amassed a group of twenty to twenty-five men at once. When all had been collected, they frog-marched the prisoners down the corridor, past the bars of our cell. We heard a door open at the end of the hall, then the loud bang as the door slammed shut. We never saw those men again. Neither did their families. We heard the shots a few minutes later, and that was that.

During my year at Changsha Number One Jail, I counted at least one hundred prisoners who were executed in this fashion. But Changsha is a medium-sized city. There are at least fifty more prisons of approximately the same size spread across China, and another five hundred cities with prisons that are smaller than Changsha, not to mention four thousand counties that don't factor into this tally at all. If you do the math, you'll come to realize that China executes a lot of people.

The government preferred not to execute prisoners over the holiday season. October 1 is National Day, the anniversary marking the founding of the People's Republic. Each year a grand parade is held. There are fireworks in Tiananmen Square on the spot where Mao Zedong first stood to declare our liberation in the autumn of 1949. Executions therefore reached a frenzy during the month of September. The government wanted people dead so as not to obstruct the festivities. The killings would resume in the spring. After the New Year's celebration, the angels of mercy came back in the form of the uniformed soldiers. They hauled you out to the prison yard, stood you up against a stone wall, pointed their rifles, and shot you. Free at last!

5

I met a lot of familiar faces in Changsha Number One Jail. One of them was my old, dear adviser, Professor Peng. The CCP had come to his home in mid-June, around the same time I fled Hunan, heading south for Guangdong. They beat him, questioned him, and threw him in jail where, despite his age, the good professor showed excellent spirit. Every day, he would shout from his cell so that everyone on the block could hear. "Why are you holding me?" he would say. "This is an abomination! I demand to be released!"

His show of resistance did not go unpunished. Since Old Peng wouldn't shut his mouth, the cadres pulled him out of his cell and shackled him onto the *menbanliao*.

Over the next few days, we heard his cries, a wandering scale of tones. First outrage, then childlike confusion, then fear, then pain, then outrage again. A call to rally. A call for vengeance. Finally, a call for aid. This last one was the worst to our ears, the one that meant that Peng's spirit was breaking.

"Let me out!" he would scream for a while, followed by lengthy silence. Then: "I need to take a bath." More silence. Then, with rising vigor. "We are not afraid! Do you hear me? We are not afraid!"

Enraged, scared, and in pain though he was, Old Peng remained quite sensible. For instance, he never spoke slogans or phrases the cadres could point to as counterrevolutionary. Sometimes, Peng would even sing that age-old communist anthem, the one they teach in primary schools. "Learn from the Good Example of Comrade Lei Feng."

Lei Feng, of course, was a common soldier, an Everyman of the PLA who died in 1962 at the age of twenty-two. The Party lionized his life, purely for propaganda purposes. Lei Feng was the PRC's Molly Pitcher, a communist Rosie the Riveter. As in all propaganda, fiction had been superimposed over fact. The Party had told blatant lies to create a People's hero. Lei Feng, they said, had been selfless, modest, and dedicated to communist thought. A Lei Feng Memorial was built in Fushun, the town where Lei eventually died. Another memorial was built in Changsha, the home of so many great communist heroes. Schools, hospitals, plazas, and roads were all renamed for Lei Fang. March 5 was declared "Learn from Lei Feng Day." T-shirts and buttons bore his image, along with the slogan "Follow Lei Feng's Example! Love the Party, Love Socialism, Love the People!"

The Party at one point even announced that a copy of Lei Feng's diary had been found. And guess what Lei Feng had written in this most personal document? He asked the youth of China to "submit unquestioningly to the control of our Great Leader." In light of this discovery, a new term was coined: *Huo Lei Feng*, which could be used as a noun or as an adjective to describe any person whose manner was legendarily selfless.

We would press ourselves to the bars of our cell, while, down the hall, Peng's voice would rise, warbling toward a crescendo. "Learn from the Good Example of Comrade Lei Feng!" he sang. To the cadre's ears, Old Peng was praising Lei Feng, the Party, and the communist system. But my ears, and the ears of all political prisoners, heard something very different. Peng was letting us know he was fine, that he was alive and had kept his wits enough to give us encouragement. He was telling us not to be afraid in that place of awesome darkness.

His voice would reach the final note and fall silent. Many of us who had known the professor crushed steel bars in our palms. Then, as we'd been trained to do as children in Chinese grade schools, we all cried out in unison, lauding this singer's selfless performance. "Professor Peng! A good example!"

Silence rose in answer.

They kept him on that damnable board for days and days on end. Old Peng's cries, like the roar of a tide, crashed forward but always rolled back out, receding to a dull background roar that was worse than if he had stopped altogether. At one point, I couldn't bear anymore. I called for a cadre and demanded that Peng be released.

The cadre looked at me calmly and said that Professor Peng was "psychologically ill," which is why he'd been kept in shackles. "For his own benefit," the cadre said, without a trace of irony.

I told the cadre I'd read the statutes. Under Chinese criminal law, the mentally ill are considered "exempt from prosecution." If Peng were in fact disturbed, he should be given special treatment, not made to endure some horrible torture strapped to the *menbanliao*. But the officer shook his head and smiled. "As yet, we have no proof of the good professor's illness. He therefore cannot qualify for the exemption you propose." With that, he walked away.

In total, Professor Peng survived three long months on the shackle board. Some days after his release, while escorted by guards, I passed old Peng in a corridor. I was being led to interrogation. He was being led away. When I saw him, I had to choke back tears and fight to retain my composure. The man I had known, the man who had befriended me and all the pro-democracy students, was gone. The thing that remained was stoop-backed and shriveled, a wasted husk of a man who walked on legs that were bamboo thin and drooled all over himself. But somehow Peng managed to look up and smile. I'll never forget the look on his face or the words he spoke to me.

"Don't worry, *Xiao* Tang," he slurred. "Everything is all right. You'll see."

That was the last time I saw him. A few days later, he disappeared.

I asked about him constantly. By then, I was being pulled from my cell almost daily to meet with pre-trial investigators. One of them became open with me, if not exactly friendly. He treated me like I was a dog who'd done something terribly wrong, but only because I was dumb, an animal badly in need of training. This man eventually told me that Peng had been taken to a hospital where he'd finally been diagnosed as having a psychiatric illness. The government said that Peng could be released. He was finally going home. I felt a great relief. But a year or so later, I learned the truth.

Peng had been released, all right, but he certainly hadn't gone home. Diagnosed as mentally ill, the Party had placed him directly in an asylum where he wasn't allowed to see his family. It was the government's way of levying a life sentence using alternative means. Soon after being admitted, Peng died. No one seems to know how.

6

Ren Jun was also imprisoned in Changsha Number One Jail. My colleague and sometime nemesis from Central-South Industrial had been arrested toward the end of June, then transferred to Changsha Number One Jail in mid-July, around the same time I arrived from Guangdong. He was kept in Cell Number 6, a few doors down from mine. I saw him each time the guards took me out of my cell and led me down the hall to the interrogation rooms. Sometimes we would exchange a few words.

"We stand together, Baiqiao Tang!" Ren would hiss at me through the bars, flashing the V sign for victory. But I noticed a change as the months went by and our hopes for an early release began to fade. Ren Jun began to grow listless and dark. His eyes, so formerly full of life, were downcast and dull, bereft of expression. I began to fear for his health.

"We stand together," I would say, hoping that he would reply. But Ren Jun often answered in silence. At times, he never looked up.

In the spring of 1990, he must have reached some personal brink. He started to shout and make big scenes—dangerous, counterrevolutionary statements. I tried to get word to him, to caution him against making such displays. I don't know if he ever received my messages. Maybe he simply ignored them. But soon, the prison officials had marked Ren Jun as a troublemaker. They started to pull him out of his cell and subject him to discipline. One of the measures most often chosen was *jiao*, a word that means "reaming." A prisoner given *jiao* is shocked repeatedly by an electric baton placed against sensitive body parts. First the cadres shock the prisoner's throat, his face, his ears, and the back of his neck. But the term "reaming" comes from how they would push live batons in a victim's mouth and twist them around as though reaming a hole, scalding them inside their heads.

My cell mates and I heard Ren Jun being tortured like this too many times to mention. His cries became unbearable, but what could we do? Ren made things worse by fighting back. It was a very big mistake. The cadres finally shackled him to the *menbanliao*, the same way they had Old Peng. They left Ren Jun on that damnable board to rot, and only took him off when they wanted to stand him up against the wall and administer more reaming. Or sometimes he was handed to a *laotou yuba* known for particular cruelty. This man would beat Ren Jun for exercise before handing him back to the wardens, who placed him once more on the *menbanliao*, and so began the cycle anew.

At some point, Ren Jun simply went berserk. Whatever was left of his mind must have cracked. Late in the evening, we'd hear his screams ratcheting down the hallway. "You bastards! I'll kill you! I'll kill you all!" he'd say. Then: "Let me out of here! I'm so angry, I could die!"

Sometimes we heard him bark like a dog or quack like a duck. At other times, he crowed like a chicken or talked to himself through the night, into daybreak.

Once again, I called for the cadres, begging that Ren Jun be freed. The cadre shook his head and said that Ren was bringing these "treatments" upon himself. "This facility has rules," he said. "And Prisoner Ren Jun has stirred up his fair share of trouble. It's essential that he be punished. How would you like to join him?"

That threat was enough to make me step back and contemplate other strategies.

Eventually, Ren Jun lapsed into a state not unlike catatonia. His body no longer responded when the cadres used their electric batons. It took a few days, but the wardens finally seemed to recognize something was amiss. For a while, they stopped the reaming. By then, however, Ren Jun had become a sack of meat with arms and legs. He could not stand up on his own. They placed him in different cells where the other prisoners could torment him. The *laotou yuba* stuffed dirty socks or cloths in his mouth, and doused him in freezing cold water. Sometimes, for sport, they would kick him. All the while, Ren Jun would lie there, his eyes wide open and staring ahead. Three months went by like this.

The prison officials got scared then, I think. Word of excessive punishments had already started to leak outside the walls of Changsha Number One Jail. The public had endured the crackdown that followed Tiananmen Square, but unrest was still in the air. The last thing the government needed or wanted was more discontent, especially over a young student leader who'd been savaged by government officers.

Ren Jun's punishments halted at once, replaced by intense "ideology work." Mind you, the cell gods continued to bully him, drawing blood whenever they pleased. But none of it seemed to affect Ren Jun. By that point, he was a lifeless husk, his spirit departed, like wind. Later, I heard that his torments continued right up until his release in late 1990.

7

As prisoners, we were forced to make matchboxes. You know the kind—they're two inches long and one inch wide. Each box is made of two pieces that fit together, a hollow rectangular shell as well as the shuttle that fits inside, both made of lightweight cardboard. You can find them in bars and good hotels and quality restaurants from coast to coast across the United States.

The cardboard for the boxes arrived at our cell each morning. Guards would bring in great stacks of the stuff bound together with twine. Each prisoner helped himself to a stack, along with a tiny bottle of glue and a tiny squared-off wooden dowel to help with shaping the boxes. We'd find a place to work on the floor, sit down with crossed legs and spines flagpole straight, and set to work.

Our fingers moved under the watchful eyes of the guards. The cardboard came with slight perforations that helped you know where to fold. The dowel assisted in making crisp edges. Folding the matchbox shell was simple, you just followed the perforations and used a tiny bit of glue under the friction strip—the place where matches are struck—to hold the shell together. The shuttles took a bit more time. We fiddled with the tiny tabs that folded into each other. Used another touch of glue. Then we had to make sure the shuttle would fit inside the shell. Once it did, we tossed it aside. A pile of finished matchboxes grew like the bricks of a tiny pyramid. We would get to work on the next one fast, or the guards might get ideas.

A prisoner's normal daily quota was five hundred finished boxes. This could take up to sixteen hours, sometimes more, but rarely less. Prisoners who didn't meet the quota were punished in stages like this: First, the guards would keep them awake until they had finished their ration. If that meant they worked straight for twenty-four hours then started again on a brand-new ration, so be it. If they still weren't meeting their quota, the guards would deprive them of cigarettes, which was worse than being deprived of food. The smoke withdrawal was a physical pain, like getting a case of the flu.

If having no cigarettes didn't inspire them, the guards resorted to torture. They would enter the cell and make the prisoners kneel, then start the "electro-curing therapy," or sometimes they would use *jiao*, the "reaming." In cases of more extreme abuse, the guards might take the prisoner out of the cell to the privacy of the hallway where they could execute these tortures and more, out of sight from other inmates.

After about two weeks of folding matchboxes, I noticed I didn't need the dowel anymore, nor did I have to watch my fingers as they worked. My hands knew what they were doing, which allowed my mind to drift. I often thought of my family and wondered how they were doing. As a government detainee, I was not allowed to get mail or to receive visitors or to have any communication with the outside world at all. I wondered how my mother and father were getting along in Yongzhou. I worried sick about them, and thought they must feel the same about me.

One day, the guards brought in many more stacks of cardboard than was usual. They said a big order had just come in. Do these boxes immediately, or else. No one bothered to ask what that meant. We sat down and got to work, and did not sleep for the next three days. We folded. Crimped. Glued. Finished. Tossed the matchbox aside. Started again. Folded. Crimped. Glued. Finished. Tossed the matchbox aside.

I don't know how many boxes we made during that one long stretch.

Thousands apiece, I have to assume, and no one ever complained. No one said a word. What would have been the point? Words could not help you to fold, crimp, glue, or finish. Words only got you in trouble.

As it turned out, a good thing arose from this exercise. Once forty-eight hours had passed, I realized that I was wide awake, clear in my thoughts and feeling good. After that, it was easy, and that's when I had a realization. You can always go farther than you think at first. Do more. Get better. Set your sights higher. Farther than you've dared to dream.

The boundaries we perceive in ourselves are mostly self-imposed. You can push them back if you want to. Make space for the power of the spirit. Let go of that which is dragging you down, and you can reach a new level inside. It doesn't have to be some great religious epiphany. Religion doesn't have to be involved at all. You can find how strong you really are by folding thousands of matchboxes. The challenge lies within you. It has always been there, and nowhere else.

8

I was finally placed under formal arrest on November 28, 1989, nearly five months after being captured in Jiangmen City. The guards took me out of my cell and brought me into a tiny room where officials leveled four charges against me: Spreading counterrevolutionary propaganda. Inciting counterrevolutionary activities. Defection to the enemy. And treason.

The first three charges were no surprise, but treason? I had a violent reaction to that.

"What does this mean?" I asked. "Treason?"

The officials said, "You are a traitor to the motherland."

I rose from my seat and began to shout. "You bunch of gangsters and crooks! A traitor to the motherland? *You* perpetrate treason, I do not! *You* are corrupt. Not me! You won't get away with this, damn you!"

The officials stayed very calm, as if they were watching a theater show. My tirade seemed to convince them that their accusations were justified. They took notes on everything I said. No doubt my damnations would later show up in a nice, new transcript they'd ask me to sign—evidence to be used in my case whenever my trial rolled around.

I was escorted back to my cell by guards with electric batons. That night, I awoke as rough hands grabbed me and picked me up and threw me against the wall. The beating began. I had spoken too loudly. Too boldly. I had disrespected the cadres. The *laotou yuba* had their orders and were eager to show their loyalty.

Six months passed during which no one paid much attention to me. I was grateful. Going unnoticed is the best outcome you can hope for in a Chinese prison. I spent my days making matchboxes. Eating. Sleeping. Avoiding trouble. Because I refused to confess, I was thought to be an "instigator." The cadres frequently transferred my quarters, moving me from cell to cell in hopes that the constant shuffling would keep me from forming alliances. And they were right. Each time, the *laotou yuba* knew who I was before I arrived as a new refugee in their domain. They subjected me to various tortures for no good reason at all. Their punishments grew even more severe whenever I dared to "speak wild thoughts." In my case, that meant speaking at all. I learned to keep my mouth shut, to move my fingers. Make matchboxes.

Now that I'd been officially arrested and charged, I was finally allowed to receive mail, as well as occasional visitors. Letters from my mother and sisters began to pour in, but not from my father. This worried me. I wrote to my sisters and mother and asked why I hadn't heard from my father. They wrote back and told me not to worry. My father was very busy, they said. "He sends his best. He wants you to concentrate on staying healthy and coming back to us."

I started to grow suspicious. I'd been in prison for more than a year. No word from my father at all? I demanded to see the warden. The guards took me out of my cell and down to a room where the warden came in and listened to what I told him. "Something is wrong with my father," I said. "Please. I must see my family."

The warden shook his head. "That's not what prison is for," he said. "You shouldn't be thinking about your father. Right now, you should think about yourself. The crimes that you have committed."

I persisted, knowing the dangers. Prisoners don't demand things of wardens. Prisoners have no rights. I was an outcast, a pariah. But once, while I was pressing the issue, the warden gave me a shock. He spoke very softly, almost kindly, as though he were addressing a friend. "Listen," he said. "I have no idea why your father has not written to you. Perhaps he is angry at you for disgracing your family name. Perhaps he has divorced your mother out of shame. Having a relative in jail takes a very big toll on a family. I've heard terrible stories throughout my years."

The warden said this so flatly that it started to make perfect sense. I began to believe what he'd said. Perhaps my father *was* angry with me. Look at what I had put him through. Changing my major, the whole ordeal. He'd leveraged contacts to help me. And then to end up wanted? Hunted by the Party? Perhaps I'd disgraced my family, indeed. Placed strain on my father and mother's marriage. Perhaps they had parted. That would explain my father's absence. My mother and sisters were probably too embarrassed to tell me that he'd left.

I felt an awful shame right then, a gnawing, black sensation. How could I have done this to my family? To my father? I gave up asking his whereabouts. I didn't want to know. He would contact me when he felt ready. For the moment, the warden was right. I needed to think about what I had done. I resolved to focus on that.

9

My case was finally brought to trial on July 17, 1990, more than a year after I'd been arrested, and far beyond the legal limit for holding me. I was given no notice at all. Guards came into my cell one day. They pulled me out and placed me in fetters and dragged me outside to a vehicle.

It was the first time I'd seen the sun in months. Blinking hard at the baleful eye that was hot like a giant ember. The doors *clunked* closed. The car sped off. I was driven to Changsha Intermediate Courthouse and led into a room where a judge named Tang Jikai (who was no relation to me), two *peishen yuan* (or jurors), two prosecutors, and a lawyer sat primly up on a rostrum. Waiting.

The only people in the audience were my two older sisters, Yan Ni and Yan Zhen, and they were there by luck. Yan Zhen was an officer in the public security bureau. She'd heard about the trial at the very last minute. Connections at her office informed her, otherwise she would have missed it. Gathering up Yan Ni, Yan Zhen had dashed to the courthouse. So now the two of them sat there, nervous, watching me from the back of the room.

None of my fellow students from Hunan Normal were present. No one was there to testify on my behalf. I'd been told I'd be given a court-appointed lawyer when it came time for me to stand trial. The lawyer was there, but we'd never met. How was it possible for him to defend a man he had never spoken to? During the course of my trial, he didn't even look at me.

I protested, calling these oversights of law egregious. I said that, based on this awful misconduct, the trial must be invalidated. The court completely ignored me. Then the judges and prosecutors read the charges against me. The charge of "traitor against the motherland" had been dropped. Thank goodness for small favors. But everything else remained.

As part of my indictment, the following passage was read:

> Our examination shows that defendant Baiqiao Tang was chief leader of the illegal organization, Hunan Students Autonomous Federation. From May 1989 on, he organized and participated in illegal rallies and demonstrations on many occasions.
>
> After the quelling of the counterrevolutionary rebellion in Beijing, defendant Baiqiao Tang attended, in the evening of June 7, a meeting called by Ren Jun, Zhang Xin, and others. At that meeting, they plotted to hold a memorial meeting on June 8 for the counterrevolutionary thugs suppressed in Beijing. Defendant Baiqiao Tang instructed Li XX, a student in the department of Chinese of Hunan Normal University, to draft a "memorial speech." That speech invented the story of our martial law troops having massacred students, workers, and citizens, and of having killed thousands of them. It was most pernicious.
>
> On June 8 of the same year, defendant Baiqiao Tang co-chaired, with Zhang Xin, the "memorial meeting" held on the square in front of the Changsha railway station. Liu Wei, Lu Qing, Zhou Ming, and Zhang Xin (all prosecuted in separate cases) spoke at the meeting. They venomously attacked the party and government, and incited antagonism. On June 12, 1989, the People's Government of the City of Changsha issued a public notice outlawing the Hunan Students Autonomous Federation and the Changsha Workers Autonomous Federation. Defendant Baiqiao Tang refused to register with the authorities.
>
> On June 15, together with Yu Zhaohui and others, he absconded to Guangzhou and Xinghui, and made telephone contacts with people outside the country. They accepted 92,500 yuan and HK$4,500, as well as a book of secret codes for communication sent from Hong Kong. Baiqiao Tang passed out his calling cards, bearing the title of Executive Director of the Hunan Students Autonomous Federation, and copies of the memorial speech delivered at the June 8 "memorial meeting," to people outside

the country. At the same time, defendant Baiqiao Tang absconded to Muzhou Township in Xinghui County, attempting to cross the border at Zhuhai and sneak into Macau.

The above-mentioned facts of his crime are attested to by witnesses' testimony, criminal scientific techniques, as well as photographs, telephone receipts, and evidence of confiscated booty. The defendant also admitted as much in his recorded confessions. The facts are clear and the evidence is solid, complete, and sufficient to prove the case.

In the opinion of the procuratorate, defendant Baiqiao Tang planned and organized illegal demonstrations and presided over the June 8 "memorial meeting." His activities violated Article 102 of the Criminal Code of the People's Republic of China, and constituted the crime of counterrevolutionary propaganda and incitement. In order to consolidate China's political power of the people's democratic dictatorship, defend the socialist system, and punish counterrevolutionary crimes, and in accordance with Article 100 of the Criminal Procedure Law of the People's Republic of China, we indict the defendant, and request that your court judge him according to law.

Once the reading was finished, the judges and prosecutors began to ask me questions. I answered them all as best I could, though it was an exercise in futility since the questions they asked had nothing to do whatsoever with me or any actions I took. These men had already made their decision and were tapping about for the sake of appearance. Finally they asked if I had any questions.

"Yes," I said. "Why have none of my fellow students been allowed to speak as witnesses?"

The judges seemed puzzled by this. One of them said, "Let your campus mates come?" He shook his head. "Oh, no. No, no. That would not do."

So I asked to read a letter that I had taken great pains to write in my defense. I'd worked on it for months knowing my trial would come eventually. The five-man court started laughing as though this were the most naive thing they'd ever heard. They told me to sit down.

There followed a brief adjournment, after which Judge Tang Jikai stood up and announced that I was a sinner against the people. Then he levied my sentence: three years in prison, with two years' subsequent deprivation of political rights. And that was it, my trial was over. The entire hearing took less than two hours, which, coincidentally, is about the same time it takes to watch a Marx Brothers movie.

I was immediately presented with sentencing documents that the court had drawn up before I was given a chance to defend myself. I refused to sign them. Judge Tang Jikai came over to me. He was about twenty-seven or twenty-eight years old, and very polite. Quietly, he said, "Listen, Baiqiao Tang. Your guilt and the length of your sentence were determined in meetings that all took place long before this trial. Several months ago, in fact. That is why the court refused to admit anyone. And look at what month this is."

"July?"

"Yes. Summer vacations have already started for colleges and universities. A coincidence? Do not think so." Judge Tang Jikai smiled and shrugged. "This is a very good sentence," he said. "Be happy with it." And then he left.

So now I was formally a convicted criminal. Since the Chinese government never admits it incarcerates political prisoners, I was officially no different from the countless rapists, robbers, murderers, and thieves with whom I had spent the past year. The guards came again and took me away.

I'd been living in Changsha Number One Jail so long, the cracks in the walls and floors were familiar to me as lines in a favorite book. But after fifteen months, the government uprooted me and sent me to Changsha Number Two Jail. This was an unofficial punishment since conditions in Number Two Jail were much worse than those I'd grown accustomed to. To say nothing of what a burden it was to start all over again. I had to make new friends. I had to fight new battles for territory, to protect myself from marauders intent on testing my mettle at every moment.

No matchboxes were made at Number Two Jail. Instead, we inmates assembled cardboard boxes used to store Chinese medicine. These boxes would hold the little vials of tonics, tinctures, and traditional potions used to clean the blood or move the Qi—the vital energy—through a sick person's body. Some of the medicines we made boxes for calmed the Five Dragons, emotions said to jeopardize health: *Fear, anger, excessive joy* (which is often referred to as *mania*), *grief* or *sadness*, and *worry*.

Four of those dragons live here, I thought. In Changsha Number Two Jail. All are present in this awful place, save for excessive joy. You would have to look very hard indeed to find joy in a Chinese penitentiary.

I only spent a month at Changsha Number Two Jail. After that, I was finally sent to a prison, a place called Longxi, also known as Hunan Number 6 Provincial Prison, also known as the Shaoyang Marble Factory, the place where my formal sentence began.

10

Longxi Prison. Picture a low button of stone surrounded by walls about 150 miles south of Changsha. Picture remote terrain raked by the granite noses of mountains. Picture desolation in all its natural splendor: scrub pine, scrub grass, living things disdaining growth, knowing in their secret ways that this land is forsaken.

Now go behind the stout stone walls. Walk through the shadows thrown by the guard towers and witness the massive operation that's taking place inside. The prison is actually a large-scale marble quarrying plant. The workforce is entirely made up of Longxi inmates. When I was there, the population totaled some two thousand convicts, about seventy of whom were political prisoners serving sentences ranging from two years to life. The majority, however, were common criminals serving terms of ten years or more.

My first day there, I was called to a room with a handful of other new inmates. This was my freshman class (as it were) in the inmate training program, also known as Ideological Education for Criminals, a course that was scheduled to last three months. I wasn't looking forward to it, though joining the general population seemed even less appealing given how violent and inhumane it was reputed to be. At that time, Longxi was known as one of the worst prison hellholes in China.

"Attention!" a prison cadre shouted. My fellow inmates and I snapped to. The cadre swaggered in front of us, grinning, drunk on the wine of authority. He started to call out the rules.

"Welcome to Longxi Prison!" he said. "If you do not feel welcome here? Too bad! You are part of a prison induction team. If you do not want to be part of this team? Too bad! You and your fellow inmates are criminals! Therefore you will undergo our program: Ideological Education for Criminals! If you do not want to undergo this program? Too bad!"

He laughed. As did the guards, on cue. Small apes mimic the big ape.

The moment this meeting was finished, a guard took hold of me and led me away down a hallway, alone. The guard stopped in front of a door and knocked. The door swung open. The guard led me in. A uniformed officer a few years older than me motioned for me to take a chair. "Thank you," the officer said to the guard. "Leave us and close the door."

The guard complied. The cadre and I just sat there, face to face. Alone.

"Baiqiao Tang, do you know who I am?"

I had no idea, but I needed a friend. So I lied, putting confidence into my voice. "We went to the same high school together," I said.

The officer threw back his head and laughed. "You're desperate, aren't you?" He grinned. "My name is Zhao Yuen.* And no, we didn't go to high school together. But I was in Changsha during the movement. I heard about your exploits. We even met during a demonstration. Frankly, I was very impressed."

Zhao Yuen told me he was a mechanical engineer. I thought I'd misheard him at first. "A mechanical engineer who works at a prison?" But Zhao Yuen reminded me that this particular prison was also a marble quarry. As such, it had lots of equipment for cutting, shaping, and sanding stone—equipment that broke down a lot. As such, men of his expertise found themselves in high demand.

"I've been following your case," said Zhao Yuen. He saw the look on my face and laughed. "Does that surprise you? You should know, Baiqiao Tang, we all looked up to you during the movement. In fact, I consider it my honor to stand before you."

I cannot tell you how this felt, to have made a friend in such a dark place—a friend in power, no less.

Zhao Yuen glanced toward the door to his office and lowered his voice a notch. "This is the way it will work," he said. "You will call me Officer Zhao when the other guards are present. In private, however, please call me Zhao Yuen. Whatever you need, you will come to me. I will try my best to look out for you."

Over the next few months, Zhao Yuen made good on his word. He would smuggle food into Longxi Prison. We always ate it together. He even brought bottles of fine rice wine, a surreal indulgence in prison and one that, if discovered, would surely have cost Zhao Yuen his job. Or worse.

At first, we kept our activities quiet. I was adamant in protecting our secret. I wanted no harm to come to my friend. Zhao Yuen was the one who finally told me, "Relax. No one is watching."

He worked it out so I could bring one or two trusted friends to our "meetings." Some colleagues who came were Zhang Jun,* Tang Liang,* and Zhou Rong.* I hadn't known any of these men before arriving at Longxi. They came from different cities throughout Hunan, and all were political prisoners. They had worked as teachers of high school or college and, though still in their early twenties or thirties, they each had a greatness of character that reminded me of my father. And of course they'd been part of the movement in the spring of '89.

It's hard to believe, looking back, but eventually my friends and I were laughing and joking and playing cards with Zhao Yuen in the prison's education office. We'd eat food and drink beverages that put the prison kitchen to shame. It was quite a strange, alternative life to the suffering all around us. Not that we ever forgot where we were. Whenever our meetings were over, the suffering was always right there, waiting for us.

Zhao Yuen took all these dangers in stride. How I still remember him! Relaxed, smiling, carefree Zhao Yuen. I worried about him constantly. He was taking such a large risk, putting his very life in danger. I vowed that I would never take his generosity for granted.

11

My political reeducation was an exercise in the absurd. Each morning, my fellow teammates and I were forced to sing three songs, our warbling jailbird chorus. The first song would be "Without the Communist Party, There Would be No New China." It was a bouncy, jaunty, doo-dah rhythm. Perfect for manual labor.

Our second song was that grand old chestnut "Socialism Is Good." The lyrics go:

> *Socialism is good!*
> *Socialism is good!*
> *In socialist nations, the people have high status!*
> *Overthrow the reactionaries!*
> *Imperialism flees with its tail between its legs!*

Finally, we'd close out our session with "Learn from the Good Example of Comrade Lei Feng." I thought of Old Peng each time we sang it. Where was my friend the professor now?

After each song, the Swaggering Cadre would shout three questions at us. "Who are you?" he would demand.

We had to respond, "We are criminals!"

"Where are you?"

We had to say, "In prison!"

"Why are you here?"

We had to shout back, "We are here to reform ourselves through labor!"

As well as to learn to sing, I thought.

Once the singing and shouting were finished, my teammates and I performed parade drills that were staged for the wardens' and officers' pleasure. These drills were actually a chance to degrade and humiliate us. The guards would kick out our feet as we marched or tickle our ears with feathers while ordering us to stand at attention. They would demand that a man step forward, then strike him for breaking the line. And so on. Bullying games played by low men with little imagination or character. It was smartest just to play along, but sometimes I found that I couldn't. Every man has his limits, the days where he must stand up for himself, even when it is dangerous.

On one occasion, the warden ordered new inmates to repair fishnets. I refused because Chinese law is clear: working prisoners must be paid—a paltry sum, barely pennies a day, but we had to be paid this sum nonetheless. And we new inmates weren't getting paid at all. When I objected, the guards brought me to see the prison director in his office. He was very angry with me.

"What do you think you're doing?" he said.

"I'm not sure what you mean."

"You were ordered to repair the nets."

"Yes," I said. "That's true."

"And yet you refuse."

"That's right. I do."

"Why? What makes you so special?"

"I don't think I'm special at all. I just want to get paid. It's the law."

"Didn't the guards give you cigarettes?"

"Yes," I said. "But that's not being paid."

This director was very bright. He'd instructed the guards to pass cigarettes out in lieu of deposits to our prison accounts. No one knew where that money went, though of course I had my suspicions.

"Fine," the director said. "Cuffs and fetters."

"I think this is very simple," I said. "You're breaking the law. I'm protesting that."

The director snorted and shook his head and recited a popular Party

The Tang family. Photo taken at Tang Rentong's high school in Yongzhou, approximately 1977. *Top row* (*from left to right*): Tang Yanni, Tang Jiezhen, Baiqiao Tang, Tang Yanzhen. *Bottom row*: Tang Yanhong, Tang Rentong, Luo Huaying, Tang Yanfei. *From the personal collection of Baiqiao Tang.*

Baiqiao Tang as a student at Lingling Number Four High School, Hunan Province, 1984. *From the personal collection of Baiqiao Tang.*

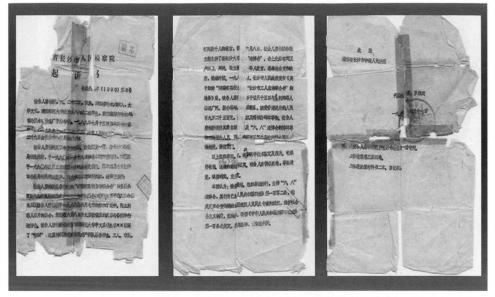

Copy of Baiqiao Tang's indictment from the Changsha Attorney's Office issued ten months after Tang was detained for the crime of being a counterrevolutionary among others. *From the personal collection of Baiqiao Tang.*

Photo taken at Baiqiao Tang's *Huangsong* (farewell) party at the home of Robin Munro in Hong Kong, 1992. *From left to right*: Sheng Feifeng, Scott Bellard, Tang Jun, Li Wei. Sheng Feifeng and Tang Jun were students who supported Baiqiao Tang in many ways during his stay in Hong Kong. *From the personal collection of Baiqiao Tang.*

The UN's *Palais des Nations* in Geneva, Switzerland, in June 1992, one month after Baiqiao Tang arrived in the United States. Beside Baiqiao Tang is Harry Wu (*left*), the noted human rights advocate and author who was imprisoned in China for nineteen years.

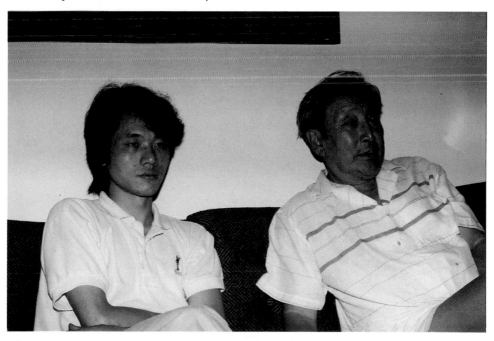

Baiqiao Tang sitting beside the well-known writer Lui Binyan in autumn 1992 at Liu Binyan's home in Princeton, New Jersey. At the time, Liu Binyan was the chair of the China Society in Princeton. *From the personal collection of Baiqiao Tang.*

Photo taken at Luo Huaying's home in Yongzhou, approximately 1995. *From left to right*: Tang Yanhong, Tang Yanzhen, Luo Huaying, Yang Mohui, Tang Jiezhen, Tang Yanfei. *From the personal collection of Baiqiao Tang.*

After a hearing on the human rights abuses of Chinese prisoners by the House Subcommittee on International Operations and Human Rights. In the Rayburn Building of the US House of Representatives, 104th Congress, First Session, April 3, 1995. *From left to right*: Father Chai Zhongxian, who was imprisoned in China for over thirty years; Congressman Chris Smith (R-NJ); an unknown human rights advocate; He Kailing; Liu Xinhu; Baiqiao Tang; Tibetan lama Bandan Jiachuo, who was imprisoned in China for over twenty years; Harry Wu.

Felicity Lung and Baiqiao Tang following Tang's graduation ceremony, spring 2003. He earned a master's degree in international affairs from Columbia University. *From the personal collection of Baiqiao Tang.*

International conference held at Soochow University in Taiwan, 2003. *From second-left to right*: the conference host, Professor Xie Zhengyu, director of international development for Soochow University; Baiqiao Tang; Ruan Ming, former adviser to Hu Yaobang.

Baiqiao Tang and Felicity Lung, taken in Central Park, New York City, on the day of their wedding, November 15, 2003. *From the personal collection of Baiqiao Tang.*

Baiqiao Tang and his groomsmen. *From left to right*: Feng Congde, a student leader during the 1989 democracy movement; Zhang Xianzhang; Han Dongfang, former spokesman for the Beijing Workers Autonomous Federation; Baiqiao Tang; Han Shaohua, a student leader during the 1989 democracy movement; Robin Munro, noted human rights expert. Central Park, New York City, on the day of Baiqiao and Felicity's wedding, November 15, 2003. *From the personal collection of Baiqiao Tang.*

Sima Lu, the well-known Communist Party historian, walks Felicity Lung down the aisle at Riverside Church near Columbia University. *From the personal collection of Baiqiao Tang.*

Meeting with the Dalai Lama in New York City, 2006. *From right to left*: Baiqiao Tang; His Holiness, Tenzin Gyatso, the fourteenth Dalai Lama of Tibet; the Dalai Lama's translator.

US Capitol during the campaign to protest the CCP's persecution of Falun Gong practitioners in the summer of 2009. Several US congressmen attended this event. Baiqiao Tang's hand is still bandaged from the attack that occurred in the karaoke bar. *Photo by Lisa Fan,* Epoch Times.

From left to right: Baiqiao Tang with his friends and colleagues Yi Rong, chief of the Falun Gong association in New York, and Li Dayong, executive director of the Global Service Committee to Quit the CCP. This photograph was taken at a rally intended to call attention to eleven years of Falun Gong persecution, held in front of the Chinese Consulate in New York City, 2010. *From the personal collection of Baiqiao Tang.*

mantra. "*We live in a Marxist, classless, totalitarian regime.* And what are you? A prisoner. And one who wants to be paid? This is shameful."

"It's not shameful, it's the law," I said. "You can look it up. Stop breaking the law, I'll repair the nets."

"We don't have to listen to you. It's the other way around."

"I won't listen to someone who breaks the law. For that, I wouldn't listen to Deng Xiaoping," I said, regretting those words at once since they were a blasphemy in China.

"Oh ho!" the director said. "So! You won't even listen to Deng Xiaoping? Well, we'll see about that."

I was placed in cuffs and fetters as punishment for my insolence and left like that for the rest of the day. But that was just the beginning.

The director called a meeting that night: all guards and wardens, cadres and inmates. My fetters and cuffs were removed, and I was placed on display in front of the group. When everyone was assembled, the director stood before the crowd with me beside him, the chastened schoolboy.

"Everyone!" the director said. "This evening we have a very unusual person among us. This person thinks he is better than us! This person thinks he is better than China! Better than our laws! In fact, this person seems to think he's better than our Communist Party, sturdier than our history and stronger than our culture! He will not listen to me. I wonder if he will listen to anyone! While in my office, you know what he said? He would not listen to Deng Xiaoping! He told me this to my face! He would not listen to Deng Xiaoping! Now what do you think about that?"

The officers all began to shout, the way that they had been trained to. Meetings like this were a legacy of the Cultural Revolution. By tradition, everyone got a chance to stand up and speak his mind, so long as they used their allotted moment to criticize or mock me. This went on for some time while the prisoners sat there, glum.

"You know?" the prison director said. "I've worked at this prison for thirty years and managed thousands and thousands of inmates. Never have I seen such audacity! Well, my comrades. Don't you worry. Everyone listens eventually. Baiqiao Tang will be no exception!"

With that, the director adjourned the meeting. He knew it had served its purpose. I was ostracized at once. No one would talk to me. No one dared risk association. The prison hierarchy readjusted, putting me at the bottom, but it wasn't such a bad place to be. At least I knew that I couldn't fall further.

12

Two months into my stay at Longxi, Zhao Yuen pulled his most daring stunt yet. He called me into his office and said, "I have a surprise for you." Then he handed me his prison guard's coat, a very big garment, thick like a cloak. Warm in cold weather. Intimidating. Like the greatcoats of Nazi storm troopers in Germany during the 1930s. He also gave me his prison guard's hat, which had a low brim and was perfect for hiding a person's face. Also very intimidating.

"What should I do with these?" I asked.

"Put them on," said Zhao Yuen. "Let's go for a walk."

"A walk?" I said. I began to get nervous. "A walk *where*?"

"You'll see," Zhao Yuen said. "There's someone I think you should meet."

He helped me put on the prison guard outfit and led me outside his office. My brain was on fire with fear and excitement. Here I was in the enemy's costume, feeling his uniform's power. We went down the hall and out a door and into the courtyard beyond. That's when it started to dawn on me: we were going outside the wall. Leaving Longxi Prison. I couldn't believe the audacity.

It was winter by then, and very cold. Drizzle fell as though heaven were melting, the gray sky turning to liquid, saturating the lungs. It made sense that I wore an overcoat, made sense that my hat was pulled down low with my chin tucked into the notch of my neck. Man Who Wants to Stay Warm Gets Bundled Up in Bad Weather. We walked as quickly as possible, which also stood to reason.

Zhao Yuen hustled us past two guards who barely looked up. They appeared to be just getting off their shift, and wore the same look of consternation I'd seen on butchers, builders, factory workers. A long day done, now let me go home. Like anyone else, I thought. The cadres' fearful ambiance faded. I would never look at them quite the same way.

We hurried through another wet courtyard. The cobblestones lay slick with cold rain, the sky above us had gone the color of gunmetal. There were more guards here, but none of them looked. No one spared us a glance. However, at one point, we passed the director, the same man who'd called that damnable meeting and stood me up in front of the prison and did his best to humiliate me. My nerves began to sing arias. My spine went stiff. My hamstrings tightened. Zhao Yuen, I saw, was also affected, but what could we do? We kept walking, getting closer. No way to turn back now.

The director looked up from the talk he was having with some other officer. He nodded to us while in mid-conversation. Zhao Yuen nodded back. I took my cue and nodded as well. The click of Zhao Yuen's boot heels sounded impossibly loud on the cobblestones. The swinging hem of my guardsman's coat was a hoop around my legs.

Keep walking, I thought. Just keep walking. Walking.

We went through the gate and nodded to a final guard, and then we were outside the wall. Neither of us dared to speak. Zhao Yuen appeared distraught.

"That was too damn close," he hissed, when I thought we were safe. "We're never doing that again."

That was the last he spoke for a while. His lighthearted attitude had evaporated, merging with the drizzle.

We walked to Zhao Yuen's apartment. It took us ten minutes. He lived in a nearby dormitory reserved for the prison cadres. Zhao Yuen opened his front door and ushered me inside, saying, "Here. I hope this was worth all the trouble."

I wasn't sure what he meant until we stepped into the next room and a woman rose from the chair she'd been sitting in. I couldn't believe my eyes! It was my sister, Yan Ni! We were both so shocked to see each other. I asked her what she was doing there. She told me to sit down at once.

"Zhao Yuen says that we don't have much time. I made you food so we're eating dinner. That's what you're doing here."

The smell from the kitchen was spicy, familiar. One of my mother's recipes. Fish and pork and chicken with herbs. My stomach began to groan and twist itself into knots.

How long were we together that night? The minutes and hours flew by like seconds. I ate until my belly bulged and the waist of my pants grew tighter. At one point, Zhao Yuen got to his feet and said that we had to go back. How could I argue? He'd given me such a tremendous gift. I rose as well, said good-bye to Yan Ni, and climbed back into my prison guard outfit.

On the way back, on the darkened road, Zhao Yuen bent his head toward mine. "Please, Baiqiao Tang," he said. "You must understand. I don't think we should do this again. Meeting the director like that was *jiangxian*!"

Translation: a little too close for comfort.

I thanked Zhao Yuen for what he had done. We never went back to his house again, but that visit with Yan Ni is something I've come to regard as one of the greatest gifts I shall ever receive. Zhao Yuen had been my hero before. Now he was more like an angel, a light to guide me through places of darkness, leading me back to the world of the living.

We made it back to Longxi Prison. To Zhao Yuen's office, and then to my cell. All without incident. Thankfully. But every gift has a price. My little taste of freedom made me more defiant than ever. Over the next few weeks, I found myself acting out again and again. Refusing to work. Refusing to obey orders. The wardens finally had no choice. They put me in solitary confinement.

Sometimes I think this was all for the best. It helped me maintain equilibrium. I found I was more comfortable alone, in a physically awkward space than out on an open parade ground with guards and officers shouting obscenities, placing bets on which inmates' thighs they could shoot with a slingshot. Who would hop highest or scream loudest in pain. Their tired, awful shenanigans.

I was in solitary confinement for two days. Strangely, I enjoyed it. You couldn't call it comfortable, but at least it was quiet, something I hadn't experienced much since entering Chinese prisons. I tried to use it for what it was: a chance to get away.

13

This is how Longxi Prison worked. Prisoners were divided into six brigades of two to three hundred inmates each. Brigades 4 and 5 were "field brigades." Each day they went up in the mountains to the quarries and cut or blasted marble from the living breast of the rock. After which, they transported massive raw blocks to the plant and handed them off to the first three brigades who cut, ground, and polished the stones using outmoded, jerry-rigged equipment. Brigade 6 was a support crew. They did mechanical and electrical work.

The finished products became goods used in building and construction. Marble floor slabs. Marble wall tiles. Marble decorative plaques. But also paperweights, table lamp bases, vases, ashtrays, pen stands, and signature seals. These products enjoyed brisk trade in China, though prices for items varied wildly from one province to the next. I remember one Longxi product, a six-inch-long, character-inscribed paperweight that retailed for less than one yuan when purchased at the prison sales office or in the nearby towns. I'd seen the same item sold for thirty to forty times that amount during my travels to China's larger cities.

As part of my course in Ideological Education for Criminals, I was taught the government's labor reform policy, which the cadres made a frequent mantra. "Reform first! Production second!" A blatant falsification. At Longxi, as in so many other Chinese prisons, production always came first, second, and all the time. No one cared about reform. In the end, it all boiled down to prisoners being used as slave labor to maximize government profits.

I wasn't at Longxi very long when a meeting was called. All inmates were ordered to come. Swaggering Cadre was back, this time performing in front of a larger audience, all two thousand prisoners. He said, "Criminals! Would you like to go home? I'll bet you would, and you can! Today, I will outline our facility's merit policy. I know you will find it flexible, as well as exceedingly generous!"

In essence, here was the "merit policy": inmates were pushed to encourage their families to broker sales on the prison's behalf.

"Foreign exports of marble goods are the most ideal!" said the Swaggering Cadre. "They yield the highest profit!"

As an average Chinese citizen, meaning I'd never left the country, I could only imagine a world where people from other nations clamored and screamed and paid crazy prices, desperate for marble paperweights. Then the Swaggering Cadre read from a list of rules drawn up by the government. "If a prisoner or his family can arrange for a sale of marble goods yielding net profit of 8,000 yuan,* the prisoner will be awarded one minor merit point! Each minor merit point earned will reduce the prisoner's overall sentence by ninety days!"

It sounded almost too good to be true, so of course it was. Was this policy truly flexible and generous? I couldn't really tell you since political prisoners were exempt from participation. But other inmates took advantage of it, like one of my cell mates, a man named Zeng Qingxi.* Zeng had been employed by a Shenzhen import/export business when he was arrested and convicted for various economic corruptions and sentenced to

---

*At that time, about $1,500.

ten years in prison. Zeng, after the meeting with Swaggering Cadre, tipped me a sly wink and said, "This is a blessing from heaven. Watch and see what I make of this."

The merit system was child's play for Zeng. He already had the connections. Through family and friends, he quickly arranged for massive overseas sales. His contracts totaled several hundred thousand yuan, which created an instant problem. According to merit policy rules, Zeng's sales had utterly wiped out his sentence, entitling him to an instant release, which the prison couldn't abide. It was one thing to offer a merit system aimed at remitting a sentence. But a policy that allowed crooks to buy their way out of prison? That cut a bit too close to the bone, even for the Communist Party. And so a deal was eventually struck.

Prison officials thanked Zeng Qingxi for his family's contribution. Zeng was guaranteed parole after serving five years of his sentence. Meantime, he became a highly privileged guest of the prison. He was removed from the general prison population and placed in living accommodations far in excess of the low-level prison officials living on site. Zeng ate better food and took frequent trips home. Worked whenever he wanted (never). He spent a great deal of time reading books that his family sent him or lounging in front of his cabin, ignoring our stares as we trudged to work.

"You see?" he later said to me. "A blessing from heaven. What did I tell you?"

The rest of us weren't so lucky, of course. Our lives continued to muck along from day to deadly day. We worked under strict daily quotas. A failure to meet your daily quota resulted in an increased sentence. Repeated failure to meet your quota saw you wind up in solitary. And the number of days you spent in there would be tacked to the end of your sentence as an additional penalty.

At Longxi, there was also something called the *yanguandui*, or the "strict regime unit." The *yanguandui* was often used in place of solitary confinement. It was justifiably famous for a series of awful ordeals called "Playing the Three Deadly Games."

The first game: "Clinging Gecko." In this, a prisoner was made to kneel facing a wall with his hands raised over his head and his arms pressed up to the bricks. He was told to hold that position for hours, never moving a muscle. Imagine the strain on his body, the excruciating pain he felt. Even the strongest prisoners collapsed and often went into spasms. He might be spared further torture, depending on how long he held the pose.

But then again, he might not. Perhaps the wardens felt fit to subject him to deadly game number two.

The second game was called "Golden Chicken Stands on One Leg." It was a bastardized version of a common martial arts pose. It started when the guards cuffed the prisoner's wrist to his opposite ankle. His other hand was cuffed as well, hauled straight up, and fastened to a pipe or a grommet set into the ceiling. In essence, the prisoner would be made to stand on one leg. His posture would sag as exhaustion set in. Excruciating pressure would be placed on his arm, his shoulders, his hips, prompting him to stand up straighter, which only exhausted him faster.

The third game was called the "Pillar Standing Feat." Guards ordered the prisoner to climb a pillar about three feet tall. The pillar had been set close to the base of a wall. The prisoner's hands were cuffed behind him and chained to a grommet set into the wall, at which point the prisoner would be left alone. Within a few hours, he would tire of standing and start to shift his weight. He'd search for a more comfortable pose where no such pose could be found. Eventually, he would doze. But, nodding off, he'd lose his balance and start to fall off the pillar. This would jerk his arms back roughly, jolting him wide awake once more. The wardens would leave him that way, waiting and smirking, knowing the outcome and desperate to see it happen. No matter how hard the prisoner tried, he'd eventually fall back asleep. Each time he did, his arms would be wrenched from their sockets, waking him up. And the process would start all over again.

14

The members of Longxi Brigades 4 and 5 used dynamite to quarry rock. Every day, they cut shafts with handpicks and tools, laid in the sticks of dynamite, stepped as far back as they could, and triggered a detonation. The earth would shudder, and flames would leap up from the breast of the rock. Chunks of granite would fly like shrapnel. It was dangerous work, and sometimes fatal. Prisoners suffered injuries. Some were crippled permanently.

Since Longxi was a Chinese prison, it had no medical facilities to speak of. Minor wounds got treated with basic first aid and common sense. Anything worse than a minor wound was left to be what it was. Assuming the injured man survived, he resigned himself to a life of disfigurement, incapacity, or both. The authorities often refused to provide medical care or emergency leave on the grounds that the prisoner's wounds were "self-inflicted." Evidently, the cadres saw a prisoner's maiming as acting out against authority.

"Stop shirking!" the guards and wardens would say. "Get back to work!" At one point, I was assigned to work as a teacher in the prison's education section, which got me excited! As a teacher, I wouldn't do heavy work. I would be out of harm's way. Joining the education section was the best job I could have hoped for. But I never got to teach a single class.

One day, seventeen fellow inmates and I were huddled around a radio, a common thing in prison. Radios weren't allowed, but visitors smuggled them to us in pieces. We'd assemble the parts, keep the radio hidden, and listen to it whenever we could until the guards found it and smashed it and meted out punishments. Then we would start all over again, waiting for parts to arrive. Or we would rely on other prisoners whose radios still operated, getting our news from them, secondhand.

My colleagues and I often listened to the Voice of America network, from which we learned of an organization called the Federation for a Democratic China. It had been founded by Chinese dissidents in Paris and the United States as a reaction to June 4th. My group of colleagues decided we wanted to join the Federation as the Longxi Prison branch. And so we held a few meetings, making sure to keep our gatherings small so as not to call attention to ourselves. But the guards found out what we were up to, and a warden pulled me out of my cell and accused me of having organized a "counterrevolutionary rally." I looked at him, half-stunned and half-amused.

"A group of us have been talking politics," I said. "But nothing counterrevolutionary."

To the warden's ears, that was damning enough. He called a hasty meeting. The prison staff fingered seven of us and called us the rally's instigators. As punishment, we were all consigned to the strict regime unit.

Our little group of seven joined another group of approximately the same size that had been in the strict regime unit for a very long time. One inmate in particular had been there over two years. He looked the part.

For the first three days, we were all forced to mount tiny platforms measuring a little more than two feet square and sit on tiny wooden stools that were less than seven inches tall. An awkward position, to say the least. Our feet were flat on the platform floor with our knees sticking up like the folded wings of a locust. Our hands were at rest in our laps and our spines were straight. The guards assigned to the strict regime unit told us to stare straight ahead at the blank wall on the other side of the room. They forced us to maintain this posture—a pose of "introspection," they called it—for ten hours a day, during which the guards and wardens wandered among us, beating us with an iron rod if ever we slouched or sighed or dropped our gazes or moved at all. For repeated offenses, they dragged us down off our stools and took us to a door where we were handcuffed and beaten again.

For meals, we were herded together for fifteen minutes to half an hour. We chewed the rice we were given as fast as we could. We chewed the tiny chicken bones since something was better than nothing. Then we were herded back together and made to remount our platforms. At night, we were locked in separate cells, which were unbelievably tiny. Each cell measured less than six feet square with a cement slab "bed" about a foot wide. It was as though the prison was somehow trying to kill us all in miniature: tiny stools, tiny portions of food, tiny moments of cruelty that were bright and hard as diamonds.

By that point, winter had reached its coldest point. Hunan was a plain of ice. The cells were freezing. We had no heat. We watched our breath form clouds in front of our faces and stared at the patterns. When left alone, we tried to sleep, but it simply wasn't possible.

By the fourth day, my fellows and I had decided we couldn't take anymore. The next time we met to eat, I spoke to them, quickly and softly, keeping my head down. Staring at my portion of food, I kept my chopsticks moving. The guards couldn't see. The guards couldn't notice. "Hunger strike," I said.

The idea was not met favorably.

"Hunger strike to protest these deplorable conditions."

An inmate snorted. I looked up. It was the man who'd been held in strict regime for over two years. I don't know his name, I never learned it, but his mind was clearly gone. He was a being more animal than human, a slouching beast that picked cigarette butts off the floor and smoked them, a practice the guards found hilarious. They treated Butts like their personal jester, the pet dog for the unit.

Now Cigarette Butts was looking at me and rolling his eyes like bicycle wheels. Clearly, he thought me ridiculous. Clearly, he thought my idea even worse. I had to act before his rebuff could taint the rest of the crew. "If we go on a hunger strike," I said. "Maybe they'll let us out of here. Or maybe we end up like him." I pointed to Cigarette Butts.

"Your choice."

Everyone sitting around the table looked at Butts and nodded. They got the point right away. Compared to such degradation, a hunger strike would be nothing. Cigarette Butts got the point, as well. He grumbled and walked away. I didn't worry about him. What was he going to do? Butts didn't talk to anyone—not the guards nor his fellow inmates. The walls were his silent companions, the sky his vigilant, frowning God. Cigarette Butts had already left us. He'd gone to a place that everyone knew but no one wanted to visit.

Our hunger strike lasted the rest of the week. The guards watched us, derisive at first. Then blinking. Uncomprehending. Confused. We heard them muttering. They scurried away, running to get the wardens. "What do you want us to do? Beat them all?"

The tension over the next few days pulled tight but was also delicate, like a silk string being unwound from a cocoon. We prisoners forced our heads to one side as food was placed before us. Each time was a greater challenge to spirit. Our stomachs were roaring. Salt sweat broke out all over our skin. Our bodies had begun to engage in their very own revolution.

But something miraculous happened at the end of the third day. We were all released from the strict regime unit and sent back to the general populace. I was tempted to think that our strike was the cause, but experience taught me to wait for the answer, which came in the form of a summons to stand before the prison director.

"You are being awarded parole," he said.

Picture me. Open-mouthed. Gaping. Astonished.

"This is only parole," the director said. Clearly, it chafed him to speak these words. "You will come straight back to jail if you violate parole mandates. Leave this facility. Proceed directly to your hometown. Once there, you will not leave. You will not contact turmoil elements. Will not make counterrevolutionary instigations either in print or in speech. Under no circumstances will you contact or meet with other counterrevolutionaries."

I couldn't believe it. I'd been behind bars for eighteen months, in sixteen cells within seven penal facilities in five locations in three different provinces. I'd been interrogated by representatives from at least ten separate security bureaus. Dozens of people had been implicated as possible suspects in my case, including every member of my family, their colleagues, and officials from my provincial security department who'd clearly "let me escape," not to mention several individuals who'd given me aid and succor during my flight. The Ministry of State Security had twice sent investigators to Hong Kong to search out the people I'd contacted there. The government's case against me had cost a staggering sum of money.

And now they were letting me go. Paroled only seven months into my three-year sentence. What was going on?

Later, I learned the truth. The central authorities had fallen under tremendous international pressure. The world had risen up against the atrocities of Tiananmen Square. In the end, the CCP had claimed that three or four hundred people were killed. Not so, said various independent groups. After completing autonomous research, they verified that the number of deaths was actually more like three or four thousand, ten times the Party's official tally, a major political gaffe. By trying to wipe away its tracks, the Party had made its position worse.

The Party had dug their grave deeper by sentencing Wang Dan, the student leader of the cadres I was once nearly forced to admit I had contacted. During my eighteen months in prison, I'd learned a bit more about Wang Dan. I knew that he wasn't a girl, for instance; another prisoner and fellow dissident set me straight on that. Wang had been a student leader at Peking University. He'd joined the organizing body of the pro-democracy movement as Peking University's representative. In other words, he'd been right there at the heart of the matter, leading the fight in Tiananmen Square. A very impressive figure. He was later quoted in *HK Magazine*: "Until the army began firing their guns, I simply couldn't imagine the government would order a massacre. The officials I talked to had guaranteed that there would be no violent suppression."

After June 4, Wang Dan had fled, hunted by the Party. The CCP caught up with him on July 2, 1989. They put him on trial a year and a half later in January 1991. But, bowing to international pressure, the courts came down with a lenient sentence. Wang Dan was given only four years, whereas other pro-democracy figures were sentenced to ten or fifteen. It was another CCP mistake, one that created a glaring discrepancy between the punishments handed to activists. It showed that the Party was willing to buckle in order to appease the world community. It was a tacit admission of guilt for a crime too heinous to comprehend.

My parole was part of the Party's flailing attempts at damage control.

They were scrambling to free student leaders as quickly as they could. That way they would appear more humane, more civilized in the eyes of an increasingly vigilant global community.

It made perfect sense, but I can't say I cared. Paroled or not, I was finally going home. I might have felt tremendous relief if I wasn't so eager to see my family.

15

They released me from Longxi Prison in the early morning hours of February 14, 1991. It was New Year's Eve in China. Early on, my family had put some money in my prison account. I'd spent it on cigarettes and bribes for radio parts, but not much else. Now I withdrew what was left to pay for a bus, and then a train. I chose not to call my family. Preferred my arrival to be a surprise. Good tidings for a brand-new year.

The journey back to Yongzhou took ten hours. I slept for most of the way. My body was exhausted, close to collapse, but my mind swam around and around in circles like a carp that was trapped in a tiny canal, searching for outlets that didn't exist.

It was evening when I pulled into town. Awful weather. A freezing rain fell hard, like a palm slapping flesh. The storm was constant. It didn't let up.

My head was shaved from being in prison. My clothes were soaked, and clung to me. I traipsed through the wet streets. Squishing shoes. Finding my mother's apartment, I knocked on the door and braced myself for the moment I saw her.

The door creaked open. Some man I'd never seen before was staring back at me. "Yes?"

"Huaying Luo?" I said. My mother's name.

"Huaying Luo? No. She doesn't live here. Not anymore."

A round of questions came next, followed by quick explanations. My mother had changed jobs and moved away to another school with another apartment. I asked the gentleman where it was, and he said that he didn't know. Apologizing. Hesitant. His eyes darted up to my stubbled scalp. Back to my face. To my scalp and back. No one in China shaved their head. He struggled to keep his composure.

Our interview lasted less than a minute, during which I began to see how far I'd really fallen. Once a man with a promising future, I was now a fearsome outlaw. I thanked the man and left.

With no other choice, I walked the wet streets. Eventually, I aimed my steps toward the local police department where I knew my sister worked. Her apartment was on the security campus. I went to her door and knocked. No answer. So I tried the neighbors. Same thing. Well, I thought. It's Chinese New Year. Everyone's gone for the holiday.

It was late. I tried the police station. Found it empty and silent. There was only one old doorman on duty. I recognized this man. We were distant relatives, third or fourth cousins.

"*Xiao* Tang!" he said, and his old eyes went wide. He stared at my shaved head, my wet clothes, my face. He might as well have stared at a ghost from the shock that showed on his features. "How did you escape from prison?"

I showed him my papers. The old man read them quickly, his lips mumbling out the characters, his eyebrows rocketing north. "Approved for parole. You are very lucky." He folded the papers and handed them back. "So. You want to know where your family is."

"My sister is not here," I said.

"No, *Xiao* Tang. She isn't. She moved to another apartment last year. Your mother did as well. I happen to know that your mother now lives and works at Yongzhou Number Three Primary School. Do you know where that is?"

I did, so I thanked the old man and set off, stepping through puddles that held my reflection, heels striking wet coin smacks on the pavement, walking away through the night and the rain. I was at home but felt more lost than ever, like a sleeper who wakes from a dream to find that the world has moved on without him.

At Yongzhou Number Three Primary School, I found the building reserved for faculty apartments and wandered the courtyard, searching for some kind of sign that would indicate where my mother now lived. I passed a door that stood open to let in a breeze. I looked through the doorframe and froze, feeling happy and nervous and fearful at once. Water dripped off the hem of my coat and formed a puddle beneath me.

The apartment I saw was small but cozy and warm, like a battered box for favorite shoes. It had a small front room, which stood empty. Toward the back, through an arch like a window onto another world was another room, a small dining area, lit like the set from a movie. Nearly a dozen people sat at a table. They were eating and laughing and talking at once, their arms reaching out like a game of cat's cradle, criss-crossing, pulling back platters, their plates piled high with food. The smell of spices hit me again, as they had in Zhao Yuen's apartment. The air had gone moist and vibrant with the scent of my mother's cooking.

My family. Home.

No one noticed me walk through the door, slow and surreal like a walk through a dream. Another step, and another. I'd nearly made it halfway across when two or three heads at the table looked up. Smiles dropped off their faces at once, replaced by shock and wariness. Then something else settled into their eyes, the glimmer of recognition.

"*Xiao* Tang?" someone said.

"*Xiao* Tang?" said another. "What are you saying? What of *Xiao* Tang?"

Everyone turned at once to look, and suddenly all their eyes were on me. My mouth dropped open but nothing came out. What could I possibly say? I wasn't given a chance to speak. In an instant, everyone leaped to their feet and came rushing toward me in a solid wave. They smiled, observing the Chinese way. No outbursts of emotion per se, though my youngest sisters, Yan Hong and Yan Fei, began to hop up and down and scream.

I felt everything. I felt nothing. I was alive. I was numb. I was home.

part six
Exile

1

My mother was still a beautiful woman, but she'd aged ten years in eighteen months. Her eyes had the furtive look of a person who's suffered a terrible anguish. My sisters had also changed, I saw. They looked older, wiser, more taut, and sad beneath the smiles they rallied in order to greet me. I began to feel overwhelming grief for what I had put them through.

I looked around. The new apartment was smaller than the one my mother had lived in years ago. Another instance of miniaturization. It was as though the world were collapsing inward, shrinking away from June 4. If this trend continues, I wondered, will there be anything left of China at all?

My coming home was auspicious. Dinner on Chinese New Year's Eve is the most important family event of the year. Loved ones congratulate each other on passing another turn. Everyone wears red clothing to ward off evil spirits. Black and white are shunned for the evening as colors that signify death and mourning. I had interrupted a feast of ten dishes that are sacred in Hunan Province. Taro with yam noodles. Pigs' feet with seaweed. Braised pork. Chicken. Vegetables. Prawns. Steamed fish. Egg soup with tofu. Dumplings boiled in water to call back a single, lost good wish for the family.

Tradition dictates separate courses, but my mother had them all out at once. Plates steamed like circular islands in the brown wooden sea of the table top. Why not? It was easier that way for her, and tradition be damned. I took this as another shred of evidence that my family had been through enough. The framing of our lives had been reshaped to accommodate new forms.

The New Year's Gala was jangling on CCTV; the reception as bad as it ever was, the aerial not doing its job, as if it really mattered. In those days, you didn't go out in the evening. Electrical wiring wasn't so good. At night, people stayed inside, turned off the lights in the houses, and sat in their living rooms staring at TVs as though at divine apparitions. You could walk around any city in China, even the bigger ones, like Beijing, and witness nothing but ghostly blue flickers of TVs coming from darkened apartments.

Once the joyful riot had passed, a dozen sets of hands seized hold and dragged me toward the table. They pushed me into a chair. There were wails and moans at how thin I was. Fingers rubbed my stubbled head like the belly of the Buddha. A plate was set in front of me, heaped with food.

Chopsticks were thrust into fingers gone numb. I started to eat, my eyes darting around, alighting on faces I did not know. All five of my sisters were present, as well as men whom two had married, my brother-in-laws in the flesh at last, materializing from descriptions set down in letters I'd read in my cell. It was a satisfying magic trick, a feat of great transmogrification, but something was wrong. My father was missing. I did not see him anywhere.

I did not ask where he was right away. The spell of finally being back home, as well as seeing my mother's face, allowed for temporary delusions. My sisters swirled past me. Everyone smiled and laughed and cried and ate, talking at the same time.

At one point someone got up from the table and went to a neighbors' and tattled that I was home. Soon, I was bombarded by more unfamiliar faces. Who were these people? I did not know them. They weren't the neighbors I'd grown up with; they were replacements, the neighbors who came with my mother's new home in her new life teaching at a new school. But, strangers or not, they came right up to me, seized my hands, and clapped me on the back, crying as though we were kin.

"My, how you've suffered, *Xiao* Tang!"

"You're back at last! You see? Heaven is just!"

"Everything will be all right now! This is a new beginning for you!"

One of them told me a story about how a former county magistrate came to see my mother and father very soon after I was arrested. This man had been very old and had walked with the aid of a stick. He'd tried to console my mother and father, both of whom were sick with grief. "Your son is an excellent student," he said. "Remember? He never failed to win the Three Outstandings at school! Keep your spirits up! Be sure to tell him how good he is. What a fine, outstanding young man!"

I was also told about rumors. Shortly after June 4, stories had spun like eddies in water throughout the town of Yongzhou. The most pernicious tale said that I had been killed in Tiananmen Square, along with the other martyrs. In fact, so many people believed this that a memorial service was held in my honor. Only later did so many learn that I was alive and in prison.

"*Xiao* Tang! You missed your own funeral!"

Everyone cackled at that, the jest that the living can make at the dead, quite appropriate for that moment since another grand illusion was about to be dissolved.

My new brother-in-law held out a cigarette. I took it gratefully, asked for a light, touched the flame, and drew in the smoke. But this drew a scolding from my sister, Yan Zhen—one that changed the course of the evening.

"Young brother, do not smoke," she said.

A strange request, I thought. It was my first cigarette as a man of freedom, and it tasted outstanding. "Why?" I asked.

"It makes you look like a convict," she said.

"I *am* a convict," I said. Planting a hand on top of my head, I stroked my stubble and grinned. Yan Zhen winced and looked away.

"Young brother," she said. "Please stop."

"What's the problem?" I said. "I smoked before I went to jail. Why should I be different now?"

She stared at me. I stared right back. Knowing how I must look to her. Bedraggled. A drunk coming out of the cold, my clothes still damp from the rain. And gaunt, my cheeks like hollowed out cups. Eyes too sharp, like filed steel points. The insouciant slouch of the damned.

My sisters must have gotten off work late that afternoon. Yan Zhen hadn't had time to change. She still wore her security uniform. I suddenly became aware that a policeman sat before me on the other side of the dinner table. But this one had features resembling mine, a very surreal realization.

Yan Zhen had joined the CCP but was not a militant member. She'd had no choice, she had to join in order to keep her job. It was an occupational hazard, and one that I'd never before held against her, though I suddenly found myself changing my mind as charity lost its grip on my spirit and dropped to the floor like a curtain slipping off its rod, revealing some picture long hidden.

"Please," said Yan Zhen. "Obey your sister."

I held her firmly in my gaze and, playing the part of a dragon, exhaled twin plumes of blue-gray smoke from my nostrils. "I've had enough of obeying police."

Her head rocked back as though I had struck her. It was exactly what I'd intended. I'd been home for less than half an hour. Already a fight was brewing. Everyone at the table went quiet.

"Young brother," Yan Zhen managed. Her body, stiff as a carving. "Why do you say such a thing to me?"

Cracks appeared on the dam, then broke. The tide rushed out in a howl. Months of protests. Sleepless nights. Soaring hopes soon dashed to pieces, mocked by little minds. My flight. The hunt. My hiding. Capture. Eighteen months of torture. Prison. The mental abuses. Flies alighting in rancid rice. Water that tasted like rust. The lies. Deceits. Injustice. Farce. It all rushed out in a wave. The barrier, finally broken.

I slammed my palm on the table. Plates jumped. Bowls shivered. Chopsticks rolled and hit the floor, clattering. "Have I insulted you?" I demanded. "Well! I beg your pardon, officer! I have been insulted, too! Over and over again. It was my insult to be thrown in prison. Doubly so to be released and have to call it a kindness. Licking boots and calling them candy. All for the sake of thinking?"

I looked around the table then. My eyes were fully open. I rose from my chair. Scared faces looked back. "Where is my father?" I asked.

No one spoke. All eyes rolled toward the table.

"Why do I not see him here? And why does no one speak of him? Tell me the truth. Where is he?"

Right then, my mother began to wail. My younger sisters rushed to her side as another dam burst, though this one was different. The water was no flood of rage but grief. "Do not be angry," said Yan Ni. "Please do not be angry, Baiqiao!"

My mother wailed. "Don't blame us for not telling you! You were already going through so much, we couldn't bear to tell you!"

That's when I knew that my father was dead.

2

It is a facet of Chinese culture that we do not speak of the dead, or death, or dying. These subjects are a kind of taboo, as though speaking of them works like a summons, calling black angels to bedsides and cribs, inviting them to cause accidents, violence, sudden illnesses. My mother and sisters had followed the custom and kept me enshrouded in ignorance. Traditionally, death is only discussed in private meetings held among male members of a family. I would have such a meeting the very next day.

My sisters, my mother, and I took a train to visit my father's old home. We wanted to pay our respects at his grave, but the trip would also afford me time to speak with our family patriarch, my father's older brother. My uncle looked a lot like my father, though cast in a different clay, the features altered ever so slightly. The craftsman had kept the cheekbones intact but made the nose more crooked, for instance. The forehead higher. The point of the chin a bit sharper.

I had not seen this uncle in years and was very anxious to meet him, to unlock the secret denied me so long. Until then, the Chinese way said that we should act as though nothing had happened, the same way the people I met pretended that nothing had happened on June 4. Their silence was bitterly disappointing. I found that most Chinese harbored great sympathy for the movement, for what I and my fellow leaders had done, the students and workers alike. But few ventured far beyond that. They paid lip service, nothing else. One or two words. A grunt and a shrug. Then mouths would close and heads would turn. Eyes would look away. People were simply too afraid. The risk of saying more was too great. By this point in Chinese history, the Party had mastered the art of reprisal.

Everyone seemed to feel that what I had done was morally right, but in practice very stupid. I see the same thing in America when people talk to a veteran who comes home from the wars in Iraq or Afghanistan. There is a tone of respect, the deferent nod, then they quickly change the subject. No one wants the details. Nobody wants to know. Ignorance, isn't that easier? Forgetting is so much better. Human virtue is like a mirage, more beautiful when viewed from a distance.

Our train passed by my father's old school. I looked out the window and saw it, the one where I had lived as a boy back when my father had caught the carp and slipped it in the canal. I remembered how we had capered around it, the ecstasy of the catch. And later the meal. Delicious fish. Roasted, buttery flesh. My father watching my family eat. His eyes shining bright as summer stars, reveling in his little joke.

I remembered him making a show of thinking. *You know? If I'm not mistaken. This fish is so big, there should be enough for all of your families to eat. Share and share alike. That's what good neighbors do for each other . . .*

The chorus of children's cries that it caused. Yes, we had said. My father was wise. Share and share alike.

I couldn't help it. My grief rose up, and I began to weep. My sisters and mother cried as well.

Father, I thought. Have I made you proud?

Not knowing whether I had was the most awful thing I had ever felt.

But then my mother tapped my hand. I looked at her and stopped crying, then turned to see what she was staring at. The whole train was watching us. Passengers whispered, nodding toward me. Some of them weeping as well.

The people riding the train were locals, most of whom knew each other. They knew my mother and sisters. And . . .

"They know," said my mother. "They know who you are."

Our train pulled into the station. My family and I got off. So did a lot of other people. Murmuring cross-talk. A gathering crowd followed us like a pack of dogs, curious, sniffing the air. Gawking is not an unusual thing in certain parts of China. The populace has perfected the art. Shame gets eclipsed by fascination, a phenomenon like a spontaneous cult.

The crowd began to follow us wherever my family and I went. Some people ran ahead of us, into the village. They came back quickly with family and friends. The crowd began to grow like a smoke cloud, billowing, roiling, expanding from within. At one point I turned to ask them to stop, but some people knelt down in front of me. This is the ultimate sign of respect in China, an ancient token still used in certain provinces. It is the gesture reserved for prayer to the Buddha, as well as for heroes and royalty.

I could not think of a thing to say. I turned back around, and we kept walking to my father's grave, a scrap of land on the outskirts of town that was bordered by a rice paddy.

The spot had been marked by a simple stone on which was written my father's name. Elegant characters were etched in the rock, along with the dates of his birth and death, and names: my mother, my sisters, and me. Beside his grave, there was one other mound for my father's great uncle. This sparseness was not so unusual. It was strange that my father was buried at all.

In China, it's public policy to cremate the dead. Land and resources must be saved. Only those of noble lineage or very high station are buried. Interment is considered both an honor and an award. My father, however, was common stock, which is why I struggled to understand. Why had his remains been placed in the ground instead of burned?

More and more questions required answers. We left the plot at the edge of the paddy and went to visit my uncle.

3

The old man sat me down in a room with several cousins and uncles whom I knew vaguely, having met them many years ago when I was still a child. The atmosphere in the room was tense. Afternoon shadows grew long on the walls.

My uncle sighed. "It happened November 30."

"In 1989," someone added.

My uncle nodded. "This is what we know. Someone called Tang Rentong on the phone and evidently invited him out. To go someplace for a visit."

"Who called?" I asked.

My uncle shrugged. "No one knows. Not us. Your mother. It could have been a friend. A coworker, perhaps. We only know that he left his apartment in the early evening, maybe five or six o'clock. We assume he went to someone else's home, but we don't know that for certain."

His tone made the implication clear: *nor will we ever know.*

"A few hours later, Tang Rentong was walking down a street in Yongzhou when a car lost control, jumped a curb, and hit him."

My uncle paused and glanced at me, as though to make sure I should hear the rest. I said nothing. Did nothing. Barely breathing, I stared at him and waited for him to continue.

"His body was blown through the air, *Xiao* Tang. Several feet. He landed on the ground and lay there while someone summoned an ambulance. He was taken to the hospital. They say that he lived for an hour or two. They say that he called your name several times. Then he expired."

"The car?" I asked. "The one that hit him."

"What about it?"

"Has it been found?"

"It stopped at the end of the road. The driver did not try to flee."

"I want to talk to him," I said. "Was it a man who was driving? Did you talk to the police?"

My uncle gave me a look that was difficult to interpret. "The police have done all they can," he said.

"What does that mean? Something must be done. Who is this man? He killed my father."

I darted my eyes from face to face. Everyone in the room looked supremely uncomfortable.

"It was an accident, *Xiao* Tang." My uncle shook his head. "That's all it was. An accident."

I could not parse my feelings. I didn't believe my uncle. Why? Because what he said wasn't believable? Or because I did not *want* to believe? There is a difference, of course.

"How did he come to be buried?" I asked. "Why was he not cremated?"

"Huh," my uncle grunted. "That is another story."

He said that my father's passing had left my mother and sisters bereft. In the first place, his death had been sudden. In the second, I was in jail and therefore unavailable to lend my support, to say nothing of handling arrangements.

My mother had refused to allow the body to be burned. She said that I, his only son, should be able to view it. This was hardly a rational argument under the circumstances. At the time, my case had not gone to trial. The prospects of my release were slim, and so my family petitioned the government. Let Baiqiao Tang out of jail, they said. For two or three days, that's all. Let him come home, bid farewell to his father, and go back to jail after that. But the government refused this request, which sparked an incredible protest.

My uncle told it like this. "For a while, I thought the whole city would riot. Everyone got up in arms. Your father was very well-liked, *Xiao* Tang. People took the government's denial personally."

Thousands of people had written letters, swamping the offices of Party officials. Visits were made and phone calls, as well as impromptu speeches pleading to have my father buried. But the Party held the line and insisted on cremation. That's when the demonstrations started. Even my sister, Yan Zhen, got involved—Yan Zhen, who worked for the police.

"People started collecting weapons, primitive implements—knives and poles, for the most part. But knives and poles can still take a life when wielded by angry people."

My uncle showed me photographs of my father's funeral. I was astonished. Thousands of mourners marched across the camera frame. Some stared directly into the lens, shouting with furious faces. They seemed less bereaved, more like an angry mob whose passion rivaled the kind I had seen on display in Tiananmen Square or the demonstrations I'd led through the spring of 1989. I was horrified.

"They could have thrown you all in jail!" I said.

My uncle shrugged, not disagreeing. "It didn't come to that."

Resistance of this kind is growing in China every year, inflamed by various programs. A good example is the CCP's practice of eminent domain. Millions of Chinese citizens are thrown from their homes each year to make way for new roads, high-rise apartments, and government-sponsored businesses. The Party calls it progress, but some people refuse to leave. They stay in their homes and shut themselves in, while, around them, the rest of the neighborhood crumbles away, hewn by wrecking balls, eaten by backhoes and bulldozers. A term has evolved for these holdout homes. The Chinese call them "Nail Houses," or sometimes "stubborn nails." Because that's what these homes resemble in spirit: nails that cannot be pounded from wood no matter how hard the hammer strikes. In 2009 alone, Party official statistics reported approximately eighty thousand uprisings like the kind my family had nearly led.

"In the end," said my uncle, "the government acquiesced. They didn't want to risk another row, however small. Especially one that had to do with the relative of a dissident, a man who'd been killed rather suddenly, under very unusual circumstances. In the end, they told us to bury your father. 'Do what you like,' they said. 'It makes no difference to us.'"

When it became clear that I could not attend the funeral, my family had conspired not to tell me my father had passed. They thought the shock would be too much. I've often wondered if they were right.

"With your father buried, your mother thought you'd at least have a grave to visit."

"Was it murder?" I asked.

My uncle's face darkened like falling dusk. "Whatever it was, it's over now."

But it wasn't. Not for me. "Who would call my father?" I asked. "He didn't go out a lot, and certainly not to drink alcohol. He rarely drank. Perhaps a glass of *mi jiu*," I said. "For the holidays. For the New Year. But always with family, Uncle."

My uncle's face became a full-on eclipse, his light tucked behind the moon of frustration. "I know," he said. "I know. Everyone knows, *Xiao Tang*."

"He was only fifty-four," I said.

To which my uncle said nothing.

4

Part of me died to think that my father had left this world in despair over me. There's an old saying: *No parent should ever be so cursed as to bury his child.* How true, but the saying is not complete. No child should ever be so cursed as to bury his parent without mending a rift. Yet plenty of children endure this sad vexation. It is far too often the legacy of a family's black sheep.

I resolved myself to investigate my father's death. With no idea how I should proceed, I started by asking questions, trying to find out exactly what happened. I wanted to know the name of the man who had driven the car that lost control, but no one would surrender it. In fact, no further information came forth beyond what my uncle had told me.

Eventually, however, word must have spread that I was looking for answers. The phone rang at my mother's apartment a few days after the New Year. A woman I hadn't seen in years had called to reintroduce herself. Her name was Jiang Xiuying,* and we had gone to high school together in what seemed like another life. Now she worked in government for the city of Yongzhou. Her father was well placed in government but wasn't a party official, a strange situation at best, and one that deprived him of any real power.

This happens from time to time in China. Here is the way you should think of it: there are two systems of government. First, the so-called regular system, which is also called the "official" system, run by the CCP. The Party is home to most government workers. Officials. Politicians. Bureaucrats. They join to advance their careers. They join the winning team.

Occasionally, however, a regular government man abstains from joining the Party, or he participates in a tangential fashion. This was the case with Jiang Xiuying's father. No one ever discusses their reasons for taking this difficult path. It's understood that political suicide comes in many forms. Some choose the death of a thousand cuts—expiration by willful disenfranchisement.

"Baiqiao," said Jiang Xiuying. Her voice was hushed. She whispered into the phone. "Can we meet someplace? I have something important to tell you."

I suggested a local restaurant—an old shack both of us knew. We met there, had some tea and pork that was spicy, greasy, good. We spent a while catching up with each other since so many years had passed. We were no longer children who looked toward the future. Now we were more intrigued by the past.

After we ate, Jiang Xiuying suggested that we should go for a walk. I could see she had something to tell me and the restaurant wasn't the place. We got up, dropped some yuan on the table, and walked out into the street. Jiang made a rambling, circuitous route. The boulevards were mostly empty. A few cars passed. Not many, however. Traffic was slow at that hour.

"You cannot repeat what I tell you," she said, not looking at me, just walking. She was certain that I was attuned to her every word, and I was. "Mention this, and I fear for myself. I fear for my father and his position. My family, and their well-being."

I assured her I would tell no one.

"Your father was struck by a car," she said.

I nodded. "Yes. I know."

"Your father had been drinking." Jiang Xiuying was being direct, a tactic seldom employed in China but one I now appreciated. Again I nodded. "The warrant for your arrest, *Xiao* Tang, was found in your father's shirt pocket."

This was news. I looked at Jiang Xiuying. She did not look back. She nodded and kept on walking.

"As best I can tell, the warrant arrived by mail perhaps a day or two before he was killed," she said. "I feel certain he felt despondent over the charges leveled against you."

That was putting it mildly, I felt, but I sensed that something else was coming. So I walked beside Jiang and waited.

"Your father was walking down a very quiet street at approximately 8 p.m.," she said. "A car came out of nowhere. Sped up. Your father had reached the corner. The car left the road and went up on the sidewalk. It hit him."

"I was told the driver lost control of the car," I said, though without much force in the words. I thought I could see where this was going. "That it was some kind of accident."

Jiang Xiuying shook her head. "That car was driven by a man named Song.* He works for the mayor's office."

A man who worked for the mayor's office? Now I began to get angry.

"What became of this man named Song?" I asked.

Jiang Xiuying shrugged, her face downcast. It was all the answer I needed.

It's been over twenty years since that day. I know I will never have proof that my father was murdered. I'm resigned to that. But I know.

I know.

5

I was now twenty-four years old. I stayed with my family in Yongzhou for half a month, through the end of the Chinese New Year. While I was there, the Year of the Horse ended, and my birth year, the Year of the Sheep, began. Birth years are very important in Chinese astrology. They roll around every twelve years. Some say that something either very good or very bad will happen when your year comes up. The Year of the Sheep is typically marked by change, as well as the characteristics of creativity and struggle to overcome obstacles. Well, I thought. We shall see.

Struggling to overcome obstacles certainly seemed very likely. June 4th had dealt the CCP a blow but hadn't killed it. Not by a long shot. Quietly, I took a new oath: for the rest of my life, I would share weal and woe with my nation. I'd dedicate all that I had to my vision of China as a free and democratic country. The people who'd suffered so much for that vision deserved nothing less, I thought. Among this number, I counted my father. May his soul rest in peace.

Once the New Year's Festival passed, my mother took me aside. "Here," she said, and she pressed a wad of cash in my palm, a roll that, once unfolded, turned out to be several hundred yuan, a small fortune for a teacher.

"What is this?"

"It's yours," she said. "I saved it while you were gone. I knew that you would need money when you finally came back to us."

I wept then, knowing the cost of this gift. She must have scrimped for months, depriving herself of basic things while cleaning the house and humming old songs. I could visualize her stalwart face, waiting for me to return.

This was so indicative of my mother. During my first year in prison, she traveled each month to visit me, long journeys lasting many miles on a rickety, burping bus. She was turned away by the guards the first time and told she should not come back, but she did. And each time, she waited outside for days, thinking the wardens would change their minds when confronted with a woman's resilience, a mother's undying love. They didn't change their minds, of course. She always went home but came back again. And again. And again.

One time, the bus she was riding in turned over when its tires slipped on unpaved roads. Two of her ribs were broken. Shattered glass cut through her skin. My sisters brought her back to Yongzhou where she lay bedridden for weeks. Her doctors said that she had to be careful lest she succumb to infection and pneumonia. My mother refused to listen. The moment she felt herself fit to travel, she got on the bus and came back to see me, only to be turned away once more. I knew nothing of this in prison.

"Mother," I said. "I cannot accept this." And tried to press the bills back in her hand, as futile as catching rain with a sieve.

"You must," she said. "You will need it now. To start your life over again."

Which is when I felt that I had to tell her. "Mother, I cannot stay here. I cannot stay in Yongzhou."

This shocked her, as I'd imagined it would. "But this is your home," she said. "I've waited so long for you to come back."

How could I explain to her that, no, this wasn't my home anymore. I had a different calling; I knew it deep in my bones. Call it karma. Call it destiny. Call it whatever you will. But I could not remain in such a small place. The world had pulled me too far away. It had shown me that my earliest dreams were too small and another path awaited me. I did not know where this path would lead, but I knew that I had to follow it, though it led me away from my family, and, worst of all, from her.

"Mother," I began to say, but nothing more would come out. She is such a selfless, loving woman, despite all that I've put her through.

"Your parole," she said. "You cannot leave. You are only free to stay here."

She was right about that. My parole was clear. I had to check in with police each week. The locals wanted me under their thumb to assure themselves that I hadn't been meeting with other "turmoil elements," inciting them to action. A laughable demand. I never once stopped by the local police station, and nobody came to look for me.

But my mother never gave up. She kept warning me over and over again. And a few days later, she followed me down the platform at Yongzhou station. She never believed I would do it—leave—but I did. I broke my parole and went to Changsha to visit my former classmates.

6

Liu Shao put me up. He and his roommates allowed me to stay in their dorm at Hunan Normal. It felt so strange to be back there. We tried to keep my presence a secret, though word got out very fast. I met old friends and new ones, too. All of them told tales of how the university had made me a scapegoat, saying the unrest in Hunan Province had mostly been my idea.

In the wake of the June 4th incident, all Chinese universities showed their allegiance to Party and country by holding special *zheng zhi xue xi*, mandatory meetings in so-called political studies. Essentially, these were Marxist reeducation seminars hosted by Party officials who were also, conveniently, faculty members. Students and teachers had to attend or be punished. This was hardly a shock. At Hunan Normal, we'd had to attend *zheng zhi xue xi* every week, on Fridays. The curriculum, if you could call it that, was about what you might expect: lectures on why socialism was such a perfect system; stories about the great Lei Feng, but also cautionary tales—horror stories that centered on how China was before Mao. It was also an opportunity for the Party to disseminate copies of its newest policies and propaganda. You were expected to review these items and express your deepest admiration.

"Your grandfathers were so poor." The speakers would strut and bellow. "But look at you! You all have shoes! You all have food and clothing! You're getting an education! You'll leave this institution and be guaranteed a job. Now I ask you: isn't China better than it was in the day of your grandfathers? Who here says that it isn't?"

Evidently, these meeting had quickly turned into anti-Baiqiao Tang rallies, especially once I'd been captured and thrown into prison. "Baiqiao Tang is a counterrevolutionary," the speaker for that day would trumpet. "Baiqiao Tang does not appreciate his parents or his grandparents. Baiqiao Tang is a criminal. His delusions deserve to be punished."

Party officials forced poor Sun Dan to say awful things about me, chief among them was that I had physically abused her. They used this bogus testimony to further undermine my character. I was a despicable character, they said. My behavior was emblematic of a counterrevolutionary. Lies told to preserve a lie.

While I was staying with Liu Shao, emissaries from the dean of students' office sought me out and told me the dean would like to speak with me. They asked me to come to his office.

"If the dean would like to speak," I said. "Tell him he will find me here. I'm sure he knows where the dormitories are."

The emissaries frowned and went back to counsel the dean, who eventually came to the dorms. A polite man. Somewhat nervous. If I had to guess, I'd say I was the first ex-convict he'd ever seen face-to-face. He made me an interesting offer.

"Come back and study here, Baiqiao Tang. You were so close to graduating. Why not finally earn your degree?"

I thanked the dean but told him that my focus had changed. Oddly, I couldn't care less about earning a Hunan Normal degree. Moreover, I found his visit strange. From what I had heard, the college had consigned me to a form of moral cancer. "Why would you want me back?" I asked.

The dean looked very glum. "Please, Baiqiao Tang. You must understand the position you put us in. The nation was in turmoil. You were leading the resistance. What did you expect us to do? You spoke of the Party so violently."

This man was possessed of such astronomical hypocrisy, it was hard to be angry with him.

"But now things have changed?" I asked.

He brightened. "Oh, yes! You have paid your debt to society. The Party has forgiven you. How could we not do the same?"

"I deeply appreciate this," I said. "Unfortunately, one small matter remains."

"Yes?" the dean said hopefully.

"I have not forgiven you."

Liu Shao and I were on a bus one evening at about 11 p.m. We were heading back to the dorm after visiting friends who'd worked for the prodemocracy movement. The bus was very crowded. Liu and I were standing in the back. I heard a sound like a *put-a-put-put*, looked out the window, and saw a scooter following us with a sidecar. In China, scooters with sidecars are the chosen vehicle of local security forces.

The bus was moving ponderously through the streets of Changsha. It stopped every few blocks or so to let people on and off. Every other car and scooter swerved to move around us, impatient to be on their way. The sidecar scooter, however, stayed with us no matter where we went. I sighed.

"What is it?" said Liu.

"Don't be afraid," I began.

But Liu Shao was full of pluck. If anything, he'd grown bolder since June 4. "I'm not afraid of anything!" he said. "Not even dying!"

I nodded. "Great. Well, in that case, I think the police are following us."

Liu's face fell. "Oh," he said. "Really?"

"See for yourself." I gestured toward the window.

Liu looked out. Sure enough, the scooter was still there. The bus made a turn toward campus, and the sidecar scooter followed.

"The next stop is ours," I said.

"No, it's not."

"It is now," I said.

We got off at the stop before our dorm. The scooter stopped and hovered nearby. Liu Shao and I started walking. The scooter followed us, corner to corner, maintaining a distance of fifty yards or so.

"You think that's the police?" said Liu.

"Would you like to go over and ask them?"

He turned pale again, dropped his eyes, and kept walking.

That incident soon became part of a grand routine. Plainclothes policemen tailed me day and night. How did I know they were plainclothes police? For one thing, it was a little uncommon to see men in China wearing suits, looking physically fit, all with the same dead look in their eyes behind you each moment you turned around, day after day after day. And they were always the same men, more or less. I named them after a while. There was Pig Nose. Anvil Chin. Melon Head. Scar. Sometimes they worked in combinations. Pig Nose and Melon Head. Melon Head and Anvil Chin. Scar with Pig Nose. And so on.

They didn't bother to hide themselves, so I didn't bother pretending I didn't see them. Quite often we'd make direct eye contact and hold it there for a moment. A challenge between the hunter and the hunted. *Yes*, they were saying. *We're here. We're following you. So what are you going to do about it?*

They knew I couldn't stop them. At first, I was apprehensive. Then I got angry. Then the whole thing settled down to the rhythm of stock comedy.

During this time, Sun Dan sought me out, which provided an awkward moment. Our breakup during the spring of 1989 was now a matter of public record, the retelling as grounded in truth as a myth, salacious details concocted like the lyrics of a pop song. I'd heard through friends and former classmates that Sun Dan had started dating again, which was fine by me. We'd ended things, I thought. I probably would have started dating again, too, if I hadn't had other things on my mind, like surviving my stay in prison.

It was hard to feel angry about the stories the Party had pulled from her. The CCP had used Sun Dan, which was to be expected. Her father, after all, was well placed in the government of Hunan Province. Directly or indirectly, she'd been coerced to make choices. And who would she support in the end? Me, her former boyfriend? Or her family and its way of life, as well as the system that kept them wealthy, employed, in power, and connected?

She apologized when we met. Said that she wanted to come to see me but felt conflicted. She'd joined the Party in my absence, which complicated things. I said that I understood, and I did. The Party was the only world Sun Dan and her family knew. She was under tremendous pressure to maintain tradition.

"I haven't seen anyone else while you were away," she said. This contradicted hearsay, but so what? It didn't matter. Not knowing what else to say, I thanked her—another awkward moment. She said, "I respect very much the stance you took. Your willingness to suffer the repercussions."

I thanked her again. It was nice to hear that from anyone, especially an old friend.

She said that she wanted to try again and what did I think about that? Not such a good idea, I thought. Too complicated. To say the least, a lot had happened in nineteen months. But I thanked her and said, "You are still my good friend."

She got what I meant and did not seem pleased. I was careful not to mention where I planned to journey next, Guangzhou, to look up my old friend and jail mate, the Party official Fu Jintao.

7

I hadn't seen Fu Jintao since the week we'd spent in *Huang Hua Jian Yu*, but I'd heard about what had befallen him. The grapevine grows very long in prisons. Fu Jintao was detained for ten months before the Party released him. Then, to everyone's great surprise, he refused to work as a cadre. He also refused to go back to work at the import/export business he'd managed. Instead, he'd contacted friends in Singapore, financiers who'd advanced him some money to start a new business, an industrial cleaning company called Teng Fei, Limited. I'd heard that the firm was based in Guangzhou, with sister headquarters in the resort city of Zhuhai, which is sort of like the Marseilles or Nice of the Pearl River Delta. Zhuhai lies north of Macau in the blustering, honking hub of the fast-spinning Guangdong SEZ.

I went to see Fu Jintao at his office. He was pleased to see me and gave me a job on the spot. With Fu Jintao's financial support, I got an apartment in Guangzhou, but I practically never saw it. It was a place to hang my clothes, nothing more. I was constantly on the road taking trains, buses, more trains, taxis. Over the next half year, I traveled all over the country, ostensibly working for Teng Fei. My job was to visit factories and demonstrate the Teng Fei industrial machinery cleaner, a device like a shampoo or dry-cleaning unit for large-scale machines. It was my day job, as I saw it. I had another, more secret mission: to motivate a new group of people toward democratic values. To reignite those partisans whom the June 4 incident had convinced to abandon the cause of change for China.

Slowly, I built up a network, starting with colleagues from 1989, contacts I knew from their voice on the phone, the word of someone I trusted, or sometimes just a fax number. "I'm dropping into your town on business," I would say. "Could I meet with you and anyone you think might be interested?" Talking like that left the invitation vague enough so as not to be damning. There was no such thing as being too careful.

Shui Lianan, my old colleague in the SAF, was especially helpful in providing contacts, numbers, and advice on how to do business in even the most remote provinces. I could not have functioned without him. He introduced me to lots of new faces, all of them eager and ready to feed the overall effort.

"Call here when you get to this city," they would say.

"You'll stay with him when you get to this town."

"Call this number when you arrive."

"I know the restaurant's owner. He is very sympathetic and will let us use his back room. He'll also give us a break on the meal."

Strand by strand, my web spread out, the locus growing tighter and stronger, able to hold more weight. Old friends met new friends. New friends brought in newer friends. The weaver's art is a curious thing. Strength results from many connections, from a pattern repeated again and again. City by city. Town by town. Train ride by train ride. Bus by bus. A web is a vibrant, living thing. Strands of mine reached clear across mainland China, and more were being added each day. Eventually, my web needed a name. I decided to call it *Zhongguo Minzhong Tuanti Zizhi Lianhehui*. Loosely translated—the All China's Civil Organization Autonomous Committee.

Looking back, it's tough to estimate, but I'm certain I met over a thousand people during those crazy six months. Probably closer to two thousand. By day I would visit the factories and follow my scripted itinerary. I'd demonstrate the Teng Fei, Limited, industrial machinery cleaner. Then, at night, I'd attend private parties: small rallies, really, of about fifty or sixty people. Some were students, but many were not. Many were ordinary folks in their thirties and forties. We'd talk about what rights we thought the people of China should have. We'd talk about democracy, the fact that all people everywhere deserved to live in freedom.

Sometimes I met people on the trains where I found myself free to act as I pleased, so long as I wasn't overt. It wasn't hard to strike conversations. People wanted to talk. It's common to meet new friends on long journeys. Part of the fun, in fact. Someone sitting across from me might spot the book I was reading. "Oh. What's that you have there?" he would ask. I'd show him the book and tell him if I enjoyed it or not. Gradually, conversation would turn toward why we were on the train, what provinces we were from. What town. How our families were doing. And then: how the country was doing. Where we thought it was headed. And so on. By then, we were talking politics.

Once I had their confidence, I would introduce myself and tell them a bit about who I was. When they heard I'd been in jail for June 4th, they'd say, "Oh, my! Were you in Beijing?"

So I'd tell them the story of that. I soon discovered that most of my countrymen wanted to talk of Tiananmen Square. They wanted to know more about it. How it got started. Who had begun it. Why it had ended the way it had, and what we should do to move forward. Most of the people I talked to were very antigovernment. They couldn't believe what had happened. By and large, these people were outraged by the Party's corruption, fed up with the hypocrisy. It didn't matter what province they came from. Even the smallest villages had been tainted by CCP influence. In some towns, people were starving, but the cadres lived like kings. They drove a Lexus. They drove a Mercedes. They lived in five-story luxury buildings while everyone else lived in huts.

People saw how the system worked. The Haves and the Have Nots. Those who worked for the government had, while everyone else had not. A riptide of unrest was brewing. The nation, the swimmer, was feeling the pull, soon to be sucked underwater and drowned.

I once met a man from Hangzhou, a city famous for rich and luxurious teas, the very best in China. This man and I started to talk, and it turns out he was wealthy, an executive for the most famous brand of tea in China. He was well connected to CCP officers—had to be to do business, he said. That was the way of the world, though he hastened to add that he wished it weren't so. He gave me a packet of very fine tea and said, "Take this. We only serve it to Chinese leaders. I want you to have some, Baiqiao Tang. And next time you come to Hangzhou, please come visit with me. My home will be your home. And we will have much to discuss."

This brand of tea was the same brand my father had once made me try, pilfered from some grand teacher's conference and stuffed into his courier's sack. To me, this gift was a small bell that rang loudly. This man had legitimized my mission. He was saying, in essence, that I was worthy to lead in the cause I had chosen. He was showing support for democracy and showing support for me.

Fu Jintao was aware that I was meeting dissidents while working for his company. I would make appointments with him each time I returned to headquarters in Guangzhou. Quite often, he took me out to dinner or sometimes brunch. He wanted to know how the Teng Fei industrial cleaning machine was faring in demonstrations. He listened to what I had to say and asked many questions, then made suggestions on how to improve my sales, after which our conversation would always turn to less formal matters.

Fu Jintao was a very smart man and tremendously circumspect. He never insulted a problem by confronting it head on but chose more subtle angles by which to conduct himself and his business. The waiter would bring a carp to the table, and Fu Jintao would strip back the skin to expose the meat and organs. "Try this part here, *Xiao* Tang," he would say. "Taste how sweet it is! My favorite. You will see." Fu Jintao could not lend me support on the surface. But his contributions were there. Much deeper. Always hidden.

"Boss," I would say.

"Yes, *Xiao* Tang?"

"I do not wish to cause problems for you. If the government or the Party or the police come to see you. If they said, 'We know what Baiqiao Tang is doing . . .'"

Fu snorted and cut me off. "They cannot touch me. I make so much money and pay so much tax. If they want to come and arrest me, so be it. I've been through all that before." He picked up a prawn and bit off its head and sucked its innards out.

In appreciation of Fu's largess, I resolved to do the best job I could for him, to further his aims however he asked. But at one point, I could not.

8

Fu wanted to set up a branch of Teng Fei in Hunan. Changsha would make the perfect city, he said. It was far enough north to expand his company's operations but still close to Jiangxi Province in case Teng Fei pushed eastward later.

"*Xiao* Tang," he said. "You know Changsha like the back of your hand. Go to the government offices there and secure the proper permits. Everything must be by the book. I want Teng Fei doing business there soon."

I did as Fu bade me and went to Changsha and applied for the permits, but resistance followed wherever I went. The municipal clerks I met were disdainful. "We cannot allow you to do this," said one.

"But why?" I asked. I was shocked. These permits were routine.

"You would know better than we would," he said, his nose in the air like a dog sniffing beef.

"Let's assume that I don't," I said. "Why don't you bring your superior here? I'd like to speak with him."

I would climb the ladder higher and higher and find no explanations, only hints that grew bolder and bolder, as when one department director said, "There are political reasons why you will not be doing business in Changsha."

"Political reasons?" I asked. "Can you be more specific?"

The man rolled his eyes and twiddled his fingers. "I'd rather not go into detail."

"And yet," I said, "I'd rather you did. We find ourselves at an impasse."

The director rolled his eyes again. He was bored, not caring to hide it. "What would you guess would happen," he said, "if a known political dissident sought to implant himself in the Changsha business community?"

Aha, I thought. There it is.

"I'm glad you asked," I said. "Assuming this person had gone to jail and paid his debt to society? I would hope that you would afford him every chance for his business to succeed and for the country to profit."

The director twiddled his fingers again. "Alas," he said. "Not so. The civil servants you spoke to on previous occasions gave correct information. Thank you for your time, Mr. Tang. We cannot allow you to set up this business. Good day."

Humiliated, I took the train back to Guangdong and reported this news to Fu. He wasn't put off in the least. He smiled and chuckled and shook his head, then rang his assistant and ordered tea. "Do not worry, *Xiao* Tang," he said. "You and I will return to Changsha. Together, we will straighten this out."

"I'm not sure how," I said. "You were in prison, too. Another political dissident."

"Then you don't understand Chinese politics." Fu smiled.

A week later, Fu and I took another train to Changsha. We checked into a lavish hotel from which I thought we'd leave right away to visit municipal offices. But Fu shook his head and picked up the phone in his room. He punched the keys while humming a tune, making call after call, barking into the mouthpiece. That was all we did for two days. I read the papers. Drank tea. Watched television. Played basketball on the hotel court. Mystified.

Two days later, I found myself at a very expensive restaurant. Fu and I shook hands with ten high-level Changsha Party officers, prefecture-level secretaries who comprised the power base for the city. Their influence lay in many places scattered throughout the province.

The restaurant was what we in China call a "corpse house"—a private place, with only one table and only one seating for dinner each evening. Each dish that was served got stranger, more exotic than the last. Snake meat was an early course. Monkey meat was another. The sauces were rich in spices that cost more than a month of my salary. The wines cost about what I made for a year. I had spent years in Changsha—as Fu had said, I knew the city like the back of my hand—and I still had never heard of this

214

place. Later, I learned that it had no name. You either knew where it was and how to book it or didn't.

After dinner, Fu took us out to a dance club at a five-star hotel. Red neon lights. Velvet ropes. A red carpet leading into the maw of a beast whose heart was a thumping bass rhythm. The liquor flowed and women appeared, their bodies writhing on the parquet floor. All this under the twinkling light of the hovering disco ball moon. I watched those Party officials behave in ways I'd have never supposed.

This second part of the evening became another adventure that was stratospherically expensive. But it barely dimpled the plush cushioned walls of Fu Jintao's upholstered wallet. As provinces go, Guangdong was quite a bit wealthier than Hunan. Guangdong was an SEZ, after all—one more reason why Hunan Party officials were eager to help a man like Fu Jintao. No one mentioned business throughout the course of the evening. But within two days, the permits appeared, the very same permits that I'd been denied, now offered with courteous smiles and congratulations. "Best of luck on your new venture."

"You see?" said Fu Jintao. "Now you have learned a lesson, *Xiao Tang*. This is how communism really works!"

I thanked my employer again and again for teaching me many new things.

9

In early May of 1991, I called my mother's apartment and heard her voice, a nervous warble on the other end of the line: Woman under Great Distress Relays Bad Tidings.

"Baiqiao Tang!" she said. "Police keep calling, demanding to know where you are. They say that you haven't checked in with them. They tell me they will arrest you for violating the conditions of your parole."

Let them try, I thought. It sounded like a bluff to me. The CCP had begun to strike me as a gambler with too much money on the table for the meager cards in his hand. The stakes in this game were too high. He was starting to sweat. The CCP couldn't risk making waves anymore lest another uprising occur. The Party had nearly lost control of the country in

1989. I thought of the way they had handled my father's funeral and doubted they'd move to arrest me. Why risk another carnival sideshow to bring me back to Hunan?

"Mother, do not worry," I said. Like telling a pigeon not to coo.

"Where are you, son?"

"I'd rather not say. It's better you that do not know." I said this feeling certain that someone had bugged the line. "I will come home when I can. I miss you."

About a week later, I went to visit Shui Lianan. Though a prominent student leader, he'd never been arrested in the crackdown that followed June 4. Evidently, the CCP considered Shui Lianan too young to be any threat. If only they knew! Hunan University had leveled its own brand of discipline by giving Shui Lianan a written warning and telling him to abandon his pro-democracy work or else he would be expelled. Shui Lianan had played the game and made a big show of stepping down. He acted callow and contrite, a perfect supplicant, carved in wood, but really he surrendered nothing. Instead, he guarded his contacts, his power, and his work, conducting his business on the sly. His politics were like seeds that could sprout in darkness, unseen by the naked eye, but firmly taking root. Like the organization I'd built, it was a rare sort of tree, one that could flower and flourish entirely underground.

When I went to see him in 1991, Shui Lianan was twenty-two years old and taking his final tests for a degree in engineering. I went to Changsha and stayed at his dorm on the Hunan University campus. We spent a few days trying to contact other student leaders, many of whom refused to see or speak with me. They feared the Party's reprisal that much. Shui Lianan shook his head and snorted at those who thought the risks too great. "Change cannot come without risk," he said. "A person who will not risk is a person who is too comfortable."

I told Shui Lianan about the call my mother had received. How I'd laughed it off. But Shui Lianan was sober. "Listen," he said. "Don't do that. Don't underestimate them. Putting you back in prison might look very good for the Party. They're flexing their muscles. Showing their strength. I think you should take this seriously."

"I won't go back to prison," I said. Once had been enough.

Shui Lianan understood. He nodded. "If they come for you, you have no choice. You must go to Shenzhen, in Guangdong Province. When you get there, call this number." He passed me a slip of paper.

"Who is it?" I asked.

"My friend Li Feng,* an old classmate of mine. You can trust him. He's an engineer, too. He earned his degree last year, then went to Shenzhen to work in a factory. Li Feng will help you however he can. He is very active."

Very active. The meaning was understood. "Thank you," I said.

I took the paper and folded it twice and slid it into my pocket. There was no reason to ask *how* Li Feng would help. In those days, dissidents only went to Shenzhen for one reason: Hong Kong lay just across the bay. You could look across the water and see the beckoning, wooded hills that marked the northern reach of the New Territories. If I thought I had no other recourse, Li Feng would help me to flee the country.

During my visit to Changsha, Shui Lianan and I went to a movie together. It turned out to be the last film I ever saw in China, a period piece based on a true story. The film was called *Long Yun and Chiang Kai-Shek.*

Long Yun had been a warlord. Throughout the 1930s, he and his private army of more than a hundred thousand men had controlled a southern portion of China based in a province called Yunnan, which borders Laos and Vietnam. Long Yun was known for his craftiness, as well as for his tenacity. People called him the King of Yunnan, or sometimes Yunnan's Old Dragon. General Chiang Kai-Shek, who was leader of the GMD, had great respect for Long Yun, but he saw the Old Dragon as threatening the power of the Guomindang. So Chiang Kai-Shek made a plan.

In 1945, he ordered Long Yun to attack Japanese forces along the sweet-smelling banks of the upper Salween River. This order was hardly unusual. The Sino-Japanese War was raging. Japan was the enemy and was losing. Long Yun did as he was ordered and sent his troops into battle. While they were gone, Chiang Kai-Shek betrayed him. He sent a force to capture Long Yun in the Dragon's home city, Kunming.

Long was eventually exiled, sent to Hong Kong in disgrace. Chiang Kai-Shek stuck a GMD flag in the soil of Yunnan and claimed that he'd unified southern China, a fanciful claim at very best, and one that didn't last long. The Communists had just unified the northern parts of China. A showdown was brewing: Chiang and the GMD on one side, Mao and the CCP on the other. There could be only one victor. One true ruler of China. That was where the movie left off.

"What did you think?" asked Shui Lianan. The movie had just ended. The credits were rolling. The lights had come up. Audience members were rubbing their eyes and heaving themselves to their feet.

"Well," I said. "At least we know how it ends."

Meaning, who was the final victor, the CCP or the Guomindang? But I confess that, in that moment, I was also thinking of stories in general. My country's. My own. The world's. All of them sat open-ended like the mouth of a flowing river, a movement that never ceased its flow, regardless of who is watching.

10

That July, I returned from a trip to the western reaches to find a tiny pile of paper slips on the barely used desk I kept at the Teng Fei office in Guangzhou. They were phone messages, scratched out by secretaries. Most of them were marked URGENT. I checked the dates. Some were as old as a month.

Pangs gnawed in the pit of my stomach. I knew what the messages said before I read them. I picked up the first one and stared at it. CALL A MR. SHUI LIANAN. HE SAYS IT IS URGENT.

Yes, I thought. The mouth of a river, emptying into the sea.

I grabbed the receiver and punched in a number and heard the burr of a dial tone ringing a few hundred miles in the distance. The phone picked up. I heard Shui Lianan's voice. He sounded guarded. "Yes?"

"My friend," I said.

A pause. "My friend." We were on the same page at once.

"You called?" I said.

"I did, to tell you some news. I wish I had reached you sooner."

"So do I. Is it good news or bad?"

"Very good. You will be pleased."

My heart sank. We were using a simple reversal tactic. For this conversation, good was bad, and bad was good. Therefore, Shui Lianan was saying: brace yourself, hard truths to follow.

"Your friends remember you fondly here. They're throwing a celebration in honor of your anniversary. Invitations are everywhere. Everyone's got them. Congratulations."

"Thank you," I said, my voice barely a whisper.

At Longxi, when the explosions went off, you could feel the heave and plunge of the world, the roar as great as an earthquake, the rumble of rocks and tearing stones. But shifting lives make no sound at all. Great changes are marked by silence.

My friends. Translation: the CCP. A celebration: a gathering. The Party was trying to find me. My anniversary: June 4. For which invitations were everywhere.

I stared straight ahead at the blank office wall and pictured Changsha in my mind. The posters bearing my image. Police and soldiers clogging the streets. Running from door to door like dogs. Officers barging in on my mother. Dragging old friends to the precincts. Interrogations in windowless rooms. The same show of force they had put on before, the first year after the massacre. I'd been in jail then. Now I was not. Now I was once more a target.

Shui Lianan had been right when I'd gone to see him back in May. I had been glib. Obtuse. The CCP was flexing its muscle. Showing off its power. Now they were rounding up dissidents like cattle, stuffing them back into pens for slaughter. Not me, I vowed. Not me.

"My friend?" Shui Lianan was still on the line. Waiting.

"Yes?"

"Will you attend this party?"

A moment passed before I decided. "Yes," I said. "I think I will."

Truth is often found in opposites. *Good-bye, Shui Lianan*, I thought. *And thank you.*

He sighed. "Then I look forward to seeing you. Safe travels until I do, my friend. Be well."

"Be well. I'll see you soon."

I hung up the phone and stared at my desk, at the pile of messages waiting. Then I turned and left the office. By the end of the day, I had packed my belongings, called Fu Jintao, and resigned my post. He understood, of course.

"Be careful, *Xiao* Tang."

"I will," I said. "And thank you. For everything."

That night, I left for Shenzhen.

I had the number for Shui Lianan's friend but didn't use it right away. When I arrived, I looked up an old friend and colleague from the SAF, Lu Qing, formerly of Central-South University. Ren Jun's friend, and a man who'd been labeled a co-conspirator in my indictment the previous summer.

Two months before, during my trip to Changsha, I had asked around about Lu Qing. The reports I got were conflicting. Some students said that Central-South had expelled him for his work on the SAF. Others said that wasn't true. They'd heard that Lu Qing had been stricken with a case of tuberculosis that required him to be bedridden in a university hospital for a year, unable to leave or see visitors. Which others claimed was a ruse. Lu Qing wasn't sick at all, they said, he was under house arrest. This was a common tactic the government used. They would tell the world that a student was sick and then take their time debriefing him without any risk of damaging his reputation.

No one in Changsha seemed clear about whether Lu Qing had earned his degree. Most, however, thought it mysterious that Lu had somehow avoided a prison sentence. From Changsha alone, over twenty students had gone to jail for their work in the movement. Most of those had been underlings, but Lu Qing, like me, had been active, influential, and visible. Yet I had gone to jail and Lu Qing had not. How?

I knew that Lu Qing was alive and well and living in Shenzhen. He was working for a factory that manufactured electronics parts and kept an apartment in the dormitory for factory employees. I had the name of the factory, so, when I got to Shenzhen, I took a cab to the dorm, got out, and read the listing placard. I found Lu Qing's name right away and called up to his apartment. His voice through the intercom sounded tinny and stupefied. He was clearly surprised to hear from me, and he wouldn't come down. He told me to meet him out in front of the factory a little while later, so I did.

"How are you?" I asked when he finally appeared.

"Fine, fine," said Lu Qing, but to me, he looked anything but. He was fidgety. Scared. Avoiding eye contact. "So. You're here in Shenzhen."

"I am."

"I see. And where are you staying?"

"I was hoping I could stay with you."

Lu Qing nodded as though he'd been expecting this but wasn't happy about it. "Well," he said. "I suppose you can."

His demeanor was a puzzle whose pieces refused to fit. Why was he so unhappy to see me? I started to ask him that very question, but he suddenly grinned and said, "You know who else is here? Ren Jun."

"Ren Jun?" This came as a total surprise. I'd lost track of Ren Jun after the government had me transferred to Changsha Number Two Jail. "What is Ren Jun doing here?"

Lu Qing shrugged and looked away. "I invited him," he said. "In fact, I introduced him to some people at the factory. Got him a job. We live in the same dorm. I told him you were here. He's coming down in a minute."

Sure enough, Ren Jun arrived moments later. I couldn't believe my eyes! This was not the broken, hollow-eyed wretch I'd last seen skulking about his cell in Changsha Number One Jail. Ren Jun had put on weight. His hair was well managed and shiny. We shook hands. Ren Jun did not smile, but he met my eyes, which is more than I could say for Lu Qing.

"Come upstairs," Ren said.

We went to Lu Qing's apartment. The atmosphere there was more tense than I had ever imagined it being. The three of us were behaving like friends attending another friend's funeral. No one knew what to say.

A stilted conversation followed. Long pauses. Half-hearted chuckles. Recollections of two years before were offered in clipped and coughing tones, as if the price we had paid for those days had infected us somehow, making us ill. I felt very uncomfortable.

At one point, Lu Qing got up and said, "Here. Come with me."

I followed him outside, into the hallway where he had me stand against the painted brick wall and took out a camera and snapped my picture.

"What was that for?" I said.

"Don't worry. You'll see."

After which he left me in Ren Jun's company and went to run some errand.

11

An hour later, Lu Qing returned to the apartment with a brand-new government ID, the kind that, by law, every Chinese citizen must carry. The ID had my picture on it and a name I did not recognize. "There," said Lu Qing. He handed me the ID. "This will help you get around."

"Where did you get this?" I said. Turning the ID over, I examined its every contour. To my eyes, it was a genuine document, exactly like my own, save for the name, of course. I was amazed, but also taken aback. I had not asked for this fake ID, and I found it very strange that Lu Qing had produced such a crafty forgery in only an hour.

He shrugged. "I know someone who makes them," he said. "It cost about three hundred yuan."

This was also very strange. Three hundred yuan was a lot of money. Why was he being so generous?

His eagerness put me on edge. In the course of my dissident days, I'd received help from plenty of people, but even the ones prepared to give it usually had to be asked a few times. Suspicion crouched at the base of my spine. Without warning, Lu Qing got up again and gathered his clothes and said he was sorry, he had to go back home to Hunan, a distance of nearly two thousand *li*.

"But please," he said and smiled. "Stay here. Use my apartment. Ren Jun has a key."

With that, he left, which left me in shock. His reaction flew in the face of our friendship, as well as that of common courtesy. Ren Jun and I found ourselves alone, a fact that appeared to make Ren Jun supremely uncomfortable. We began to talk more intimately, acknowledging the experiences we'd shared working side-by-side in the movement. Then what had befallen us, the dark times in Changsha Number One Jail. Which led Ren Jun to make a confession: he no longer wanted to play any part in the pro-democracy movement.

"I just want a normal life," he said. "A good job. An apartment. I want to make money. Be a good citizen. What's wrong with that, Baiqiao Tang? Seriously, you should consider it."

I couldn't believe what I was hearing. "But what about our work?" I asked. "You know that the CCP is corrupt. You know that it can be brutal. You told me yourself right before June 4. Democracy is the answer, you said. 'Democracy has its share of problems, but none like China's dealing with now.'"

Ren Jun made a face. "I was wrong," he said. "There's no point fighting it, China won't change. You're wasting your life. You want my advice? Get a good job and settle down. Make money. Marry a good woman. Have children. There's no shame in doing that, Baiqiao Tang. No shame whatsoever."

I asked Ren Jun if he'd had any contact with former SAF colleagues. He shook his head and said he hadn't heard from anyone, nor had he reached out to find them.

"And Lu Qing?" I said. "I suppose he shares your views?"

Ren Jun nodded. "He's the one who convinced me that what we did in Changsha was pointless."

His words impaled my brain like hot steel barbs. Now I was more convinced than ever that Lu Qing and the CCP were somehow working together, that the ID he had given me would mark me the moment I used it. Also that his "trip to Hunan," as sudden as it was, held dangerous implications for me. And one more thing: there was nothing left to discuss or pursue with my old friend Ren Jun.

I only stayed in the apartment one night. The very next morning, I went outside and found a pay phone and took out the folded slip of paper I'd been given. I called the number written down. A man picked up and said, "Hello?"

"Yes," I said. "I'm a friend of Shui Lianan. From Changsha. He and I worked together in college."

The voice did not speak for a moment. Then: "Where are you?"

"Shenzhen," I said.

"Just you?"

"Yes."

"How can I help?"

"I'm not sure yet. Can we meet someplace and discuss it?"

The voice on the other end of the line quoted me an address. I hung up the phone and left immediately, making my way across Shenzhen, stopping often to ask for directions. The address I had been given turned out to be in Shekou, Shenzhen's waterfront district. And that was a problem.

In 1991, the entrance to Shekou was heavily guarded by police and army troops. The waterfront lay on the Pearl's northern shore, but the river was poorly named. It had no luster. It didn't glisten. The water was brown and caked with pollution. It served as China's Berlin Wall. Even though the Pearl was wide, any person in decent health could swim across. The far shore marked the border of Hong Kong and freedom. The river was therefore a prize for any who wished to escape mainland China. The government understood this allure and posted troops along the shore to stop the refugees from fleeing, telling the soldiers to shoot on sight if their orders were not obeyed.

When I got to the gates of Shekou, there were guards wherever I looked. I hadn't planned for this problem. In order to pass through the gates, I would have to show an ID, but which one? By that point, I felt certain my name was on a list. A guard would read my state ID and see I was Baiqiao Tang from Hunan Province and arrest me on the spot. However, what if I was right about Lu Qing? Suppose he was working with the CCP? I would also be arrested if I offered my fake ID. The guards would have been briefed on that, told to watch for a fake name linked to a dissident on the run. I would flash the fake ID, and they'd smile and sound the alarm. Either away, I'd be under arrest. And turning back was no longer an option.

The devil I knew and the devil I didn't. I weighed them fast in my head. I could not use my real ID—of that much I felt certain. My only chance was to get in line and force my hand to stop shaking. When I reached the inspection point, I held out Lu Qing's false ID.

The guard took the card, held it up to his face, and read the name. He lowered the card and looked at me. I thought I saw a glimmer of recognition in his eyes. He looked back at the card, then back at me. Back at the card. Then back at me. He handed the card back and leveled his eyes. "I know who you are," he said, very quietly and direct.

My heart slammed the inner wall of my ribs, a wild animal caught in a trap. I waited, expecting alarms to sound, expecting the guard to hit me, shoot me, slap me in chains and drag me away. It was over. Finally over. My heart settled down and my body relaxed. Surprised, I felt relief.

"Go through," said the guard. He waved his hand, the same way he'd done for tens of thousands of others during his shift. "Go on. Hurry."

There was no hesitation. No poignant moment like you might see in the movies. I offered no word of thanks. Just did as he said and moved quickly past him, entering Shekou.

That guard saved my life. But more than that, he showed me the true face of China. Yes, he worked for the CCP, and yes, he should have arrested me. That was his job, after all—the thing that he'd been ordered to do, but he didn't. He said that he knew who I was. Therefore he must have known what I'd done. Evidently, he had approved. In his own quiet way, he was fighting back.

I still remember the face of that guard. I see it sometimes when I close my eyes. I think I will see it the rest of my life.

12

Li Feng was a short man by Chinese standards, wiry and fit, with arms as long and ropy as an orangutan's. He had developed premature crow's feet from the engineer's tendency to crinkle his eyes while mentally adding sums. The spectacles he wore had round lenses that always needed a polish. I never saw how he smudged the glass, but he managed to do it just the same. Li Feng had a habit of smiling an apology whenever he spoke, as though he felt certain that whatever he was saying couldn't possibly be of interest to anyone, and yet he was obligated to say it anyway.

I stayed with Li Feng for a week in Shenzhen, during which time he came to a grand decision. "There is nothing left for me here," he said. "If our movement has failed, if men like you are fated to spend the rest of your life being hunted, then I don't feel a part of China anymore. I will go with you, Baiqiao Tang."

It took Li Feng that whole week to cut a deal with a man he knew, the captain of a ship that routinely went to Hong Kong. For the princely sum of six thousand yuan, this man would let Li Feng and me hide in his cargo hold. The money came from a special fund donated by pro-democracy advocates for use in cases like these. The crossing was dangerous and illegal, of course, but hardly uncommon. Especially in Shenzhen.

Back then, Shenzhen wasn't the glimmering modern cityscape you'll find today. It was more like a shantytown, the waterfront slumping and rat-ridden, festooned with barnacles, drunks, and garbage. The water carried the sweet-sour reek of petrol mixed with puke. Fish heads bobbed in the brine, staring up at the sun with their dead, milky eyes. It was a place where humans were smuggled like silk crates, packed into cubbies and steel ships' bellies where they huddled, blind as moles in the darkness and cold.

At that time, Hong Kong was still a colony and entrepôt of Great Britain. The Party could not operate there—officially, at any rate. So Hong Kong carried a strong allure, especially for young Chinese. The level of human trafficking was high, and the CCP tried to crack down on it. I suppose they succeeded in many cases, but the numbers working against them were large, and one brick placed in a streambed cannot stop the flow of water.

Li Feng told me the conditions of our passage. "We cannot take anything with us," he said. "Just the clothes on our backs. After paying the fare, we'll have about a hundred yuan and some Hong Kong dollars between us. That's it."

"I don't care," I said. "When we get to Hong Kong, we'll call some numbers." I held up my notebook, my constant companion, in which several coded entries were written—information that would help us contact pro-democracy activists in Hong Kong. "They will aid us," I said.

Li Feng nodded. "Assuming the CCP doesn't intercept our ship. Assuming we land safely in Hong Kong. Even then, the trick will be to contact the movement before the Hong Kong authorities find us and throw us in jail as illegals. If that happens, they'll send us back to China. And who knows what will befall us then."

"Best not to think about that," I said. "Let's look to the future with hope."

We left Shenzhen on July 28, 1991. The ship was a medium-sized cargo vessel, a hulking shadow that loomed against the black curtain of night. I remember the deckhands surrounding us, hiding us in their foul-smelling ranks. They jostled Li Feng and me up the gangplank and herded us into the cargo hold, away from the prying eyes of inspectors.

"Okay," said one of them. "Stay here and don't make a sound until we come to get you."

We weren't alone. When the hold hatch opened, a sliver of light from the ship's deck lanced forward into the darkness. I couldn't believe my eyes. Some thirty other passengers stood upright, frozen, pressed together like an army of mannequins in some demented dressmaker's shop, none of them over twenty-five years of age. Their frightened eyes blinked at us. I remember thinking how odd it was that I wasn't scared at all.

I've already been in jail, I thought. Compared to that, this is a pleasant boat ride, nothing more.

We got inside, and the hatch swung shut with a squeal of unoiled hinges. The sliver of light grew narrow again, collapsing into itself until it disappeared altogether, leaving only the cold, the darkness, and the smell of mollusks and gasoline.

The trip took about four hours. As I look back, it seems that we took an odd route, perhaps to foil authorities. I know for a fact that we sailed southwest down the Pearl River into Shenzhen Bay. From there, we entered the South China Sea and skirted the western edge of the New Territories before docking briefly in one of Hong Kong's central ports. All this I saw through a tiny slot, a rectangular porthole set in the hull through which we exiles looked in turns, snatching glimpses of where we were going.

At one point, I looked through the porthole and saw a landscape out of a fairy tale. Mountains lit by powerful lights against the blue-black velvet sky. Hills that lay under carpets of forest that marched off into the night. A placid semitropical bay, the waves like tongues of foam that lapped against the lamp-lit shore. And the skyline, so majestic! A tall collage of twinkling jewels rising against the midnight sky. Like none I had ever seen in my life. Back then, tall buildings were alien things. There were practically none to be found in China.

"It looks like Manhattan," I said.

"Like what?" In the black of the hold, I could almost hear the crinkle of Li Feng's crow's feet.

"New York City," I said. "I've seen pictures of the skyline. In books."

I was hoping the captain would let us off near the skyscrapers, but he didn't. For reasons I guess I'll never know, we turned around and headed back west, returning toward Shenzhen. I remember thinking that something was wrong. Why hadn't we disembarked? Had our ruse been discovered? Were police outside with clubs and electric batons held high, waiting to be brought down?

No. An hour later, the ship docked again. Again, I looked out the porthole, and this time I saw the tapestry of night spread across the sky. There was a dingy waterfront lit by floodlights. It boasted no tall buildings or skyscrapers, only shacks that sighed to one side, rickety things with holes in their roofs, and wharfs that stood on cracked wooden pylons, skeletal in the gloom. My eyes followed shadows of rats running round, and men who looked like rats. Unshaven. Filthy. Lounging against low buildings drinking rice wine from paper cups, none of them caring for anything more than to further the depths of intoxication.

I had no idea where we were at the time, though later I figured it out. A town called Yuen Long, a destitute place that I hear has changed a lot since then, and so much for the better.

The next thing I knew, I heard the scream of the cargo hatch being pulled open, saw the dark forms of deckhands crouching above us, black against the purple night sky. They waved their hands and shooed everyone out as though we were flies alighting on meat. "Go!" they hissed. "Get up. Get out! Go quickly! Welcome to Hong Kong!"

It must have been four in the morning, possibly five, but no later. Dawn still lay an hour off. The cover of night was a blessing. We moved quickly down the gangplank on legs turned to rubber from the rocking of the sea. Hitting the docks, our little group scattered. The baleful eyes of the drunkards watched us, sneering. The first low crackling words we heard were all phrased in Cantonese.

Li Feng grabbed my arm, and we started to run. We hadn't gone far when the first whistles shrieked, followed by shouts from behind us, sharp in the night. "Freeze! Police! Hey! You there! Stop!"

Were they shouting at us? I didn't know, and what could it possibly matter? By then, the only trick was to run. Li Feng and I bolted, gasping. We cleared the untended waterfront gates and surged into the twisting streets of Yuen Long. Mingling with rodents and slinking stray cats, we hid among piles of trash in the alleys, wincing at the stink of rot. Long hours lay behind us, but many more lay ahead.

"We'll be safer up in the mountains," said Li Feng. So that's the direction we headed.

The higher we traveled, the more the district thinned out into neighborhoods like quiet little villages. We walked the streets and kept a sharp eye out for anyone passing by. When a car approached, we got off the road and hid ourselves very quickly. The car would pass us on churning tires, music from the radio wafting out open windows, its headlights washing the asphalt. The moment it passed, we returned to the street and kept walking until the next car came.

We repeated this process over and over. A little while later, we watched the sun rise, but that was no comfort to us. In daylight, things were more dangerous. Two refugees were more easily noticed.

A taxi approached, and I flagged it down. The driver stopped and said something in Cantonese. Li Feng nodded and offered translation. "He wants to know where we're headed."

"The center of town," I said. Thinking that was the best place to look for people who'd help us.

Li Feng nodded and told the driver, who narrowed his eyes at us. Looking back, I know what he must have been thinking. The center of town? There's no such thing as a center of town in Hong Kong. The territory spreads out like a quilt with one district abutting another, like patchwork. The fact that we didn't know this certainly marked us as refugees.

Besides, Li Feng and I wore T-shirts and trousers gone filthy from the hold of the ship. And we were wearing beards, a common thing for mainland men while everyone shaved in Honk Kong. In short, we must have borne a striking and painful resemblance to that which we actually were: illegal immigrants. Trouble on legs. Calamity waiting to happen.

It's a testament to the driver's courage or the laxity of Hong Kong immigration at the time, but the cab driver finally sighed and motioned for Li Feng and me to climb in his car. Li Feng later told me the driver's words. "You have money?" the driver said.

"Yes," said Li Feng.

"Hong Kong dollars? I don't take the damnable yuan."

"Yes," said Li Feng. "Hong Kong." He showed the driver the bills.

The driver sighed again and shook his head and put the car in gear. "Okay," he said, and he started to drive. "The center of town, huh? Here we go."

He took us around the southwest edge of a mountain, into the district we'd seen from the ship, the one with all the skyscrapers. Straight to the heart of Kowloon.

13

We got out of the cab and paid the driver and entered a coffee shop. The shop's owner was just opening the place. He kept wiping his counter and motioned for us to take chairs. While Li Feng ordered, I found a pay phone, consulted my notebook, and called an old friend whom I only knew as Mr. Li.

I'd never met Mr. Li in person. We'd only spoken over the phone. For all I know, that wasn't his real name. We'd worked together a lot back in the spring of 1989. He'd told me he was a student leader at Hong Kong Chinese University, one of the two largest and most famous schools in Hong Kong. Mr. Li had been one of my connections to funding. I would call him and ask for money from the coffers of pro-democracy unions based in the Hong Kong free zone. He had sent it whenever I asked. In fact, it was thanks to Mr. Li that I'd had enough money to flee Hunan during the CCP crackdown.

He was shocked to hear from me. We hadn't spoken since the spring of 1989. He'd heard about my sentence but hadn't heard that I'd been released.

"I thought you were still in jail," he said. "Or dead."

In China, very often, the two went hand in hand.

"No," I said. "I'm still alive."

It was one of those strange moments where I realized I probably shouldn't be.

"Where are you?" asked Mr. Li.

"In Hong Kong," I said.

He couldn't believe it. "What?!"

Very quickly, I'd told him what happened. He told me to just sit tight.

"Congratulations on getting this far. Now don't move! Don't say a word. Just take a seat in the coffeehouse. If police stop in to check your papers, don't try to run away. They'll catch you."

This was a real concern. The illegal immigration problem had gotten so bad in Hong Kong that police were on patrol everywhere, checking IDs at random. They were also gaining a stout reputation for shooting people who ran away.

"What's the address?" said Mr. Li. "I'm coming to pick you up."

I looked across the coffee shop at Li Feng. "I have a friend with me. He has to come too."

Again, Mr. Li was astounded. "Does your friend speak Cantonese?" I told him that Li Feng did. "Good. Have him order some beverages, then both of you shut up and sit tight. Don't move. I'm coming to get you."

We hung up. I looked at the clock on the wall. It was just before eight in the morning.

Mr. Li arrived by cab a half hour later. He wasn't alone. A young woman was with him, another student leader in the pro-democracy movement. They took Li Feng and me to the offices of the Hong Kong University Student's Association where they sat us down and gave us more cups of coffee. Again, this fascination with coffee! That day was the first time I'd tried it. In China, we'd all drank tea.

Now I sipped the stuff in my cup—a dark, exotic, bitter taste. I liked it right away. I lit a cigarette and inhaled. Sipped the coffee again. What an excellent combination, I thought, a coffee with a cigarette. What could be better than this? And on top of it all, I was free.

"Well," said Mr. Li. "Congratulations, once again."

"Yes," I said.

"Thank you," said Li Feng.

"Unfortunately, now you must go to jail. Both of you. As quickly as possible."

We were shocked, but Mr. Li explained there was no way to get around it. Li Feng and I had entered Hong Kong as illegals. Eventually, someone would check our papers, place us under arrest, and send us back to China.

"It's better this way," said Mr. Li. "The process goes like this: You turn yourselves in of your own accord. You'll go to jail, but you won't be there long. I still have quite a few phone calls to make. But I doubt you'll be incarcerated for more than forty-eight hours. At which point, I'll have both of you freed with status as legal residents."

"How can you do that?" I said.

Mr. Li said not to worry and went to find a phone.

He had many powerful contacts. One was a man named Lau Chin-shek, who was very high up in Hong Kong's government, sort of their secretary of state. Lau Chin-shek had started his political career as a famous leader of a worker's union, then went on to become an activist on behalf of human rights. He was close to several elected representatives in the Hong Kong parliament.

We met Lau Chin-shek, who took us around and introduced us to so many people, their faces started to blur in my mind. They all seemed happy to shake my hand, as well as the hand of Li Feng. And all of them sounded confident they could help us in many ways.

"You see?" said Mr. Li at one point. "Don't worry about going to jail. We've done this more than a hundred times with other political dissidents."

And so it was all arranged. Along with a man named Chan Yaochang, the most famous student leader in Hong Kong, Lau Chin-shek himself would bring Li Feng and me directly to jail, all for the sake of good theater. By bringing us to the detention center, Lau Chin-shek and Chan Yaochang were in essence telling authorities, "See? We're doing right by the law by bringing these two gentlemen in. However, rest assured that we are working to have them freed. And thank you so much in advance for your kind and speedy cooperation."

The police at the detention center knew who we were. They fingerprinted Li Feng and me, and gave us prison uniforms. Everyone was very respectful. Mr. Li had told us quite plainly, "Say nothing unless you are spoken to. Keep your answers short. The police are doing their jobs, so don't argue with them and don't get upset. Don't talk to anyone if you can help it. We'll have you out very soon."

Li Feng and I were placed in a cell. No window. No beds. No furniture. The room was fairly large, but utterly empty. The walls facing out on the cell block were barred. The other three were made of brick, painted white, and bare. The cell had one sink and one toilet. Both were open. There was no privacy.

At one point Li Feng shook his head and snorted. "Awful," he said. He was looking around.

"No," I said. "It's not."

We waited. We had nothing to do, so we smoked our cigarettes and dozed. We had no pillows. No bedding. When we got tired, we lay on the floor, stretched out, and got some sleep. Then we woke up and repeated the process: smoking, dozing, staring at nothing. Sometimes the guards brought us food, which was good, much better than what I'd been served in any Chinese prison.

Li Feng and I both agreed that the guards were behaving quite strangely. It was like they were just pretending to treat us like normal prisoners. Gruff voices barking orders. Postures rigid and ramrod straight. They maintained the pretense of holding command when, in essence, they would defer to us. They would ask if we wanted more water, more tea. Another helping of food.

14

Everything went according to plan. Li Feng and I were released as expected and given papers proclaiming that we were welcome in Hong Kong. This was nothing like a green card or any kind of official status as legal residents, more like ad hoc dispensation, a special arrangement made with the Hong Kong government that allowed us to live and work in the colony as long as we pleased.

Lau Chin-shek and Chan Yaochang took us on more and more rounds. They made sure that Li Feng and I knew several key members of the Hong Kong Chinese University's student association. They asked these students to look after Li Feng and myself, to help us through our transition, they said. A good word, I thought. *Transition*.

Li Feng and I were each awarded 3,000 HKD a month for the next six months. Funds for living expenses, they said, for which we were very grateful. It wasn't a lot of money, but a pauper is thrilled by pennies and a wise man sees the intent as the actual value in any gift. Three thousand HKD would certainly get us started as Li Feng and I set out to look for ways to support ourselves.

A week after our release, Lau Chin-shek brought us out to dinner as sort of an official welcome. Many student leaders from Hong Kong Chinese University were present. I was impressed that everyone knew Lau Chin-shek. He was a real Hong Kong celebrity.

At one point, Lau Chin-shek stood up and raised his glass to make a toast. "We have among us two brave men," he said. "Two men to whom we shall offer aid as thanks for their daring and sacrifice. Let word go forth that men are free. That freedom is here, in Hong Kong. And for those martyrs who gave their lives, our gratitude forever."

The owner of the restaurant refused to let him pay for the meal.

Over the next three months, I saved money by living in the office of the Hong Kong Chinese University's Student Association. My bed was a table in a meeting room; it was very broad and sturdy. The office had a bathroom with its own shower. Li Feng stayed in the office, too. He slept on the floor at the base of the table. Why not? We were young men without a country. Our lives were one big adventure. It was summer, and we were new to this land. Roughing it proved no inconvenience. Compared to sleeping on the floor of a cell with forty or fifty other men, my arrangement in Hong Kong was heaven.

We ate in the university cafeteria where food was cheap and plentiful. Often, we strolled the school grounds and let our thoughts wander. The campus of Hong Kong Chinese University is way up in the mountains and so beautiful that we didn't want to leave. Li Feng and I entertained dreams of staying forever.

Eventually, Li Feng found work as an editor for *Open Magazine*, a political publication with outright pro-democracy leanings. I arranged that job for him, having corresponded with the owner and founder of *Open* during the spring of 1989. He was happy to take Li Feng on, and Li Feng was happy to have a job.

As for me, I'd begun to feel the incessant pull of the pen. The office of the Student's Association was well stocked with books and magazines, like living in a library, a very quiet, contemplative place. I started to write down all the things I remembered about my adventure, not wanting to forget a single thing, a single person who'd given me aid, or how they'd worked to advance the cause of democracy in China.

A month or so later, Lau Chin-shek asked if I would accompany him on an errand. His car came around and picked me up. We drove through the Jin Zhong, or "Gold Clock" district in the center of Hong Kong—in English, it's known as Admiralty. Continuing on, we reached Wan Chai, the district on the northernmost shore of Hong Kong Island. We went to an office where Lau Chin-shek introduced me to a man named Robin Munro.

In Hong Kong, Robin was *chuan qi ren wu*, a difficult term to translate into English. It means someone about whom other people possess the highest respect—a guardian of high ideals. There is drama attached to the word, as well as the status of legend. I was soon to find out that Robin had done much to earn this title. He was *chuan qi ren wu* all the way.

The first time he opened his mouth to speak was a moment I'll never forget. Robin was a *yang gui zi*, the Mandarin word for the Canton *gweilo*, white ghost among the people—Caucasian, and yet he spoke Mandarin, fluent and perfect, much better than I! He could also write in a beautiful hand. His characters sprang off the page, gorgeous in their execution. A *yang gui zi* who could write like Qu Yuan? I would not have imagined it possible.

Apart from speaking my language, Robin startled me with his kindness. He told me he was a Scotsman, that he'd come to China to study in the late 1970s, a point whose significance was not lost on me. During that era, China had granted very few foreign visas. Robin must have been one of the first outlanders permitted to pass behind the Bamboo Curtain. For many years, he'd worked as a foreign contact for Amnesty International in London. He'd been present at Tiananmen Square as an international observer and had borne eyewitness to the June 4th incident. The Chinese government deported Robin as part of the massacre's fallout, after which he'd gained justified renown by helping dozens of prominent dissidents escape from mainland China.

Now he was living in Hong Kong, working for an organization called Human Rights Watch. Among his many talents was a special penchant for succoring exiles. He befriended them and got them work and helped them to find their place in a world that was new, confusing, and strange.

Through Robin, I was awarded a grant to continue the book I'd been writing. The book had begun to broaden in depth and scope, turning into a kind of report of what I'd see in Hunan Province, the events leading up to Tiananmen Square, as well as those that happened after. That report eventually became *Anthems of Defeat: Crackdown in Hunan Province 1989–1992*, a publication of Asia Watch, a division of Human Rights Watch.

How I wrote that book is a story in itself. The main hurdle I faced was the fact that I was living in exile. I had gathered a lot of information while still in mainland China and traveling the country on behalf of Teng Fei, Limited. I knew, for instance, what fate had befallen a lot of the student leaders during the crackdown that followed the June 4th incident. I was also beginning to organize certain statistics. How many workers were sentenced to jail? How many journalists? Businessmen? Cadres? What were the typical sentences levied? How many had been sent to labor reform camps? How many had been executed? How many had died in prison?

During my travels, I'd shared what I knew with members of the underground whom I met in various cities. I asked them to find out more information, having in mind even then to assemble the facts, to create a clearer picture of what had happened. The underground groups had all pledged their assistance. Now I needed their help.

From the Student's Association offices at Hong Kong Chinese University, I began reaching out to my contacts, asking them to compile whatever they'd learned. Send it to me at once, I said. Sometimes I used a public phone that I felt could not be traced, but I also used fax machines a lot since they were easy to code and provided instant transmissions. Every business or government office possessed a fax machine. We doubted the CCP had the power to monitor them all. And faxes weren't sent through the mail. Therefore they weren't made to endure the probing eyes of censors.

Information began to pour in. My network of contacts astounded me with their willingness to contribute. Some of them even volunteered to undertake special missions. Sometimes, for instance, I needed to find specific pieces of information, and the only person who had it was serving time in a Chinese prison. My contacts would offer to visit that person. Sometimes they traveled for days on end, province to province to province. Some were turned away, as my mother once had been. But many more made it through and succeeded in their mission. The puzzle pieces fell into place, creating a shocking picture of the Chinese government's actions.

These men and women who worked for me were putting their safety at risk. The CCP was still hunting "spies," looking for any excuse to arrest more "counterrevolutionaries." But that didn't deter my old friend Shui Lianan from visiting Longxi Prison and talking to my hero, Zhao Yuen. It didn't deter them from sharing information on the number of political prisoners being held there, and under what charges. Hundreds of "agents" clear across China put themselves on the line like this. My fax machine in the student association offices would purr like a cat all day long, spitting paper.

Over the next seven months, I compiled information and verified facts and proclamations as best I could. I wrote the report, edited it, had it translated into English, and had the translation verified for accuracy.

It was a monumental load of work, but I still feel my job was the easiest. Were it not for my mainland colleagues, the true picture of the crackdown that followed Tiananmen Square might never be known.

15

During my time in Hong Kong, I discussed the strange behavior I saw exhibited by Lu Qing. Many student activists didn't seem surprised.

"He was working for the CCP," they said.

"Yes," I said. "I thought of that."

It was the only explanation. But the activists pushed me to ask more questions. To think in broader terms.

"The real question," one of them said, "is *how long* has he been working for the CCP?"

"I don't understand," I said.

"We know of Lu Qing even here," he said. "There are those who suspect he was working for the CCP before the spring of 1989."

I was stunned. I hadn't considered this, though certainly there was precedent. Reports I'd read had cited that up to 50 percent of so-called dissidents working for German reunification were actually working in some way or other for the Communist Party. When the Berlin Wall finally crumbled in November 1989, you couldn't tell who was who. Eastern? Western? Communist? Capitalist? People would serve different masters at once, doing whatever they could to survive and gain a stronger foothold on a swiftly tilting planet.

Nowadays, unfortunately, this sort of thinking is normal for me. One of our most difficult tasks in the Chinese pro-democracy movement is to identify who is a valued brother-in-arms and who is a spy for the Party. Over the course of their history, the CCP has developed formidable skills in the art of espionage. Their spies are everywhere—listening, working, passing on information. In China, we had an anecdote about General Chiang Kai-shek. We said that he was defeated in 1949 not because of the CCP's army but because of the CCP's spies. The anecdote said that CCP intelligence was so good, they knew Chiang Kai-shek's plans before he'd even concocted them.

I certainly have no evidence that Lu Qing worked for the CCP. I only mention the matter here in the interest of asking more questions, of shedding more light on the strange conditions in which we so-called counter-revolutionaries worked.

I'd always told Robin how much I wanted to go to America. Nearly a year after I'd fled China, he contacted the American government. The US State Department granted me political asylum while I was in Hong Kong. It happened so quickly, I suspect that my application was somehow expedited.

Then I was introduced to a man named Scott Bellard, a US political attaché. I had been blown away by Robin's Chinese, but Scott's was even better! He spoke several other languages, too.

This man is a genius, I thought.

I'd lived my whole life in China. My view of the world saw people with saffron-colored skin, straight black hair, and almond-shaped eyes, a norm that was now being challenged. There were other races. Other cultures. Other ideas. Hong Kong was helping me make the adjustment. Hong Kong! A polyglot's heaven. When you walk down the street with an open ear, you hear French, German, English, Portuguese, and Italian, as well as the languages you would expect: Cantonese and Mandarin. Hong Kong is a city of diversity in a diverse world. Why not another *yang gui zi* who could speak my mother tongue?

Scott and I became very close. He asked me many frank questions. "Baiqiao, why go to the United States? Why not England or France, or some other European nation? Why not go to Japan, for that matter? Stay along the Pacific Rim?"

I'd thought this over a lot. "Three reasons," I said. "The first should be pretty obvious. I plan to continue my pro-democracy activities, and the United States allows more political and religious freedom than any country I know. That goes for every country in Europe. It certainly goes for Japan. What would I do in Japan? Join the faceless, uniformed workers who have no creativity? No essence? Become the perfect apparatchik? That's what I've been fighting against. I don't want to go to Japan.

"My second reason: education. Harvard. Yale. Columbia. Princeton. The United States has the best schools in the world. In China, I grew up dreaming about them. Now I don't have to dream anymore. I want to study there. I want to challenge myself.

"Finally, the United States has the highest standard of living of any country on earth. I believe that this is no accident. The United States embraces the entrepreneur. The government tries to get out of the way of invention and competition. It tries to promote a free market by which everyone can benefit. I believe in this system. I want to work in it, to learn from it, so someday I can return to China and help my country reform."

Very shortly, I was fingerprinted, photographed, and given a medical exam, including an x-ray, all to make sure that I had no diseases to ferry across the Pacific. The doctors gave me a clean bill of health. Then Scott arranged for an interview with US immigration. It only lasted an hour or so. Before we went to that meeting, I'd been told my application had been approved.

"So fast?" I said. "How can that be?"

"Robin Munro helped out," said Scott. "He established your credentials. You just have to sign on the dotted line. Everything else is set. The United States is happy to receive you, Baiqiao. We welcome you to our country."

I couldn't believe how eager I was. I was going to live in America!

Right before I left for the United States, Robin Munro threw a farewell barbeque at his home on Lamma Island. Scott was there, along with some journalists and student leaders I'd met. Li Feng told me he was thinking of moving to London, which he eventually did. I remember sitting on Robin's terrace and feeling at home with so many new friends whom I'd very shortly be leaving. It seemed like my life since Tiananmen Square had become a parade of hellos and good-byes. Now it was time for good-bye again.

Ten months after I arrived in Hong Kong, the US Embassy flew me to Seattle. I traveled alone, which concerned me greatly. I had no passport, didn't speak English, and had no idea where I was going. As far as documentation went, I was *wu guo ji*, a man without a country.

16

Before I left Hong Kong, Scott Bellard gave me a thick yellow envelope.

"Don't lose this," he said. "When you land in Washington State, give this to the immigration officials. It will explain everything to them."

When I landed in Seattle, I gave the packet to the immigration officers. They read it and seemed confused. They took me into an office and sat me down and started talking to me, but of course I couldn't understand a word they were saying. So one of them picked up the phone and placed a call. Another official came in. I gathered he was higher up. He studied my packet, looked at me, and read the packet again. He also looked very mystified. He talked to the first officers, then picked up the phone and made a call. I didn't know what to do. I sat there, waiting.

A while later, they took me to another office. A man there greeted me in fluent Mandarin and welcomed me to US soil. He said we were going to see the director or the supervisor of some organization, I can't remember exactly. All I recall was nodding a lot. What else could I do?

We went to another office where four people were waiting, dressed in suits and smiling. One of them was a woman. A Man Who Seemed to Be in Charge walked over and shook my hand. He looked me dead in the eye and spoke. The translator parsed his words. He gave me another welcome to US soil, then inquired as to how I was feeling. Whether or not I was hungry. Whether or not I was thirsty. This man was very warm and polite, which put me at ease right away. It's one of those lessons you learn in life: the people who wield the most power tend to be very warm and polite. The people who hold very little power often act gruff and sharp.

Through the translator, Man Who Seemed to Be in Charge (henceforth called Man with Power) explained I would get on another plane and fly to someplace called Kansas. I had never heard of Kansas before. I hoped it would be like New York City.

The Man with Power took the yellow envelope Scott had given me and said that I wouldn't need it now. Again, he shook my hand. This time, he wished me good luck and said, "We'll have someone pick you up at the airport in Kansas City." Man with Power spoke confidently. "That person will see to your needs."

I landed in Kansas City on April 24, 1992. A large black man in a suit picked me up. He drove me around in his car for a while. I could see right away he was very kind by the way he tried to say hello and make a conversation. But eventually his face fell when he realized I spoke no English at all, not a single word. At which point, he turned the radio up and hummed along, his fingers tapping the steering wheel. Once in a while, he looked over at me and winked. I smiled back.

It didn't take us very long to get where we were going, a church with a bunch of buildings in back. The black man pulled into the parking lot and honked the horn a few times. A man came out of one of the buildings.

The black man and I got out of the car, and the black man pointed to the newcomer. "Fred,*" he said. Smiling. Pointing again. "Fred."

He said a few more words after that, but I'd already gotten the message. *Fred will take care of you now.*

Then the black man in the suit shook my hand, got back in his car, and drove away. Fred said something to me, more words that I couldn't understand. I shrugged and shook my head. He shrugged, too. Then he turned and walked back into the building where he'd come from. I followed him.

17

At first, I had to use sign language to communicate. When I wanted something to eat, I pointed to my open mouth like an infant asking for breakfast. When I wanted to go outside, I pointed toward the door. When I had to go the bathroom, I raised my hand and blushed. Fred would huff and roll his eyes. He tired of this quickly. I gathered he was some sort of Christian, maybe even a minister. He wore a cross around his neck and often carried a Bible. We'd had Christians in China, of course. They were a persecuted minority. Mao had effectively banned all religions during the Cultural Revolution, but Christians were singled out for attack because they worshipped in congregations, what the Communists called: "unregistered meetings." About the time I left mainland China, the government had inaugurated a brand-new crackdown on Christians. Picture the awful history. Many Christian communities had been driven underground. Others had been arrested en masse. Lines of men and women wearing crosses were paraded through the city streets, their hands and feet shackled. They were brought to prisons and tortured there while their Bibles burned in stacks and their churches were looted and desecrated before finally being destroyed.

I thought these Christians were a strange sect with their talk of *Tianzhu*, the "Lord of Heaven" and his son, whom he had allowed to be murdered so others could live free. It sounded a little strange to me, but not so strange to justify how the Christians were being treated. No one deserved to suffer like that.

Fred wore his hair and beard long and scraggly. He looked the part of a biblical prophet as I've since come to know them from TV and movies. His facial hair in particular struck me as very aggressive. It was like Fred was going out of his way to embody the *yang gui zi* stereotype my friends and I had laughed at for years—barbarians from another land, Vikings who killed their meat with their hands and ate it raw, like beasts.

Fred went to church every day, I think. Or that's the impression I got. He left the apartment we shared every morning, holding his Bible, barely looking at me. He wasn't especially cruel, but he certainly wasn't kind. I got the feeling he'd been coerced into taking me on as a roommate. He seemed unhappy with the arrangement despite that it was temporary.

The apartment we shared was small with a kitchen, a living room, and two bedrooms, one for Fred and one for me. In such close confines, we came in contact often, a fact that only seemed to exacerbate Fred's frustration. I wanted to ask him so many questions but couldn't.

Over and over, I thought of Cheng Xiashi, the brave farmer who had put me up in Xinhui, before I was captured. He'd only spoken Cantonese. I'd only spoken Mandarin. But people like Cheng are never content to let a language barrier stand. They'll gesture a lot. They'll point to things and smile a lot to show they mean well. They'll try to teach—talk louder, as if it helps. None of it really works very well, but it certainly shows good intentions. Fred could not be bothered. I started to get the feeling I was one of many people he had sheltered over the years, the latest in a long parade of faces from strange corners of the world.

Kansas must be some kind of traditional gateway to America, I thought. Why had I never heard of it before?

I spent my days taking language lessons sponsored by Fred's congregation, or so I assumed. Our sessions were held in a room in one of the buildings behind the church. I gathered it was a classroom for children. The walls were bedecked with posters in primary colors that showed images of animals and smiling cartoon figures. Everything was nonthreatening. Big balloon letters stapled to the walls spelled out words in English. As days went by and my lessons continued, I surprised myself by reading them. It was a difficult but rewarding process. English writing was nothing like our Chinese pictograms. The letters are phonetic, directions for making sounds.

C – A – T.

Cat.

In Mandarin? *Mao.*

D – O – G.
Dog.
In Mandarin? *Gou.*

Inch by inch and word by word, I built a vocabulary. Learning another language can be like walking through a dream. The images you see look the same, but the soundtrack is all wrong, and you're wearing somebody else's shoes.

Our teachers were all American. None of them spoke Mandarin. I was the only Chinese in the class. The others were Russian, Hungarian, Romanian, and Vietnamese. I know this because during break times we would smile and nod at each other. Like children, we communicated by pointing at things. Some of my classmates would pull photographs out of their pockets and pass them around, keeping an eye on the dog-eared squares of paper as though they were something delicate and alive. In the pictures, you would see elderly people who may have been parents or grandparents. Men and women. Brothers? Sisters? Children? Nobody knew.

Eventually, someone pulled a children's book off one of the shelves. It featured a map of the world, drawn like a cartoon. Everyone gathered around. My classmates started smiling and pointing, saying words in different languages, which, I assumed, all meant the same thing. *Home.*

And everyone was very polite. Very kind. We tried to ignore the look that must have settled in all of our eyes, the longing for a life we'd once lived half a world away, in the past. For loved ones dissected from body and soul. Still living? Or dead? No one could tell. From the distance of exile, both options seemed equally, terribly plausible. I thought of the lessons history teaches regarding the subject of banishment. Regardless of culture or country or era, the suffering of outcasts assumes the same basic forms. Some people are forced to leave their country without their blood being shed. Others are not so fortunate.

One thing was certain, however. My classmates and I were all alone, reborn in this strange new land. And we did what strangers always do when faced with forced companionship. We tried to forge connections—to each other, as well as to the past.

And by the way, for the record? English was hard to learn. The structure is different from Mandarin in too many ways to count. A big one for me was the notion of tenses; we have none in Mandarin. There's also the question of ordering thoughts. You have to arrange them a certain way before you can speak them in English. For me, learning English was less about words, more about relearning how to think. I had to learn to think in a way that was drastically dissimilar from the one I had come to know.

I wondered, How many people speak English in the world today? And they all think like this? This pattern of thoughts? The notion blew me away. At the same time, I heard my father's voice repeating in my head. *Learning another language is useless, Xiao Tang. Someday, everyone will speak Chinese. Hear me when I say this. It's enough to speak and write Chinese. That is all you will ever need to be a leader of China someday.*

Father, I thought. You were wrong.

I doubt I ever missed him more than I did while I was in Kansas.

One day, I went back to my apartment. Fred was in the living room, sitting on the couch in front of the TV. "How are you?" I said. Speaking English. Very slowly.

Fred looked up. He cocked an eyebrow. "Fine," he said. "And you?" He also spoke very slowly, exaggerating the syllables, and doing so for my benefit. I smiled and nodded.

"Fine. Yes. Good. Thank you."

"Want to watch TV?" He gestured to the television, which helped me out a little.

"Yes," I said. "Thank you."

I sat down beside him on the couch. We watched TV together.

18

The plan had always been that I would go New York City; that was part of the deal I'd worked out with Scott and the US government. In Hong Kong, I'd been told that I wouldn't go directly to New York. I think the US officials feared it would prove too much for me to handle at once. The maelstrom of the city. The deep dive into culture shock. Shortly after I'd landed, someone had shown me a map and pointed to where we were, one great square in the middle of so many others. They were right to send me to Kansas, I thought, a place where things moved a bit more slowly.

Apart from my need to adapt, Scott had also been concerned, I think, over how the media would receive me. What would occur if the papers got wind that a Chinese political dissident had been granted asylum in America and was now on the streets of New York City? Too much of that kind of exposure might shame or embarrass the Chinese government, which the United States seemed intent on avoiding.

I stayed in Kansas a month in all, a sort of cooling-off period. In Kansas, I got adjusted a bit. I trained my tongue in basic skills to speak a brand-new language. I ate foods I'd never heard of before. Bologna. Tuna fish salad. Macaroni and cheese. I tried my very first hot dog, whose name I still find deceiving. It certainly wasn't what I'd expected. And then it was time for me to go.

I left Kansas City one month after I had arrived, on May 23, 1992.

A young woman was waiting for me in the terminal at LaGuardia airport. She was pretty, petite, wore glasses, looked smart, and she was Chinese. I could tell by her face. She was also holding a cardboard sign that said my name in Chinese:

唐柏桥

I walked over to her and nodded. "Hello," I said. "I am Baiqiao Tang."

She nodded, and we shook hands. Speaking Mandarin, she introduced herself as Felicity Lung. "I'm glad you could read your name," she said. "I wasn't sure if they wrote it correctly."

"You didn't write it yourself?"

She shook her head. "Writing was never my strong suit."

I could tell by her accent, she wasn't from Hunan.

"No," she said. "I grew up in Hong Kong and spoke Cantonese for most of my life. Now I've forgotten most of it." She shrugged. "How is my Mandarin? Can you understand me well?"

"Yes. Very well."

"Good. Do you have any luggage?"

"Yes."

Fred's church had given me two big suitcases full of slightly used clothes. Felicity helped me retrieve them from the baggage conveyor belt.

"You have a lot of clothes for a refugee."

The way she said it made me smile. She wasn't poking fun at me; she was making a playful, ironic comment, arching an eyebrow when she did it, a gesture I liked very much.

244

"Let's hail a cab," Felicity said.

Felicity asked the driver to take us through Central Park. I remember staring at all the trees, the rolling lawns, the people strolling on footpaths or riding past on bicycles. Some were lying on blankets rolled out on the vibrant green carpet of grass. Some rode in horse-drawn carriages. Others zipped past on roller skates.

The tip of my nose began to throb as though some fist had smacked it. That's when I realized I'd pressed my face and hands to the glass, looking out on everything, like a child reborn in America.

"Does it look the way you imagined it would?"

Felicity sat beside me in the backseat of the yellow cab.

"It does," I said. "And it doesn't. The pictures don't do it justice."

Traffic had been moving fast until we reached Manhattan. Then it slowed to a crippled crawl that got even worse when we turned onto Fifth Avenue. For minutes at a time, we barely moved at all. I'd never seen such congestion. Not that I minded. By that point, Felicity and I found ourselves deep in conversation.

She said that I'd be working with Human Rights Watch. Felicity worked for a different organization called the Committee to End the Chinese Gulag, another nonprofit company with similar aims that shared office space with Human Rights Watch. After four weeks of flailing in English, I was desperate to speak Mandarin. I pushed Felicity to tell me about her family, her job, her education. She said that she'd been to mainland China—many times, in fact. Ever since she was eight years old, she'd spent summers in Beijing where she had relatives with whom she stayed.

"I have very nice memories of China."

"But how is this possible?" I asked. "I didn't know people from Hong Kong had free access to the mainland."

"Oh," she said. "The government made a sort of special case for us. It's all because of my grandfather."

"Who is your grandfather?" I asked.

She shook her head and frowned. "I don't know that much about him. He died before I was born, but he was famous, evidently. A warlord from Yunnan Province."

A warlord? I thought. *Felicity Lung.* Long and Lung are often pronounced interchangeably in China. I began to suspect something. "What was his name?" I said.

"My grandfather? Long Yun. Some people called him the King of

Yunnan." She shrugged. "From what I can gather, he had some kind of famous rivalry with the general, Chiang Kai-shek.

I blinked. I couldn't believe it. *Long Yun and Chiang Kai-Shek?*

I was sitting beside the granddaughter of the Dragon of Yunnan himself!

19

It turned out that I knew more about Felicity's grandfather than she did. I'd studied Long Yun in school, and knew that he'd left his exile in Hong Kong and returned to China in 1949, by which point Mao Zedong had already taken control of the country. Long Yun, still stinging from his defeat, denounced Chiang Kai-shek in public as an enemy of the people. Mao was thrilled by this. It fit his plans very well. He allowed Long Yun to become the head of the Guomindang Party in the new People's Republic. He then awarded Long Yun with lofty positions: vice chairman of the National Defense Committee and vice chairman of the Administrative Council of Southwestern China.

This was mostly a sham, of course—all part of Mao Zedong's plan. By allowing members of eight or nine minority parties to hold high-ranking positions, Mao was able to trumpet the virtues of his Multi-Party Cooperation system. He could claim that the Chinese government was diverse and inclusive. Everyone was represented, Mao said. Even the opposition! Though in reality, these minority groups functioned as decorative vases. Mao and the CCP retained control of everything. Long Yun seemed well aware of this, but he had struggled to maintain his values. I explained this all to Felicity.

"There was one trip during the middle '50s," I said. "Long Yun accompanied Mao to Russia. When they came back, Long warned Mao that Russia was not China's friend. Mao was not very pleased. He'd always seen Russia as China's benevolent older Communist brother."

Felicity looked at me, wide-eyed. "I think my father was on that trip! He was very young at the time. He told me about it once. The recollections he has."

I nodded. "That trip was very important. Long Yun presented his deepest fears regarding the Russian Empire. For that, Mao labeled him a rightist. This was in 1957, I think. After that, Long Yun fell out of favor. He died a few years later."

Felicity nodded. "That's right," she said. "He died in 1962, but the Communists rehabilitated him eighteen years later. By then, my family and I were living in Hong Kong."

We rode in silence for several minutes, mulling over the history that had affected both our lives.

"Tell me more about you," I finally said.

Felicity told me she'd graduated from Barnard College in 1988. "I've always been interested in humanitarian work," she said. "Specifically involving Africa. That's what I was hoping to do when Human Rights Watch hired me. But they didn't have any openings in their Africa department. So instead I took up with the Committee to End the Chinese Gulag."

"Do you like it?" I said. "Do you find it rewarding?"

"I'd better," she said. She smiled and shrugged, arching her eyebrow again. "It's full-time work with part-time pay."

The cab dropped us off on the corner of Forty-Second Street and Fifth—a building across the street from the main branch of the New York Public Library. The stone lions out front of the library, Patience and Fortitude, stared at us from the far shore of an asphalt river on which sailed a mighty armada of cabs, delivery trucks, city buses, sedans, and bicycle messengers.

We took the elevator up to the offices of Human Rights Watch, third floor. The elevator door slid open with a sound like *bing!* Beyond, I saw cubicles bunched together, a tiny lunchroom down a hallway, and one or two nice-looking offices, but the place had the feel of bustle and work, a churning, relentless energy.

Felicity handed me off to Sidney Jones, a thin, energetic woman with glasses who smiled constantly and greeted me with great courtesy. At the time, I had no idea she was one of the world's leading experts on Southeast Asia. She was just a friendly face, which I certainly welcomed at the time. Another translator arrived, and Felicity excused herself, saying she had to get back to work. "But I'm sure we'll bump into each other again," she said.

We shook hands, and she disappeared. I was sorry to see her go.

"Well," said Sidney Jones through her translator. "We're so glad you've chosen to work with us. There is much to do, Baiqiao Tang. Would you like to go to Switzerland?"

I'm fairly sure I gawked at her. "Switzerland?" I said.

She nodded. "Geneva, to be precise. There's an annual meeting of the International Conference on Human Rights next week. We thought that you should attend."

It was one of those moments I couldn't believe the trajectory of my life. I'd gone from Hunan to Guangdong. From there, to every province in China, then to the city of Shenzhen, where I was smuggled across the Pearl to Hong Kong. From Hong Kong to Seattle. From Seattle to Kansas City, and from Kansas City to New York. Now I was taking off again, this time bound for Geneva.

"But," I sputtered. "But how will I live? I don't have a place to stay. I don't have any money. Everything I own is contained in these two suitcases."

I gestured to the luggage that Fred's church congregation had given me, full of borrowed shirts and trousers, some of which didn't fit me.

Sidney smiled and held up her hands. "Not to worry," she said. "We're working on getting you a grant through the Soros Foundation. Meanwhile Wang Fan* will help you find somewhere to live."

That's when she introduced to me to Wang Fan, another student leader in exile.

20

Wang Fan was about my age. He'd been enrolled as a student at a well-known arts school in Beijing when the protests started to boil in the spring of '89. He told me he'd gotten caught up in the democratic movement and found himself in charge of the protestors' broadcasting station in the middle of Tiananmen Square. When the army broke in, he'd been one of the first students they pummeled.

"So many things were wrong with the government then," he said. "You know what I'm talking about."

I nodded. I did, indeed. "Did you get arrested?" I asked.

Wang Fan shook his head. "I fled before they could try and went directly to Hong Kong. From there I emigrated."

He said that he'd been in America over a year and knew the lay of the land pretty well. His English was better than mine by far. Clearly, he had been practicing.

"I can get you squared away," he said and laughed. "I know a place. It's pretty unique. You'll see what I mean. They call it Woodhaven, Queens."

It was Wang Fan who first showed me how to use the subway system. Leaving Manhattan, we took a train east.

"Now don't get off here," said Wang Fan. "That's Roosevelt Island. They named it after the president. We'll be passing close to Shea Stadium. Who's your favorite baseball team? The Yankees or the Mets?"

I didn't know the first thing about baseball. "The Mets?" I said.

Wang Fan made a face. "Stick with the Yankees," he said. "Haven't you already lost enough?"

I was new to the country, but some things don't change no matter where you go. The section of town we arrived in looked rough. We walked past gangs and drunks and people who were clearly on drugs. Night was falling. Street lamps clicked on. I noticed people lounging on corners as though it was their job, as though they'd been hanging around all day and were looking to put in overtime hours by hanging around through the night.

"Like I said," said Wang Fan. "It isn't the greatest neighborhood."

I shrugged. Where else did I have to call home?

Wang Fan and I each carried one of my suitcases. Trundling along, we moved block to block. I tried not to stare as we walked. I couldn't help but be fascinated by the diversity of people we passed. Blacks and whites. Latins and Asians. Jews dressed in black suits, black hats, scarves, their hair cascading in ringlets and curls. The air was like a soup that boiled over with different tongues. I caught some snatches of Mandarin and called it to Wang Fan's attention.

He nodded, completely unimpressed. "There are plenty of immigrants here. Some are even legal."

He guided me to a boardinghouse that had two vacant rooms in the basement. We met the landlord, a portly man with a sweaty mustache and jowls that appeared to more rightly belong on an ancient, grouchy Shar Pei. The landlord explained how all his tenants shared the phone. The bathrooms. Common space. Power and heat were included, he said. Water was also free.

The room cost $170 a month. I balked at the sum, since I had no cash. But Wang Fan told me not to worry.

"Human Rights Watch will cover expenses until you get up on your feet. Not that you'll spend much time here. You're leaving for Switzerland soon. Think of this room as temporary. A place to hang your hat for the moment."

I accepted the room with gratitude. I now had my first New York City address.

What would happen next, I wondered? Where will I go from here?

part seven

"Wu Guo Ji," Man without a Country

1

Once again, I was astounded by how quickly paperwork can be expedited when certain players have an interest in the results. When Human Rights Watch contacted the US State Department, I was presented with a Refugee Travel Document the same day, for which I was very grateful.

Geneva felt like heaven, such a beautiful, peaceful, modern city. The UN's Palace of Nations stands in Ariana Park, which is justifiably famous for the peacocks that roam freely there. I remember vividly how it felt to stand in the palace's lobby and look through the glass walls at the peacocks strutting about, conducting their gorgeous parade across the manicured lawns. It took my breath away to see them open their wings. Such a moving sight—I wanted to cry. Here, I thought, is what China should be: beauty beyond destruction and hate. Grace that has no self-consciousness. A relaxed incarnation of freedom and promise.

Our delegation included such notables as Harry Wu, a well-known dissident and human rights activist. While still a Chinese citizen, Wu was arrested during the brief period of liberalization known as the Hundred Flowers Campaign for the sin of criticizing the CCP. The Party imprisoned him in 1960. He spent the next nineteen years at forced hard labor, moving from camp to camp, during which time he was often tortured and beaten. He left China and arrived in the United States in 1979. Since then, he's written quite movingly of his experiences in books like *Bitter Wind: A Memoir of My Years in China's Gulag* and, more recently, *Troublemaker*. Harry and I had been invited to speak before the UN's Subcommission on Prevention of Discrimination and Protection of Minorities.

I remember standing at the podium to address representatives from the fifty-four nations present that day. Rarely have I been so nervous in all my life. After introducing myself and briefing the subcommission on my past, I began to outline some of the numerous and more flagrant violations of human rights I had seen being willfully perpetrated by Chinese prison authorities.

I talked about Professor Peng, whose harrowing time on the *menbanliao* had lasted three full months. I called into question a recent announcement made by the Chinese government stating that most people detained after the June 4th incident had been released. Not so, I said. My report had discovered that at least 170 persons were still being detained in Hunan alone. Several thousand more, I predicted, were likely being held in prisons clear across China.

I outlined some of the various tortures that I myself had suffered, as well as the diabolical *jiao*, or "reaming," suffered by men like Ren Jun and others. In particular, I called into question the fate of three Chinese citizens who had been arrested for throwing paint at the large portrait of Chairman Mao that hung in Tiananmen Square on May 23, 1989. For this transgression, each citizen had been given sentences ranging from sixteen years to life in prison. Since their arrest, two had been confined to tiny pitch-black solitary confinement cells devoid of heat or ventilation. At that moment, both men were reported to be in failing health.

"Mr. Chairman," I said. "International attention to their plight is urgently required."

I then switched focus and started to outline the plight of China's political dissidents who'd somehow been released. This was a misnomer, I said, since release from prison amounted to the beginning of their woes. "Many of those who took part in the democracy movement have found that they have become pariahs," I said. "They have become a new class of highly educated, unemployable vagrants, discriminated against by authorities because of their so-called counterrevolutionary records. They, and often their families as well, are barred from state-controlled housing. They are further barred from state-run enterprises and employment in colleges. Those who are not originally from the cities have been stripped of their urban residency permits and can only remain unlawfully as 'black city-dwellers,' or they must return to the countryside as farm laborers. The punishment for pro-democracy activities has thus become a lifelong sentence."

Finally, I noted that a strong and emerging network of independent organizations committed to individual rights and freedoms existed in China. The All China People's Autonomous Federation had recently made itself known in order to focus international attention on its existence, as well as its mission. But with increased visibility, I said, came the risk of increased danger. I therefore asked the subcommission to recognize the All China People's Autonomous Federation and to endorse and support its efforts as a means of keeping the human rights situation in China under close review.

"In conclusion," I said, "we appeal to the Chinese government to abide by its obligations as a member of the United Nations and to end its unjust practices."

I thought I had done a decent job, that I had spoken movingly and convincingly. How, I wondered, could anyone dismiss what I had just said? Before arriving in Geneva, I was under the impression that most countries followed the example set by the United States and condemned China's human rights atrocities. Not so. Though I held many meetings with subcommittee members who said all the right things and encouraged my stance, when the final vote came down, they did not amount to a quorum. Fewer than twenty countries' representatives voted to pursue the matter further. The United States and Japan were among those who supported my cause, while many nations of Africa, South America, and Asia voted against. Honestly, I was shocked and disappointed. But then, unbelievably, I had the process explained to me by, of all people, the representatives sent by the Chinese government.

I met with them for two or three hours. The representatives treated me very kindly but also with a kind of obvious disappointment. "You should not have come here," they said, shaking their heads, *tsk tsk tsk*. A moment to rival Dai Hai. "This is the United Nations, a place of respect for all countries, all peoples. You are Chinese. And yet today, you embarrassed your country in front of the world community."

I couldn't believe what I was hearing. "Do not make it seem as though I don't love my country. I fought for my country's rights," I said. "I want to see her progress."

The representatives shrugged and said, "It takes time for countries to change, especially one as large and as old as China. You must understand this."

"Was I supposed to figure that out before or after you threw me in prison and tortured me?" I asked.

Again, the disappointed sighs. "These things happen, unfortunately," they said. "A shame, but what can you do?"

Nothing, evidently. In 1994, a report was submitted by Nigel Rodley, the UN Commission on Human Rights' special rapporteur on torture and cruel, inhumane, or degrading treatment or punishment. Mr. Rodley had mounted an official inquiry into Chinese human rights abuses. My case was one of many he investigated. In his report,* he noted the Chinese government's response to my particular claims:

---

*Nigel Rodley, special rapporteur, UN Document E/CN.4/1994/31, 1994.

Tang Boqiao [*sic*], a student leader in Changsha during the 1989 protests, was held in six different detention centres and prisons in Hunan province following his arrest in July 1989. He was allegedly subjected to frequent, severe beatings from his cell-mates at the instigation of jail officials, as well as being struck with electric batons during his stay at Changsha No. 1 detention centre. While in Longxi prison, he was reportedly beaten, chained hand and foot, and confined in a cold, damp, and tiny cell. According to the Government, Tang Boqiao is now outside the country. During his internment he was never subjected to beatings, verbal abuse, or corporal punishment.

I, of course, beg to differ. And China, of course, has not changed.

2

When I got back from Geneva I found that someone had taken the room next to mine, a Chinese man whose name was Ling An,* and who said he was born in Hubei Province.

"We are practically neighbors," he said.

"I know!" I said. "I know!"

I was thrilled to have someone else in the house with whom I could speak Mandarin. English was proving harder to learn than I'd ever imagined possible. So much of what I'd been taught in Kansas didn't seem to hold up in New York. Being so busy didn't help. It was nice to have a linguistic crutch. And someone from my part of China, no less! The two of us, crammed in that tiny basement, like brothers, long-lost friends.

Ling An was very kind to me, though we didn't spend much time together. Most days, I was off in Manhattan, working at Human Rights Watch. Robin Munro had asked me to talk to the press. He'd even flown in from Hong Kong to serve as translator for my interviews. Mostly, the questions centered around what I'd experienced in the months that followed Tiananmen Square.

Robin set up an exhausting itinerary. Sometimes we did ten interviews a day. And always, whenever I came home, Ling An would be hanging around. He would glance up from his newspaper or wander in from the TV room. Smiling. Always smiling.

"You look tired," he'd say. "What have you been doing all day?"

I had no one else to talk to, and I was lonely. I told him everything.

I noticed that Ling An didn't work. Or rather, he worked at hanging around, which made me start to wonder. I asked him about it. "What is it that you do?" I said.

"Do?" he said. "What? You mean like a job?"

"Yes, if you don't mind me asking."

I was treading very carefully, not wanting to insult my new friend, my closest link to home.

"I used to work for a restaurant," he said.

"Oh?"

He nodded. "Yes."

"But not anymore," I said.

"No," he said. "Not anymore."

"What happened?"

"I lost my job."

"I see."

But of course, I didn't. Not really. Still, I didn't push. I was conscious of being new to the house. To Woodhaven, Queens. To New York City. What did I know of America? Or being out of work? Hadn't the United States once had a Great Depression? I thought I'd read that somewhere. Besides, being out of work seemed like a fairly common thing. Lots of people seemed to be out of work in Woodhaven, Queens.

"Oh!" Ling An slapped a hand to his forehead. "Didn't I tell you? I almost forgot."

"What?"

"It happened while you were still in Geneva. Some woman called for you."

"A woman? What was her name?"

"She called herself Sun Dan."

3

I couldn't believe it. I plied Ling An for information. "Where did she call from? China?"

"No. She said she was calling from here, in New York City."

I couldn't see how that was possible, and I said so. Ling An just shrugged and repeated what Sun Dan had told him. She'd gotten a job with a very powerful Chinese import/export concern, which I knew her father had dealings with. Sun Dan was very young at the time, probably twenty-three years old, but already she held a prestigious position, one that brought her to New York quite often. Evidently, most of her business was conducted in Manhattan.

"Unbelievable," I said, and it was. It seemed so strange that Sun Dan should be here, in the United States. "How did she get my number?"

Ling An shrugged. "I don't know. She didn't say." Then he looked at me and grinned. "Who is she?"

I didn't answer at first. My thoughts were racing too fast. I could understand how Sun Dan's father had helped her claim such a prized position. But what else had he done for her? How else was he involved in her life? Was Sun Dan somehow acting on behalf of the CCP? I thought this very likely.

"Well?" said Ling An, still standing there, grinning.

"Well what?" I said.

"Who *is* she?"

I found his question very odd. Even a little presumptuous. "An old friend," I said, then amended that. "An old girlfriend."

"From China?"

"Yes."

"She sounded nice. Sun Dan." Ling An repeated the name as though it were a sweet that he was rolling around on his tongue. "Huh," he finally said. Then he clapped me once on the shoulder and walked back into his room.

Shortly after that, I was in my room when I heard the phone ring. Ling An picked up and then called out.

"Baiqiao Tang? You have a call. A woman who speaks Mandarin."

I left my room and walked down the hall where Ling An handed me the receiver.

"Who is it?" I hissed. Thinking it might be Sun Dan.

He shrugged. "Felicity Lung?"

This got me pretty excited. Ever since meeting that very first day, Felicity and I had bumped into each other now and again at Human Rights Watch. But she was always consumed by her work, and I was always busy with mine. We barely got to see one another, let alone talk.

But the day before, during one of our brief exchanges, I'd asked Felicity to join me at a karaoke and dance bar in Flushing, a popular place among the Chinese living in Queens. We Chinese like to sing a lot. More, I would guess, than the average American does.

"*Ni hao ma*," I said to the phone. *How are you?*

"*Hen hao*," she said. *Very good*. And then: "I'd like to come out to the bar. It'll be fun."

I was thrilled. We met at the bar that evening and went inside. The waitress dropped off a couple of cold beers. The sweat from the bottles rolled down in beads, wetting the table beneath.

"Robin tells me you're very good at handling reporters."

It was July and hot outside, but dark and cool inside the bar, very comfortable. I smiled. "Robin is a slave driver," I said, then switched to English, eager to show her how much I'd learned. "I'm very . . . gray . . . grapes . . . ah . . . grape pill . . ."

Felicity narrowed her eyes at me. "You mean grateful?" she said.

"Hmmm? Maybe. I think. Say it again?"

"Grateful." Then, in Mandarin: "*Gan xie*. You give thanks to him."

I nodded. "*Shi, shi*." Yes. "*Gan xie*." I switched back to English, a momentous struggle, but I knew that I had to be persistent. "Grate-ful. For all he has done. For me. And for. Other dis . . . ah . . . dis . . . dis . . ."

"Dissidents?" Felicity said.

I nodded. Now I was *gan xie*. To her.

"*Shi*." I said, and sounded it out. "Diss-i-dents."

Felicity shot me a look. "Your English is coming along pretty well. Have you been studying much?"

I shook my head. "No time."

"Well." She squared her shoulders. "I could help you with that, if you like."

I shook my head, confused. "*Wo bu ming bai*."

I don't understand.

"Lessons," Felicity said. "I could give you English lessons."

"Oh," I said, a little embarrassed. "I'd love to. But. I don't have any money to pay you."

There was that look again. This time both her eyebrows shot up. "Who said anything about money?"

I have since been informed that many great romances have started with language lessons.

4

About a week later, Felicity endured an agonizing session in which I tried to conjugate English verbs. The patience she showed: the stuff of legends. Her resolve: like the infinite sky.

To further complicate matters, we discovered we didn't always have an option to fall back on Mandarin. Evidently my Hunan accent colored certain syllables. For instance, *Tang*, in my mouth, becomes *Tan*. *Hang* becomes *Han*. And *Shi* becomes *Si*. In a language as complex and tone-based as Mandarin, such tiny shifts in pronunciation can cause corresponding and remarkable shifts in meaning.

China is ripe with dialects. There are over eight hundred local languages in the southern regions alone. Where I grew up, you often couldn't understand a person who grew up the next town over. The differences in pronunciation were as different as water and stone.

"I don't think I'll ever get this," I said.

Felicity rolled her eyes. "What choice do you have? You're here now, aren't you?"

"Yes."

"Then let's get back to work. We'll try a simple conversation. Tell me how you feel."

"*Wo ganjue hen hao. Xiexie. Qishi wo e le liao—*"

"In English, Tang. In English. Tell me how you feel. Then I want you to comment on the weather. And after that, I want to do colors. So let's begin. How do you feel?"

I took a deep breath and started again. How did I feel? Overwhelmed.

I wanted to get Felicity's take on the recent invitation I'd received. I'd been asked to attend the Institute of Advanced Study at Princeton University on a grant from the Soros Foundation. Many of China's most notable dissidents were already there.

"Liu Binyan will be there," I said.

Liu Binyan was the writer who'd penned the famous piece called *People or Monsters?* which spotlighted a corrupt Communist Party official from the northern province of Heilongjiang. When published in 1979, *People or Monsters?* caused an uproar in China. Though a member of the CCP, Liu Binyan had always been one of their most outspoken critics. As punishment for his brashness, he'd been sentenced to a total of twenty-one years' hard labor in various rehabilitation camps since 1957.

Liu Binyan had been in the United States on a visiting teacher's visa when Tiananmen Square took place. After that, he made several well-publicized announcements, all condemning the CCP for its treatment of pro-democracy protestors. The Chinese government blacklisted him. Liu Binyan had been barred from ever setting foot in his native land again.

"This will be good for you," said Felicity. "Go to Princeton and meet your peers. Tell them the vision you have for China. Maybe you'll find that you aren't alone."

Princeton University turned out to be a cluster of dignified gray stone buildings in various architectural styles. Georgian: solid, squat, and brick. Greek and Italianate Revival: flat, low-pitched roofs with tall, narrow windows and doors, and pediments attached to the basic, boxy building. Then postmodern dances of steel and glass that hung in the air like birds in flight, their gentle curves and impossible angles suspended by hope and little more.

Students strolled the landscape, laughing, talking politics, arguing over theories and equations. They heaved their backpacks laden with books past the shops lined up on Nassau Street and traipsed toward the stately eating clubs that marched along Prospect Avenue. I noted brick mansions wrapped in the grip of long ivy fingers and manicured lawns lining the quiet, tree-lined streets. Princeton seemed like heaven to me, a haven for working minds.

I joined a group of about ten other Chinese dissidents, many of whom were famous. Liu Binyan was there, of course, a legend all over the world. People often referred to him as China's Conscience.

And Su Xiaokang was there, as well. In the early 1980s, Su wrote the controversial six-part television series *River Elegy*. Like me, he was hunted by the CCP in the wake of Tiananmen Square. Su had made the CCP's list of the Five Most Wanted Intellectuals. He was smuggled out of China, leaving his wife and son behind. They later joined him at Princeton after the international community protested the treatment of China's dissidents. Su Xiaokang would later write of his life in his book *A Memoir of Misfortune*.

Then there was Kong Jiesheng, famous for his novellas *Southern Shore, An Ordinary Woman*, and *The Big Jungle*. All of them had sparked vehement anticommunist dialogues when published in Chinese. Kong was considered the master of *shānghén wénxué*, or "literature of the wounded," or "scar literature." This genre took off during Beijing spring and did much to spotlight the Party's hypocrisy and corruption, with special focus on the suffering it heaped on intellectuals. Kong Jiesheng had also fled China after the June 4th massacre.

I met Chai Ling, the woman who'd been elected chief commander of the Tiananmen Square Committee. In 1989, Chai Ling had been a graduate student at Beijing Normal University. She'd worked with other leaders such as Wang Dan to stage six weeks of protests. For this, Chai Ling was awarded a rank in the CCP's Top 21 Most Wanted Students list. After the June 4th incident, she eluded the Party by having plastic surgery. She fled to Hong Kong on a ship, and from Hong Kong she went to France and finally to America where she was welcomed with open arms at the Institute for Advanced Study.

In fact, I think it's safe to say we were all quite welcome at Princeton. The sting of Tiananmen Square was fresh, a wound in the flesh of the world. We scholars who had been called to Princeton had all condemned our government's actions, as well as the Communist cause. Our group was a corps of rebellion, a living representation of history. These were men and women who offered perspectives on China, her politics, her economy, and her wretched humanitarian state.

The institute stayed true to its mission. There was no pressure on us to produce anything, so we studied, we strolled, we debated at leisure, and tried to better ourselves. I think I speak for the rest of the group when I call the experience somewhat surreal. We talked nonstop about China. Inflamed by the passion of exiles, we discussed events we had weathered firsthand, then new ones we had missed out on but read about in foreign edition tabloids, or heard about over Chinese radio.

We were children holding a snow globe aloft and shaking it back and forth, turning it upside down, then squinting at the scene composed in miniature within. We tried to make out details from the opposite side of the glass. But mostly our efforts were doomed. The storm that raged within the globe was no longer ours to combat. It was too removed from us, or we from it. One could not touch the other, or so we thought.

My disenchantment began quite early and caused me great confusion. Here I had a very important position among bright, distinguished colleagues. But I felt like something was terribly wrong.

Liu Binyan was a very warm man who perpetually smiled. By that point, he was well into his sixties. When I first arrived in Princeton, he took me for a walk. We wended our way through the institute's woods, a nearly six-hundred-acre reserve abundant with aspen trees, gray birch, and oaks.

Flowers leaped from the ground in thickets: violets, yellow lilies, beauties in pink and white and blue, a tango for the eyes. Warblers sang from the hickory limbs, throaty bursts of notes and caws. The air was clean and sweet as cane, the trails beneath our feet worn down by the soles of hikers, runners, and walkers—all those seeking refuge from the pell mell world outside the forest with its car horn cacophony, TVs, radios blaring news from all over the world.

Such as in Belgrade, Yugoslavia, where protests, I knew, had erupted against Slobodan Milošević. Or in Paraguay, where Juan Carlos Wasmosy became the first elected president in nearly forty years. A ceasefire had been called in Iraq. A typhoon had smacked the Philippines. Members of a radical left-wing paramilitary group had been arrested in Bad Kleinen, Germany.

"What are we doing here?" I asked.

Liu Binyan offered a shrug and a smile. "We study," he said. "We think. We write. We meet. We talk."

"That's it?" I said.

"That's it," he said. "Good work doesn't arise from stress. It comes from peace. From inner contentment. There's plenty of that to be found in Princeton, Baiqiao Tang. You'll see."

But this was part of the problem. I'd only been there a couple of weeks and already I felt restless. It hadn't taken me long to notice a lack of cohesion. The dissidents disagreed with me. With one another. With anything and everything. The older ones had been CCP cadres prior to 1989. Some had even held government posts. And some said they had no problem with communism. They saw their exile as temporary and longed to return to China. The differences in our ideologies began to overwhelm me.

Also, by this point, Felicity and I were dating. She came to Princeton often, or I would go to New York. The two of us spent time together on weekends and special occasions. We were getting to know each other more, and we were very, very happy.

But one time the phone rang at my place in Princeton. Felicity picked it up. She said hello in English, then again in Mandarin. I watched her listen to someone speaking and watched her eyebrow shoot up. She looked at me, still listening. Then she handed me the receiver.

"Who is it?" I asked.

She shook her head and looked away. I raised the phone to my ear. "Hello?"

"Baiqiao Tang?"

I didn't need another word. I knew who it was right away. Sun Dan.

We talked for a while. How long had it been? So many things lay between us by then—time as well as experience. But we had been friends at one point. I asked how she was and what she was doing. Sun Dan told me little more than I already knew from Ling An. She said she worked in Manhattan, for instance, and that she had a good job. Yes, her father had helped her to get it. Yes to all of these things.

"I want to see you," she said. "To have dinner, to talk and remember. I know a place in Chinatown. Who was that woman who answered the phone?"

"Her name is Felicity Lung," I said. "My girlfriend."

Silence between us.

"You have a girlfriend." It wasn't a question.

"Yes," I said.

After which Sun Dan wished me luck, and that was that. We wished each other health and happiness and hung up. I thought it was over, but it wasn't. Not by a long shot.

Felicity asked what was going on, so I told her what I knew. About meeting Sun Dan in college. Our two years in a relationship. Her father's position. The fealty he paid to the Party while mine was paid to democracy. How the spring of 1989 had driven a wedge between Sun Dan and me. How Sun Dan, who had come to America, evidently had tried to call me in Queens, hoping to reconcile, perhaps, though I frankly suspected other motives.

"But how did she get your number?" Felicity, arching that eyebrow again. "In Princeton, I mean?"

I stood there, staring. I didn't know. I hadn't even considered that. But Felicity was right. And now I was very curious.

5

began to suspect that the Party's reach was greater than I had ever imagined, that the CCP could affect my new life in America as easily as throwing a switch. They were everywhere. In China—yes, most certainly there. But also in Hong Kong and the United States. I could never tell for certain if they were pulling the strings of people I heard from now and again.

On a trip back to Queens, I confronted Ling An, who—I remembered—had talked to Sun Dan, had my number in Princeton, and knew most everything about me. I began to consider that Ling An's arrival to the Woodhaven boardinghouse might not have been the divine coincidence I once had considered it to be. Taking a chance, I bluffed him and said, "Who put you up to this?"

He looked at me with fear. "Put me up to what?" he asked.

"Spying on me. Giving Sun Dan my number. Don't lie to me anymore, Ling An. What did you hope to accomplish?"

Incredibly, he started to whine. "Please don't be angry, Baiqiao Tang! I needed the money. I had no choice! They said they would pay very well, and they did."

"Who?" I asked. "Who's *they*, Ling An?"

"Who do you think?" he said.

And so I had my answer, one that has since been proven to me time and time again. For instance, in 1994 I got a phone call from Lu Qing. Talk about a surprise. We hadn't spoken to each other since the summer of 1991 when I had arrived in Shenzhen and Lu Qing had behaved so strangely. That was the week before I fled to Hong Kong, the time when I met Ren Jun again, and began to suspect that my old friend Lu Qing was working for the CCP. And here he was three years later, calling me direct from China. To this day, I have no idea how he got my number.

"Baiqiao Tang!" he said. "I am still in Shenzhen, but I've made a decision. I want to return to the movement. I want to work for democracy."

I had no idea what to say to that. "Really," I said. "Are you sure?"

He assured me that he was. At which time, I felt obliged to point out that five years had passed since Lu Qing had last been active for democracy. I wanted to know what had changed his mind, to make certain he was serious.

"I'm *very* serious," he said. "Look. I'm going to Changsha next month. To marry a girl. Okay? After that, I want to work for democracy. It's very important to me."

"But what about your job in Shenzhen?"

"I'm quitting that. Going back to Changsha. My future wife is there, okay? So that's where we'll make our home."

I thought it over. "Fine," I said. "Go to Changsha. When are you due to be married?"

He told me the date. It was one month away.

"Congratulations," I said. "Call me once you get settled. I'll see if I can connect you with people who can get you back involved."

We maintained contact now and then for two or three months after that. One day, however, Lu Qing called and said:

"Baiqiao Tang, I want to leave China. Can you help me get to Hong Kong?"

"Wait," I said. "You just got married. You want your wife to go, too?"

"No," he said. "I don't want her to go. I don't want to be married anymore."

I shook my head. "You change your mind too fast. First you want to leave Shenzhen, go back to Changsha, and get married. Then you want to get back involved. Now you're married, you want to leave. You want to go to Hong Kong, leave China and your wife behind."

I shook my head. It didn't make sense. Lu Qing had always been flighty, but this was very unusual, not to mention risky.

"Will you help me?" he said. "To get to Hong Kong?"

"They might not accept you," I said.

"But why?"

I explained how I'd been thrown in jail by immigration authorities, how pro-democracy leaders had intervened on my behalf, the dispensations I had been granted because I had been a political prisoner. Lu Qing had no such pedigree. He'd spent no time in jail, nor had he been punished at all. The fact remained that how he got away with this was still a matter of great suspicion. I had to wonder: was he acting now on the Party's behalf? What would I risk by helping him?

"But you've helped other people do it," he said.

This was true. By 1994, I'd helped almost a dozen dissidents escape. Most had spent time in Chinese jails, arrested during the crackdown. Others had been so severely slandered, they'd never function in China again. Escape seemed the only alternative, their only chance for productive lives. But Lu Qing? What had he sacrificed? It didn't feel right. Something was off.

"I have helped others, but that's not the point," I said. "We're talking about you, Lu Qing. Every case is different, you know. Hong Kong's government might send you right back to mainland China."

But Lu Qing refused to relent. He insisted on going.

"Baiqiao Tang," he said. "If I have only a one percent chance of making it in Hong Kong, I would rather go than stay in China."

This from a man who'd just been married? I sighed. "Okay. I'll make some calls. But you understand: I can't promise."

"Of course!" he said. "Of course!"

"I'll tell a few people you're coming," I said. "After that, you're on your own."

I did as I'd said and made the calls. Arranged a few things. Lu Qing arrived in Hong Kong early in 1995. It didn't take long for me to regret that I'd helped him or ever known him. Part of me is convinced that Lu Qing is a CCP spy. Or crazy—one or the other. Either way, my helping him nearly crippled my efforts to free more dissidents.

In Hong Kong, he was caught several times fabricating information about Chinese human rights atrocities. He posted lies to the Hong Kong news wires. Then he misrepresented his academic qualifications. He told people he'd graduated from Beijing University when, in fact, he had not. Then he sent out press releases saying he wanted to immigrate to America, just like me. But he never left Hong Kong. Evidently, no one would sponsor him. So he sent out another round of releases saying he'd changed his mind. He wanted to stay in Hong Kong, he said. Hong Kong is the place to be!

His behavior was baffling, to say the least. In my mind, it boils down to this: he's either a spy or he's crazy. Either way, I consider him dangerous.

6

When talking about the Party's reach, there's another side to the coin. Within a few years of Tiananmen Square, many student dissidents who'd fled to the United States began returning to China, which, in a way, makes sense, though it pains me to admit it.

Consider that the pro-democracy movement of 1989 wasn't a drawn-out struggle. Some uprisings are glaciers. They slide along at a creeping pace. I'm thinking of Czechoslovakia's Velvet Revolution, which arguably took five years. I'm thinking of the Tibetan unrest, which occurred in

China between 1987 and 1993. I'm referring to the powerful dissatisfaction that has simmered in Burma for decades and continues even now. They're glacial movements, all of them. Inch by inch. Thought by thought. A slow buildup of actions. If the gain in ground is measured at all, one has to do it by molecules.

But some movements fall like an avalanche, striking fast, without any warning. The revolution in Hungary in 1956: eighteen days of chaos. Poznań June for the Poles: three days. The Orange Revolution, Ukraine, essentially lasted three months. Thailand's Black May: four awful days in May of 1992. Tiananmen Square was this kind of war, a flash of heat and light and flame that the subsequent CCP crackdown extinguished through brutal retaliation.

We didn't plan to be dissidents. We were following our passions, flying by the seats of our pants, making it up as we went along. Leaders were made in the moment. They rose to prominence, fell from grace, some in a matter of days. Nobody had much experience. We weren't veterans of the cause. We were caught up in the maelstrom, riding the vortex down. We did what we thought was right at the time. We hadn't much time for vision or plans. And yes, we made mistakes.

Now consider this as well: many students who marched for the cause were CCP-sanctioned cadres who changed their views in the heat of the moment, and with good reason. They disagreed with Deng Xiaoping, the way he handled the situation. But a few years later, look what happened! These so-called dissidents changed their views and returned to the communist cause the moment the system had stabilized. A fine example is Wen Jiabao, the current premier of China.

As I mentioned earlier, Wen supported Zhao Ziyang in the spring of '89. Right after Zhao met Gorbachev, Wen marched with him through the huddled masses that shrouded Tiananmen Square. Back then, Wen Jiabao was a rightist, a champion of reform. And now? He's another political tool, China's premier since 2003.

Wen Jiabao is a classic example: Man Who Changes His Views to Survive. That's the sole aim of his politics. Stay in the game and rise to the top. Stay there however you can. And no, I would hardly call Wen a rightist. Being a rightist implies he has ethics, which I don't believe that he has. He's simply the modern, smiling face of the same old CCP. Despite his call for reforms under Zhao, Wen Jiabao has led the charge to forget the horrors that followed June 4.

Here is very sad fact: more student leaders have gone back to China than have chosen to stay in the West. They claim they have made a great mistake. They say they got stuck in a moment, caught up in their emotions. They weren't themselves, they tell the world. They weren't thinking things through. The Party isn't so bad, they say. It was all just a misunderstanding.

The Party likes to play into this. They have many agents abroad. They contact these dissidents, take them to dinner, wine them and dine them, and talk about home. They tell them how the country has changed, and ask if they'd like to go back. We can make it worth your while, they say. We'll help you out in business. The Party takes care of its friends, they say. We only ask one simple thing: recant. Say it was all a mistake and you've finally come to your senses.

I understand the temptation, and I don't blame the ones who succumb, though I'm often surprised when they do. I was shocked when my good friend Wang Fan told me he'd had enough of America and soon would return to China.

This was a very big blow to me. Wang was the first student leader I'd met in the States—my host, in many ways. We argued a lot about his decision. But Wang, who once was so passionate for democracy, now said that it couldn't work in China.

"You know how the Chinese are," he said. "Treat them well, they will never respect you. The Chinese *need* dictatorship."

I couldn't believe my ears. But year after year, more leaders go back. More change their minds. More disappear.

I have not. Nor will I. Recently, a Taiwanese journalist asked me, "Do you think you'll ever change your ways like other dissidents have?"

No, I said. I've lived this way for my first forty years. I'll be damned if I'll live the next forty differently.

7

I stayed at Princeton for half a year, during which I grew more and more frustrated.

"We've heard reports of Zhao Ziyang," said a man named Shi Jinghai. He had called us together for what he had billed as a very important meeting. "I heard this from a friend who says that Zhao remains under tight supervision at his compound in Beijing. This friend and Zhao play golf now and then. They never talk of what happened. But Zhao, evidently, could work on his swing. Yes. Apparently he lacks follow-through. My friend says he rolls his wrist too much, which sends his balls off the links."

My, I thought. How exciting.

Watching a few of our little group's members engage in such conversation, I began to grow disgusted. I started to clash with certain people. Mostly with the man I've mentioned, Shi Jinghai, who had formerly worked with Zhao Ziyang at the Institute for Political Reform, and whom my old friend Fu Jintao had helped to escape from China through Guangzhou. Shi Jinghai walked like the CCP. He talked like the CCP. The grandiose airs. The pompous carriage. The booming voice that never said much but boomed just the same, for booming's sake. Shi Jinghai, from what I could tell, was desperate to return to China, the Soul of Opportunism.

Fine, I thought. Let him go. At least we'll get some peace and quiet. And finally, there will be air in the room.

I had one close friend in He Dong,* the famous labor activist, who arrived in Princeton a month after I did. The two of us were close in age, which probably helped to match our thinking. I told him that I felt stifled in Princeton and wanted to go back to New York.

"Tell me what you're thinking," he said.

The distance from Tiananmen Square to Princeton measured six thousand eight hundred miles. Here we were, the cream of China's dissident population, like koi fish kept in a pond. Koi are bred from carp, by the way. And like the beautiful koi fish, we could not survive on our own. We were just a small pool of Chinese faces, fed on a regular basis, idly paddling about in our artificial environment. We were ornamental. Decorative vases.

"I want to go back to New York," I said. "I was busy there. More effective. New York has many Chinese people and organizations for human rights. It's the gateway to the West, and I think I can be useful there."

He Dong said that he understood. So I called Felicity, talked it over, and used her as a sounding board. She said she understood as well.

"If that's what you think you should do," she said, "then do it. Don't hold back."

A few days later, I said good-bye to He Dong and took a train back to New York City and started to look for a new place to live.

I found a room in Elmhurst, Queens, that would fit my needs. It wasn't much better than the one I'd had in Woodhaven, but I didn't really care. Anyplace where I wasn't being spied on would be an improvement. I wasn't there very long. In June of 1993, I moved in with Felicity. Looking back, I find it hard to relate how it felt to be so happy, so cautiously optimistic.

But *caution* became the operative word. Later that month, I got very bad news. On June 4, 1993, four years to the day since Tiananmen Square, my colleague from Princeton, Su Xiaokang, a highly respected dissident, was nearly killed in an accident.

He, his wife, and his son had been driving to Niagara Falls. A friend had taken the wheel. The car they were riding in sped off the road and turned over, a terrible crash. A week later, Su woke up from a coma to find that his son had escaped unharmed. His wife, however, had suffered permanent neurological damage. It took her many months to regain the power of speech. She was paralyzed, never to walk again. The beginning of their woes, as things turned out.

Over the next few years, by his own admission, Su flailed through different perspectives on life. He turned away from Buddhism and embraced Jesus Christ as his savior. He experimented with traditional Chinese medicine, faith healers, *qi gong*, acupuncture, anything to help his wife. Su wondered where he'd gone wrong. In public statements, he later renounced his dissident ways. Then, in 2001, Su turned the tables once again and wrote down his deepest regrets in a book called *A Memoir of Misfortune*. Read it sometime. It's incredibly stark.

I mention this now to remind one and all that black fortunes can still befall us Chinese dissidents living in exile. We haven't escaped to a better life. We haven't escaped a damn thing. We are simply fish who swim in strange currents, trying to navigate back to the ancient shoals in which we were born, but these waters don't exist anymore, except perhaps in our dreams. They are the sandbars, canals, and estuaries where men like Qu Yuan became king. The sun never sets, and the waves speak in poems, and hurricanes never harry the bay.

Often, when I am tired of the road and feel as though no one is listening to me, my mind drifts back to the carp my father once bought with money that should have been spent on something else; the carp he slipped in the summer canal, the fish that my childhood friends and I rushed forward and caught in our tiny hands.

My fellow exiles and I have made our homes in this alien pool whose waters were never meant to sustain us. And what will become of us over the years? Sometimes the Party drops a line, the hook adorned with bait. They dangle it right in front of us, and some of us bite. The Party jerks, pulling us out as though nothing had happened, as though fish were meant to breathe air. But sometimes we dissidents don't take the bait, preferring to swim forever in circles, malnourished, hidden deep in the pond. The water never feels quite right, though it's better than dying on land. At least that's what we tell ourselves. Even the water has dangers.

We fight, but the current keeps pulling us back to what we are and what we knew before our world fell apart.

8

In Mandarin, as I have said, we have a term: *Wu guo ji.* Literally: "man without country." Which is, in fact, what I am since China revoked my citizenship and won't reissue my passport. As far as the United States is concerned, I'm a permanent resident alien. I have a green card and all the rights accorded the person who holds one. But I never applied for citizenship because I am not an American. This isn't my home. I am Chinese. I want to go back to see my family, to live in my country, to fight for my ideas for reform. But I can't. The CCP won't allow it. A fact we found out the hard way.

In the spring of 1996, Felicity was finishing law school. I was so proud of her. I have always been so proud of her.

We decided we needed to celebrate.

"We could both use a trip," Felicity said. "Why don't we go to China?"

"They won't let me in," I said.

"Have you tried?" she said. "It's been seven years."

"I don't imagine they care."

"Leave it to me," she said. "I bet I can make it work."

"How much?"

"Why don't we say a hundred dollars?"

I snorted. "You really want to lose money, is that it?"

She grinned at me. "I have a plan. I'll fill out your visa application using your Anglicized name. I'm betting it won't show up like that when they type it in the computer."

I had my doubts, but we drove into Manhattan. The Chinese consulate loomed above us, a windowless, monstrous block of a building dropped on the south corner of Forty-Second Street and Twelfth. Felicity went in alone and filled out visa applications for both of us in English. We waited the requisite number of weeks, then drove back to the consulate. Again, Felicity went inside. I waited for what seemed a very long time. When Felicity finally came back outside, she was seething. Furious.

"What's wrong?" I asked. I'd never seen her so angry.

"They issued my visa." She got in the car, slammed the door, and drummed her fists on the dashboard.

"What's so bad about that?" I said.

"They denied yours!"

It took a while for her to calm down, at which point she told me what happened. The man behind the counter had handed Felicity two envelopes, which she opened right on the spot. The documents inside told the story: one visa approved for Felicity Lung, one visa denied for Baiqiao Tang.

"Why?" demanded Felicity. "Why is my husband denied?"

She said she'd used the word *husband* even though we weren't married. That's how she'd applied for our visas, as husband and wife, together.

The Man Behind the Counter's lips had twisted into a sneer. "Ask your husband. He knows," he said. Which got Felicity angry.

"No," she said. "We don't know. Why don't you tell me what you mean? Why are you denying people visas? What are you afraid of? Why don't you come right out and say it?" She screamed like that in Mandarin, then repeated the scream in English.

The embassy workers refused to answer, so Felicity took matters into her own hands and started to move around the counter to head back into the offices. These days, even she will admit that this was a bad idea. In hindsight, here is a word to the wise: Do not raise a ruckus inside a consulate, China's or anyone else's.

Some embassy workers came out. They were men wearing suits with boxy shoulders, their arms pumped up thick in their sleeves.

"What happened?" I asked in the car outside.

"They stopped me," was all that Felicity said.

"They threw you out?"

"No, no." She shook her head, still fuming. "I mean. Well. I don't know. Maybe. I don't think so. I sort of don't remember what happened. I was very, very angry, Tang. Damn it, I'm very angry!"

She started attacking the car again, fists on the dashboard, kicking the floorboards, grunting, pounding, a symphony of frustration.

"Breathe," I told her. "Felicity, breathe!"

So angry, she was seeing red. The Grandchild of Yunnan's feisty Old Dragon had snorted fire and lost her bet.

We went on the trip regardless. New York to Seattle. Seattle to Hong Kong. In Hong Kong, I got off the plane and Felicity continued to China, landing in Beijing.

She had another plan, she said. She'd already called ahead to my mother and told her to ready herself for travel. The CCP had a brand-new policy: tourist rights to Hong Kong. For the very first time in history, Chinese citizens could apply for visas and visit. The terms of their passes were very restrictive, but no less so than Hong Kong's immigration police who roamed the streets, checking papers at will, and jailing any person caught without the proper documentation, no questions asked, and no exceptions. Hong Kong wanted tourist money, not an illegal immigrant problem.

This didn't matter to us. Felicity wasn't trying to encourage my mother to escape. The journey for her would not have been safe, and anyway, my mother has no intentions of leaving China. We thought it might be nice, however, if she and I could spend some time together while we both were visiting Hong Kong. We hadn't seen each other in years. We'd talked on the phone, but it wasn't the same as seeing your loved one and holding her close, being there in person. I wanted to see my mother again. She wasn't old, but she wasn't young, and I couldn't bear the thought of her passing without our being together once more. I did not want to lose her in absence, the way I had lost my father.

Our plan seemed simple, innocent even, but the CCP outsmarted us. They must have known my itinerary. Either that or it was coincidence that the visa my mother was granted began one day after I left Hong Kong.

I was disappointed, but I took it in stride. By now, I was used to this sort of thing. Static from meddling CCP hacks, Dai Hai and his Communist Lackey Parade, The Man behind the Consulate Counter, the Party's sniggering apparatchiks.

Fine, I thought. They want to play games? Let's see how far this can go.

I flew back to America, renewed my visa immediately, and turned right back around. But again, the CCP knew every move. They canceled my mother's visa for no good reason at all. So we waited a year and tried it again, another secret rendezvous, but again, the Party interfered. And again and again and again. One time, my mother's visa was late. Another time, it was suddenly and mysteriously curtailed. Another time, her request for a pass received no reply whatsoever.

Suffice it to say, we got the hint. After the fourth attempt, we gave up. I remember calling my mother on the phone. I'd always suspected that someone was listening. Now I was all but certain. I told my mother how much I love her, how much I've always loved her. And this is how we've communicated since. We are ghosts who whisper to one another on phone lines from opposite ends of the world. Meanwhile, between us, strangers listen and snicker, plotting to keep us apart. But of course it wasn't over yet. With the Party, it's never over.

It was always in the back of my mind to sneak my way back into China. I think the Party knew this, too. Which is why, a couple of years later, my turn came around. The Party asked me out to dinner. Curious, I accepted.

9

It happened in late 1997 or early 1998. A reporter I knew from a Chinese newspaper here in the States called me out of the blue.

"Baiqiao Tang," she said. "I hear you want to go back to China. Is this true?" That was all I needed to hear to confirm what I'd feared all along. This reporter was working for the CCP.

She'd spent a few years as an activist in Hong Kong's pro-democracy movement. Like me, the Party had branded her a counterrevolutionary, but then she'd gotten permission somehow to visit mainland China— several times, as a matter of fact, which is what had made me distrustful. I told myself there were other reasons, but only one reason fit. Apparently, someone had made this reporter an offer, and she had not refused. It was hard to know whom to trust anymore. Getting harder day by day.

"Baiqiao Tang?"

"Sorry," I said.

Stop drifting. Focus on what she is saying.

"Do you want to go back to China?"

"Yes," I said. "But why do you ask?"

"I know someone who would like to help."

"I had no idea my travel plans were of interest to anyone."

If the reporter heard my subtext, and it's hard to believe that she didn't, she didn't make any comment.

"Ying Xiguang* would like to meet you."

Huh, I thought. No kidding?

I knew about Ying Xiguang. He was posted at China's consulate, a very influential man in the Chinese community here in New York.

"And?" I said.

"Will you meet with him?"

As I said, I was curious. I said yes.

A week or so later, I walked into a very fine restaurant in Chinatown. Ying Xiguang waited inside the door, dressed in an elegant gray suit. He was a tall, upright man of indeterminate age, wearing a pair of designer glasses—Italian, I think. A cloak of aromas wrapped the restaurant foyer, the smells of garlic and roasting meat and soy floating out from the kitchen. I began to get hungry in spite of myself.

Ying Xiguang had a smile that never seemed to fade. His handshake gripped like a blacksmith's vice. His demeanor never wavered from formal. His voice was like a *guan*, the oboe of China, rich in tone with plunging pitches, an instrument of striking expression, capable of persuasion.

Ying knew who I was. He walked right up and introduced himself, smiling as though we'd been pen pals for years, though in fact this was our first time meeting. The host appeared at once, bowed low, and hurried to seat us. I noticed we had a choice table, also that we were alone. No other diners sat anywhere near us. Candles flickered. Orange flames danced, trapped in spheres of cut glass, throwing shadows across the tabletop.

Ying Xiguang began to prattle. A Man Who Is Fluent in Small Talk. He asked if he could order for us. He said that he knew the chef very well. They had an understanding, he said. The food here was outstanding, but certain dishes were available off the menu if you knew how to ask.

I didn't object. Ying smiled as if I'd made the right choice and waved that we were ready.

Our waitress approached. She was very pretty. She bowed and kept her eyes averted, her body stiff with the tension of servitude. Ying Xiguang began to command her. The waitress wrote nothing down. Her chin became a bouncing ball, nodding her constant agreement.

"*Shi shi shi,*" she said.

Ying finished his dictation. She turned and left without a word. Ying turned back to me and smiled an apology that we'd been interrupted.

He said he was very excited to have me try a certain dish. He smoothed a perfect lapel on his jacket, shook his head, and bemoaned the state of Chinese cuisine so often found in America. So many hybridizations, he said. Taking liberty with tradition.

"Not like we're in Beijing," he said and sighed, like: *What can you do?*

The waitress returned with a full carafe of *wulaing yeh*, a very strong traditional wine made from fermented rice. I felt my body tense. I have never been much of a drinker. Perhaps I inherited this from my father. I could not help but remember his fate.

It is best, I thought, if we skip these shenanigans. Get right down to business.

"Why did you want to meet me?" I asked.

Ying Xiguang caught the switch in my tone. He nodded and shrugged and unfolded his napkin, whose crease was perfect, then folded it back the same way. He cleared his throat and changed roles before my eyes. The transformation was magical, a subtle shift in the facial muscles. No longer the bubbling tour guide, Ying was now a compassionate friend who was faced with a delicate task. He had to ask another friend who was clearly in need if he could help. His body language spoke tomes: *I don't mean to pry, you see. But I'm here should you require assistance. Forgive me for any intrusion. Just wanted to make sure you knew.*

"I was talking with our mutual friend," he said. Meaning the turncoat journalist. "She said you might want to visit China. If this is true, it would be our honor to help you."

"I find that very strange," I said.

Ying Xiguang looked surprised. "But why would that be strange?"

"Because," I said. "I already tried to go back to China about two years ago. If you really wanted to help me, you could have issued the visa then."

Ying smiled as though he'd expected this and drew in a long, slow breath. His exhalation was even longer, conveying tones of regret. *My friend, I wish you could understand how complicated this is . . .*

"We really want to help," he said.

"Wonderful," I said. "I'm very grateful. You'll grant me the visa then?"

"Mr. Tang." Ying shook his head. Said *Tsk tsk tsk*. The ghost of Dai Hai had entered the room. I suddenly tasted tea.

"I don't see why it's so hard," I said. "You want to help? Just give me the visa. That's all the help I require."

"May I speak plainly, Mr. Tang?"

"I didn't know that we weren't."

Ying Xiguang took another deep breath. Again, he let it out slow. "You have a very unusual relationship with us."

"I'll say. You threw me in jail."

He shook his head again. *Tsk tsk.* "Long Yun helped found the People's Republic."

I stiffened, truly in shock. I'd braced myself to hear many things, but nothing about my relationship to Felicity.

Ying sensed my hesitancy and pressed forward, the flames from the candles alive in his eyes. "You were a student leader. You fled your homeland, came to this country and used it as a pulpit from which to launch so many aspersions back upon your native land. Upon your people. And yet you wish us to open our doors? Accept you back to the fold?"

"Since we are speaking plainly," I said. "Let me correct a few things. It's true that I was a student leader. But getting thrown in jail—that was your idea, not mine. I had a damn good reason to flee my country. The Party was hounding me—"

"Mr. Tang—"

"And casting aspersions? That isn't right. I haven't cast a single aspersion. But yes, I am very critical. I take my cue from Confucius, who said 'Be not ashamed of mistakes, and thus make them crimes.'"

"Mr. Tang—"

"China has made mistakes, Ying Xiguang. Too many to cover up. It's time to do the responsible thing. Talk of the past. Debate the present. Chart a course for our nation's future. An open process in which all Chinese people participate together."

Ying Xiguang shook his head. "Confucius also said, 'They must often change who would be constant in happiness and wisdom.'"

"Fine," I said. "Then let China change."

"Mr. Tang. I wasn't referring to China. I was referring to you."

"I know. Which just goes to show."

"What's that?"

"How little you truly know me."

Ying Xiguang shook his head and sighed. "Confucius is wise, indeed. I have always thought so. He says that 'When anger rises, a wise man thinks toward the consequence.'"

"He also says, 'Fine words and an insinuating appearance are seldom associated with true virtue.'"

Ying's perfectly manicured hand returned to smooth his lapel. For a moment, he did not speak. And then: "I have heard that you wish to study at Columbia University."

"Yes," I said. "That's true."

"If you go to Columbia, you will be a student again. And perhaps you will not have time to pursue your—what do they call it here? Your *activism*."

Aha, I thought. So there it is. We both knew what he was offering. Ying Xiguang had opened a door and invited me to walk through. All it would take was some indication that I would relent. Give up. I chose my next words very carefully.

"I'm sure," I said, "that I'll still have plenty of time in my schedule for speeches and public engagements. Being an activist. That's a very important job, you know."

"Ah," said Ying Xiguang. The way he said it, the word meant a thousand things. "Ah." Then he changed the subject.

The rest of the evening did not go so well. But Ying Xiguang was right about one thing at least. The food was outstanding.

A footnote: Sometime after that meeting, I sent a letter to Dai Hai. In it, I wrote that I didn't agree with the vision he had for China. But I felt that, when he had kidnapped me, his concern for my welfare was genuine, and I thanked him for that. I told him that my abduction must have been providence.

"Picture it," I wrote. "Had you never kidnapped me on May 4 back in 1989, the speech I delivered later that day would not have inflamed those who marched in Changsha. I would never have been elected to be chairman of the SAF, never have started my strange career as a so-called counterrevolutionary. In fact," I wrote, "without your help? I would never have lived the life I have led. The life I cherish so much. I would never have come to America. Never have met the woman I love. And never have tasted freedom."

I closed by saying how much I would welcome his correspondence. This, it turns out, was a very bad move, for later I heard a terrible thing from contacts of mine back at Hunan Normal: the Party intercepted my letter. Dai Hai was investigated, questioned, and forced to resign. Evidently, my letter had prompted suspicion. Perhaps, the Party must have assumed, Dai Hai's true sympathies lay with the pro-democracy movement.

I remember being very sad to think I had caused the man any grief.

10

eventually enrolled in classes at Columbia University to get my master's degree in international affairs. And in 1997, I founded the China Peace and Democracy Federation, whose mission I still hold dear: to fight for a free, democratic nation—the China her people deserve. But no matter how hard you fight, some people, sadly, still cannot win.

I had been in touch with my old friend Pan Mingdong, whose health, evidently, was failing. In October of 1997, at my urging, he went to a doctor whose physical examination showed that Pan suffered from colon cancer. A hospital stay and surgery were required, but Pan had no money to pay for these things. I launched a campaign to raise money for him here in the States, and began pleading with him to come to New York.

"Medical technology here is much more advanced than it is in China," I said. "Please, my friend. Come to America."

Eventually, he agreed, but the Party refused him a passport. And so I began a new campaign to write articles and hold press conferences that introduced Pan, his work, and his plight to the international community. The response was overwhelming. Quite a few organizations lent their support. Human Rights Watch and Doctors without Borders played exactly the role you'd expect they would, leading the way with incredible dignity and energy. The Party eventually acquiesced under such intense public scrutiny. They issued Pan a passport in the summer of 1998, but by then his health had deteriorated to the point where he could not travel. At that point, all we could do was wait and pray for a miracle.

I called Pan on October 15, 1998. He was at Hunan University Hospital. Friends had gathered to stay with him. Pan and I talked on the phone a few minutes. He sounded happy but tired. At one point his voice began to trail off, and I started to grow concerned. Someone on the other end of the line took the phone and said that Pan was bleeding again; they had to get off the line and call for the doctor.

"Okay," I said. "Tell him to rest and concentrate on getting better. I'll call again tomorrow."

But I never got the chance. The next day, October 16, my phone rang. It was Pan's friend, calling to report that Pan had died that morning. I was devastated.

The Party disallowed any memorial in China. Pan's father had died many years earlier in the 1950s. His mother had passed away in 1994. He never married and had no children. He was survived by his brother and lots of friends who wanted to hold a service, but the Party's ruling was clear. They threatened Pan's brother, I later heard. *Do not convene any meeting for this man. No funeral of any kind.* They were scared, I think, that people might come together to celebrate the life of such a well-known political dissident.

Furious, I held my own memorial for Pan here in New York City. Close to one hundred dissidents attended. I led a toast to Pan Mingdong's life and reviewed some of the many notable things he had done on behalf of the Chinese nation.

"The pro-democracy movement," I said, "has just lost one of its leading lights."

And I had lost a friend.

11

Over the next few years, my life began to get very busy. There were speeches to make and causes to back. I began to travel extensively to Europe, Asia, and Latin America to appeal directly to their governments and advocate that they pay attention to the human rights problems in China. I gave hundreds and hundreds of lectures and interviews, and eventually published more than two hundred articles offering political commentary for both the Chinese and English media.

The US House of Representatives passed a resolution praising me and my colleagues for writing *Anthems of Defeat*. In 2004, the New York State Assembly issued an official proclamation that I should be considered a "Democratic Warrior." I was later named the Top Worldwide Chinese Dissident by the *Epoch Times*, a newspaper that went on to win the 2005 special media prize from the International Society for Human Rights (IGFM). My efforts were recognized by the *Washington Post*, the *New York Times*, and many other international media. Using the Internet, I began to hold weekly press conferences detailing the progress of the pro-democracy China movement. I became a frequent speaker at colleges and universities across the country.

But I'm getting ahead of myself and overlooking what matters most. In 2002, Felicity and I were in our kitchen, feeding our cat, and talking about getting married. We'd held off, hoping my mother could someday visit, but by then we had to admit that it would probably never happen.

The great dissident Sima Lu asked if he could have the honor of walking Felicity down the aisle. "Please," said Sima Lu. "Allow an old man this honor."

By then, Sima Lu was eighty-four years old, a living legend who'd joined the Communist Party in 1933. He initially worked as editor in chief for a paper called the *People's Weekly*, forerunner to the *People's Daily*, but he quickly fell out of favor. As a newspaper man, Sima Lu thought it normal to publish articles critical of CCP policies.

"After all," as he told me once. "How could the Party grow and evolve unless we questioned ourselves?"

Evidently, his superiors didn't share this position. Sima Lu was punished so often and so stridently, he fled China in 1949, the year that Mao took power.

"And I wasn't alone," he said. "In my day, many intelligent people were fleeing China, as well."

He told me that intelligence is like money. It always goes where it's treated best, nurtured, and helped to grow. Because, as he and I discussed, intelligence is a living thing, as is the intelligence of a nation. And the more a country represses its people, the more it will lose its greatest minds, its artists and thinkers, its writers and scientists, ethicists and historians.

Sima Lu shook his head, gracing me with his puckish smile. "Look at how many noble minds fled the country in 1989. Is it not the very same thing?"

Felicity and I were married on November 15, 2003, in the massive gothic cathedral of Riverside Church near Columbia University. If you've never been there, I urge you to go, regardless of your faith. Riverside Church is the tallest church in the country, a feat of architecture. But more important, it welcomes all, regardless of race, nationality, or sect. Martin Luther King once spoke at the pulpit. So did Nelson Mandela. There is history in every stone. You can almost hear the final tones of speeches made in days gone by still ringing off the colonnades.

"Well!" said Robin Munro. He grinned and clapped me hard on the back, his big Scottish hand knocking air from my lungs. Robin stood straight and tall, looking dapper in his black tuxedo. A *yang gui zi* among

Asians. The man who had once befriended me while I struggled, alone, in a very strange place was now my lifelong friend and a member of my wedding party. I hid a smile each time I saw a Chinese guest look up with shock. Who is this man, their faces said? A *yang gui zi* who speaks Mandarin? And so eloquently, too! Truly, the world had changed.

"*Ni gao xing ma?*"

Robin said, *Are you happy?*

"*Shi, wuo heng xing yun,*" I replied.

Yes, I'm very lucky.

12

On the twentieth anniversary of the June 4th incident, I led a candlelight vigil in front of the Chinese consulate in Manhattan from seven to nine in the evening. Then I did something I probably shouldn't have. Accompanied by my secretary and a documentary filmmaker, I returned to the embassy after midnight. The documentarian filmed what followed. My secretary and I took cans of paint and sprayed graffiti on the consulate wall, as well as on the sidewalk out front of the building. We painted characters big and bold in red and white.

In English, I wrote: *Free China 89 6 4*. Then, in Chinese characters, I wrote: *Chong Ping Liu Si*. The closest translation: *Reassess June the 4th*. I also wrote these numbers: *200,000* and *20*. Because certain people know what they mean, and they will never forget.

The spray painting took about two or three minutes. The filmmaker shot it all. We might have added more graffiti, but security guards in business suits came out of the consulate, shouting.

"What are you doing?!?"

My secretary and the filmmaker bolted, but I just stood there, watching them come. "Arrest me," I said.

They stopped, the two of them, looking at me. The glimmer of recognition. They knew who I was. How could they not? How many times had I stood out front of their building, chanting protests, leading demonstrations, directing people who all bore signs that said: *Release Political Prisoners* or *End Religious Persecution*.

The CCP Must Stop Telling Lies.
Let China Be Democratic and Free.
"Arrest me," I said again.

But the guards would not. They looked at the spray paint. Drooling colors. Red and white rivulets streaming down the impregnable gray brick façade. The fresh smell of solvents. Pigments. Propellants. The odor of work in progress.

"Leave," said one of the guards.

He shook his head. Turned back around and went inside the building. His partner followed.

Note to self: vandalizing a foreign nation's consulate is dicey from a legal perspective, as Felicity likes to remind me in her ever-lawyerly way. Defacing private property is a Class A Misdemeanor, she says, punishable by up to a year in prison. However, the Vienna Convention complicates matters, as well as the fact that China and the United States signed a treaty on consular relations. Under international practice, foreign embassies and consulates fall outside the jurisdiction of local law enforcement. And diplomats are immune to the laws of countries to which they are posted.

Either way you slice it, swift repercussion should have occurred for the paint I sprayed on the consulate. Yet the Chinese authorities didn't report the matter to the New York City police. They didn't protest the matter at all, and I think I know why.

How could they risk the exposure? Why summon the eye of the media? Think of what that would be like. Photographers snapping pictures. Video cameras perched on shoulders. Onsite correspondents in the baleful glare of halogen lights, commenting on the graffiti after having done some quick research. Picture the TV news reporters informing the public.

"Our sources confirm: the date referenced in the graffiti alludes to the incident that occurred in Tiananmen Square on June 4, 1989. The Chinese characters confirm this. And the mysterious numbers—200,000 and 20 most likely allude to a comment made by Chinese leader Deng Xiaoping shortly before Communist troops opened fire on unarmed and innocent pro-democracy demonstrators . . ."

The CCP would never want that. They preferred to leave me alone. There would be no arrest for me, no day in court, no platform from which to trumpet my take on the Party's further atrocities. The CCP knows how the United States thinks, how most of America's people are sympathetic to martyrs who died so their country might live free.

Later that morning, at about 4 a.m., my secretary, the documentary filmmaker, and I took another risk and drove past the consulate in a car. We wanted to view our handiwork, but the message we'd left was gone or nearly so. Seven people stood outside the building, scrubbing the brick-work clean. I couldn't help but savor the irony. Here was a perfect analogy for the Chinese Communist Party. It shrinks from outright confrontation, preferring to wash away its sins under cover of night. It hopes that no one will see the truth, the evidence, and remember.

But there is another analogy here. For a long time after that day, if you walked past the Chinese consulate and looked very closely, you could still see the outlines—faint, but there—of writing that could not be washed away. The paint, like memory: indelible.

This is the spirit of China, I think. The true measure of her people. And this is what I am fighting for. This is the hope I have for my country. The spirit of Tiananmen Square. The spirit that we will prevail.

I began to grow more confident that the CCP wouldn't touch me no matter how I chose to protest their crimes. It turned out, I was wrong.

Epilogue

1

In mid-November of 2005, the CCP Politburo passed a narrow vote to create a proclamation that changed their official position and restored Hu Yaobang's reputation—just in time for what would've been his ninetieth birthday. Of course, there was a catch. China's president, Hu Jintao, was losing his political base. Since assuming office in 2002, he'd cracked down hard on the media. He'd levied stricter social policies, disempowered lawyers, and banned religions he felt encouraged free thought, free speech, and creativity. China wasn't progressing at all. It was slipping backward into the atrocities of her past. The people, shackled more tightly than ever, began to mutter and grumble.

Hu Jintao's actions made him especially unpopular with the Communist Youth League. In fact, rumor had it that some hundred million young Chinese had started to question Hu's authority. The Politburo came up with a plan. In China, a simple way to win the hearts and minds of the people has always been to rehabilitate a dead reformer. So that's what they did.

The vote, or so I have heard, was close—five members to four. I have also heard that the four who voted against the plan cited their fear of another uprising. In doing so, I have to point out, they were tacitly admitting there'd been an uprising in the first place.

A service was held in Hu Yaobang's honor. By now, I'm sure you can guess where the service was held. Of course! The Great Hall of the People in Tiananmen Square, Beijing. The ceremony was quiet and modest from every account I've read. Only a select group of three hundred people had been invited. And there were no protests, of course—that goes without saying. Who could bear the thought of another crackdown? But China— my dear China. Again you took what your leaders gave you, another cold nod toward reform. Another carp dragged up on the bank, cut to pieces, and handed out. Everyone got a mouthful, and more than a few were sated. It's easy to see one piece of fish as a banquet when you are starving.

My mother and sisters still live in China. I speak to them quite often. Sometimes we talk on the phone using prepaid calling cards. Sometimes we talk by computer, using the program called Skype. I prefer the computer. The calls are free. Calling China by phone gets expensive, but that is simply a question of money. I have found that calling China comes with other costs, as well. Recently, for instance, my mother informed me that my second-to-youngest sister, Yan Hong, has been hospitalized for many months. This is the sister who, many years ago, had the big Type 54 pistol fired close to her ear. I do not know what is wrong with her now; my mother will not say. It hurts that I cannot be there for her, to share my family's burden.

I tell my family how I've continued to fight and speak out against the Party. They are terrified for me. They think that CCP officials will come and arrest me here. They don't know what the United States is like, or any Western nation. They have no concept of freedom. For a long time, I tried to explain to them that the CCP has no power here. Sometimes, I've even scoffed at their fears, a jest I came to regret. Something happened in the summer of 2009 that changed my mind forever.

2

On July 6, 2009, a new member of my organization named Liu Dong* called me a few minutes after noon. Liu said he would like to see me after he got off work that evening. We made plans to meet around 9:30 p.m. a block away from the Broadway stop for the Number 7 train in Flushing, Queens.

This was nothing unusual. Liu Dong had been introduced to me two or three months before. He was a man in his middle forties who said he wished to see China freed from its Communists aggressors. I met him, liked him, trusted him, and took him into my confidence.

I met Liu Dong on the corner at 9:45. There was a Starbucks nearby, but I knew it would close at 10 p.m. Liu suggested we go to a bar, and I said that I knew one nearby, two or three blocks away. It was a karaoke place I'd been to several times before, one of those basement joints in Chinatown. Ten bucks got you a beer and the right to sing all night if that's what you wanted.

We walked down a flight of steps into a windowless basement room that was dim and smoky and small and loud, hardly a good place for conversation. Five or six tables stood cramped together, aimed toward a stage up front where patrons could take the microphone and sing traditional Chinese music.

The waitress brought us a couple of beers. I looked around and saw about twelve to fifteen patrons. Everyone was Chinese, and all were men, save one female customer, and the server, who was also female. I knew her to be the owner's wife.

I knew that I was in trouble the moment that we sat down. The other customers turned their heads and stared at me through the gloom. Their eyes were hostile. In Mandarin, they were *tiao xin*. Looking for a fight.

I knew that face, I'd seen it before. The police had worn faces just like it when they were hunting me back in China. In America, the face persisted, worn by some who came to my speeches. *Tiao xin* was often the look I saw on Chinese nationals living abroad. Many consider themselves good Communists who find no fault in the Party or its actions. They have come to this country for business and, as far as I can tell, care nothing for its freedoms.

My beer sat on the table before me. I didn't touch it. Didn't want to.

We'd only been in the bar ten minutes, maybe less. I remember two men stood up on the stage, butchering a popular song called *Yu Shan Ni Di Shiwo Yuan*. In English: "It's Fate to Meet You."

That's when it happened.

A man sitting behind me rocked his chair back and bumped into me hard. I turned around, thinking it was an accident. But the man sitting behind me turned around as well, and he grinned.

The bar was a bad place to search for details. Bad light. The thump of the karaoke bass. I could see that the man wasn't tall but was built wide as a weightlifter. He wore a red T-shirt and looked pretty drunk. His eyes had gone red and shiny. I'd seen his kind before, many times, men who are mean and crude and unafraid of getting in trouble—or of getting hurt. The kind of man who followed few rules, if any. The Chinese mafia was full of them.

"Excuse me," I said.

Red Shirt just leered and said nothing. I saw that he was sitting with two other men. One had hawkish features and was talking into a cell phone while looking directly at me. The other man wore a blue T-shirt and seemed very calm. Where Red Shirt was hot and surly, Blue Shirt was cool and professional. I'd seen this type before, as well. The Chinese mafia has those, too—men who are cold as steel in winter despite the fact they'd been drinking.

I moved my chair farther away from Red Shirt and continued talking to Liu. A moment later, Red Shirt rocked back and hit my chair again. He did it much harder this time. The action was clearly intentional. And this time, the back of Red Shirt's head slammed into the back of mine.

I turned around and readied myself to demand an explanation. But Red Shirt stood up. He was ready for that. His glare looked like a set of police lights, glowing red in the dark.

"You want to fight, Mr. Freedom Man?" He spoke in Mandarin.

I knew right then what was going to happen. All the threats over all the years. Now the punishment was finally coming. Now the thunderheads break.

"No," I said. "I don't want to fight. I'm going to call the police."

Red Shirt grinned. Hawk Face made a sign with his hand, and all three men got up and left the bar. I could see them standing beyond the door. Hawk Face continued to talk on his cell phone while Red Shirt and Blue Shirt watched me. The other bar patrons turned to me and jabbered in Mandarin.

"*Ni gang kuai pao ba! Yao chu da shi liao!*"

Hurry up and run! Otherwise something very terrible is going to happen!

But I didn't run. What would that accomplish in this case? Instead, I got up out of my chair and dialed 911 on my cell phone. The call went through, but the music in the basement was so loud, I could barely hear when the dispatcher answered. By that point, Hawk Face, Red Shirt, and Blue Shirt had walked back into the bar. I circled around them and walked outside and stood where they'd stood mere moments before, straining to hear on the phone.

"Hello?" I said, speaking English.

A woman's voice said, "Yes? Hello? This is 911. What is your emergency, please?"

"There are people here," I said. "They're trying to start a fight. I need the police to come."

"Okay," the dispatcher said. "What is your location? We'll send police, but I need to know what address you're at."

I knew the name of the street but didn't know what number, so I turned around and looked up at the arch that rose above the bar's entrance. The address wasn't written there, but while I was searching the waitress came out and glared at me. I asked her what the address was, and she turned and walked away. Clearly, she knew what was going on, and just as clearly, she'd sided with the men who wanted to fight me.

I told the dispatcher I didn't know what the building number was. She said, "Can you walk outside and check the front of the building?"

This seemed like a very good idea, so I started to walk up the steps to the street, but then I remembered there was a little table with a stack of business cards on it by the entrance to the bar. I went back down and picked up a card and read the address to the dispatcher.

"Okay," she said. "Just stay where you are. Police are going to come."

"Okay," I said. "I will." And hung up.

I waited, but the police didn't show. So I wandered halfway back up the stairs and paused on the landing, my thoughts moving fast. Liu Dong came out and asked what was going on. I told him that I'd called the police, and then I used my phone to dial 911 again. A different dispatcher picked up this time. She told me police had been sent and urged me to just sit tight and wait for them to arrive. She said it would just take a few more minutes. I hung up the phone and turned around. Liu Dong had disappeared, and Red Shirt was standing there in his place, grinning like a lunatic. I caught a split-second glimpse of his face before something hit my right eye. Hard.

The punch snapped my head back like whiplash. Later, I would come to think how professional an attack it was. Red Shirt knew how to throw a punch, knew how to make it count. He struck with the first two knuckles, making sure that bone impacted with bone.

Someone grabbed me from behind. I thought they were trying to break up the fight, to calm me down and keep me from counterattacking. Wrong. Whoever was behind me wrapped me in a bear hug. I struggled but couldn't break free. Then Blue Shirt stepped before me.

"Mr. Freedom Man," he said, and hit me in the nose.

I could feel the blood running down my face and knew that I was in trouble. I don't remember much about what happened after that. I don't know where the waitress went. I don't know what happened to Liu Dong. I remember getting hit a lot and trying to counterattack with my feet while wrestling to free my arms. My one advantage was that I'm six feet tall, much taller than most Chinese. I was taller than Red Shirt and Blue Shirt by far, but not Hawk Face, who, as things turned out, was the person who'd slipped behind me and grabbed me, holding me down.

At one point during the struggle, I broke free of Hawk Face and, with the use of my arms regained, tried to ward off the punches that flew toward my face. Then Red Shirt and Blue Shirt abruptly pulled back and hustled up the stairs, toward the street. Blue Shirt turned; I saw his arm move, and something flew toward me, very fast. Some kind of missile. I ducked just in time, and the bottle hit the wall behind me, shattering into a halo of shards alive with the hiss and spit of beer. The air went ripe with the smell of yeast. If that bottle had hit my head, I would have been killed. I got lucky. Very lucky. When I looked up again, my attackers were gone. I was hurt, but I was safe.

I sat down hard on the floor, pulled out my phone, and called 911. The third time I had summoned help. A new dispatcher said the exact same thing as the one before. Police were on their way. Please sit tight.

3

A few minutes later, two New York City policemen walked down the stairs and found me slumped against the wall near the bar's entrance. I was holding my wounds and bleeding through my fingers. Scarlet stains had blossomed all over my shirt, enlarging into a bushel.

One officer was Caucasian and the other was Korean. Neither spoke Mandarin. They squinted at me as though I was the problem, like I had caused the commotion. "What happened?" they demanded, and started to take my statement while waiting for an ambulance, which, they assured me, had been summoned.

These men didn't care what had happened, I could see that right away. Like most cops working in Chinatown, they thought that all violence was mob-related, the triads waging wars for turf, clashes over the opium trade. They imagined butterfly knives and kung fu moves—you could see it in their eyes. They'd seen too many movies.

One cop looked toward the bar and said, "Why would you come in here? You want my advice? Don't come back here again."

Like I hadn't figured that out already.

I sympathize in a way. At one point, I looked up with one hand on my throbbing head and watched these two policemen standing around, trying to look official. They were young men without much experience and plenty of fear who were trying to look as though they had lots of experience and no fear whatsoever. That's how it is with most police assigned to Chinatown. They don't speak the language. They don't know the culture. Everything that happens in jurisdiction is foreign to them, yet they're the ones who have to respond when things get out of line. Under those circumstances? I'd probably be trying to look hardened, too. World-weary. Bulletproof.

By that point, gawkers had started to cluster. Monday nights are normally quiet. The attack on me was the best show in town. People wanted an eyeful. I looked in the crowd and got an awful feeling in my guts. Some of the gawkers were grinning. Some of them knew who'd attacked me, I thought. Some had clearly approved.

I asked the policemen to question the owner. It turned out he was away in China. Instead, they questioned the owner's wife. Did she know Red Shirt's and Blue Shirt's names? Were they regulars, perhaps? The owner's wife just shook her head, refusing to look the cops in the eye.

"No, no," she said. "I don't know them." Too many times, and a bit too emphatic, wagging her chin like a spring-headed doll. The policemen turned to the crowd and stopped. Everyone else was doing the same. *No, no, we don't know them either.* That was all the cops wanted to see. They dismissed the incident without conducting any interviews, nor did they collect evidence, such as pieces of the broken bottle, on which I was sure there were fingerprints.

It's sad, but I had to wonder. Was Liu Dong somehow involved? My instincts tell me no. After all, I'd chosen the karaoke bar myself; he hadn't. But doubts exist to this day. Liu Dong had a strange reaction to my attack. He had nothing further to do with me. I later got word from friends that he no longer cared to see a free and democratic China, that perhaps he'd like to return there someday. After that, only silence.

But that Monday night, I was sitting in the back of the ambulance, driving to Flushing Hospital. I turned my head to reveal a cut to the paramedic who was working fast to stop my face from bleeding. That's when I saw the headlights on the road behind us, through the ambulance rear windows. A car was following us very closely, despite the fact that we were speeding, strobe lights flashing, sirens wailing. From what I could see, the car behind us had light-colored paint, white or a light shade of green, I thought, though I couldn't be sure in the darkness. What struck me as certain: the car was packed. I could make out the silhouettes of many heads backlit by a second car that was trailing behind the first.

"I think we're being followed," I said.

The paramedic smiled at me, in essence copying old Dai Hai in deed if not word. *Tsk tsk tsk, Mr. Tang. Where is this attitude coming from?* "You're jumpy," the paramedic said. "It's natural. You're in shock, you need to relax. We'll be at the hospital soon."

I kept watch out the rear windows. So much of my life has been spent looking back. There's never enough looking forward.

We made a few turns, but the cars stayed behind us, a fact I shared with the paramedic. He looked out the window and saw the car with the light-colored paint, which was practically on our rear bumper. "Okay, look," the paramedic said. "We'll make a left turn at the next traffic light. If the car's still behind us, maybe you're right. Okay? I'll accept what you're saying."

We made the left turn, but the cars stayed with us. I looked at the paramedic and saw his face change. He believed me now. He leaned his head forward and called so the ambulance driver could hear.

"Call ahead to security!"

The very last turn took us into Flushing Hospital. The ambulance stopped in front of the ER as a man came out through the thick glass doors, which rolled aside automatically. The man was in some kind of uniform and had a gun that he wore on his hip. An engine growled. The car with the light-colored paint slid past us and accelerated. The second car followed, a throaty *vroom*, then both cars were gone.

The paramedic who'd been swabbing my face helped me step down to the street. "Don't worry, Mr. Tang," he said. "We'll let them know the situation."

Meaning the guard, I thought. And others like him, perhaps, the hospital's security team. But then I thought, Really? You'll let them know? What will you tell them? Where on earth will you start to explain?

The doctor who tended my wounds ticked them off like entrees on a menu. Lacerations to head and scalp. Bruises across my body. My left hand had sustained a fracture, what the doctor called a common defensive injury. He showed me how I might have sustained it raising my hand to block a punch, or cracking the bone while punching back in an awkward counterattack.

Or maybe both, I thought, as he fit my hand with a cast. The battle for freedom is like this as well. Sometimes you work the offensive. Sometimes you have to defend.

4

Nowadays, I'm often asked to comment on certain key issues that are directly or indirectly related to the democracy movement in China. Let me begin by stating my stance on Tibet. Put simply, I believe that Tibet's destiny should be determined by Tibetans, not by the Chinese government or an international committee.

This stance differs from the one taken by many other well-known Chinese dissidents. Sadly, I've actually heard some of my colleagues call the Tibetans opportunistic separatists. I find this response both appalling and incredibly disappointing.

From what I can see, there are two key reasons why some pro-democracy activists do not support Tibet. First, when they lived in China, they were brainwashed from an early age to think that the Dalai Lama wants Tibet to be completely independent. If they took the time to research the matter, they'd see that this runs counter to the Dalai Lama's statements. In fact, since 1984, His Holiness has announced countless times that he and the Tibetan people are willing to work within the Chinese framework, provided that Tibet be granted certain accords that are necessary for the welfare of her culture and her people. Still, it's a very Chinese belief to think that the Dalai Lama is leading some sort of mass revolt. Though utterly erroneous, even some pro-democracy activists have been known to get swept up in this nonsense.

There is a second reason some activists do not support Tibet. Though they were once persecuted by the CCP, many activists believe they will one day be forgiven as long as they toe the Party line. In other words, they want to keep their options open. Someday, they may want to return to China. Or they may fear for the safety of their families abroad. And more than a few are afraid, I think, of what the Party could do to them even while they live here in the United States.

Let me state my case clearly. Tibet is a nation of peaceful religious people who, like people everywhere, should be accorded the right to live and practice their beliefs however they please. Of late, Tibet's very name has become synonymous with controversy. Why? The problem lies not with Tibet; the problem lies with China's government.

I have met His Holiness, Tenzin Gyatso, the Fourteenth Dalai Lama, on several occasions. I have always found him to be a warm, wise, intelligent, thoughtful man who would never say an unkind word to a single human being, not even those who would raise a hand against him or his nation. I wish that more people followed his example.

I recall the spring of 2008. After the Tibetan uprising of that year,* China stepped up its efforts to demonize the Dalai Lama, knowing that international attention would be focused on Beijing, which was hosting the 2008 Olympics. In Beijing, Tibetan students were ordered to renounce their spiritual leader under penalty of arrest. While blocking foreign media from reporting impartially on the uprising in Tibet, the Party-sanctioned Xinhua News Agency stated (somewhat incredibly) that mobs, initially led by peace-loving Buddhist monks, had attacked Chinese troops, killing sixteen and causing approximately $14 million worth of damage. Wen Jiabao

---

*Often referred to as the 3-14 Riots since they took place on March 14, 2008.

blamed the entire incident on the Dalai Lama, calling His Holiness the event's orchestrator, when of course he hadn't set foot in his own country in years. As reported by the Associated Press and the *Times* of London, Zhang Qingli, the Party's Secretary of Tibet, said, "The Dalai Lama is a wolf wrapped in a habit, a monster with a human face and animal's heart. We are now engaged in a fierce blood-and-fire battle with the Dalai clique, a life-and-death battle between us and the enemy."

It sounded a bit overwrought to me, more of the Party's propaganda, more of their sneaky tricks. How did the Dalai Lama respond? He urged his followers to remain peaceful. He offered to go to Beijing at once to meet with Party leaders. He even offered to step down as head of the Tibetan government in exile if that's what it took to end the violence. I ask you: when was the last time you heard of a Chinese leader offering to step down for the good of his people?

In essence, His Holiness refused to respond in kind to Chinese threats. I don't believe he would ever belittle himself, his people, the people of China, or China's government by acting in this fashion. How shameful, I thought, for China to behave as it had, and how edifying to watch a person respect his opponents in the same manner he would respect a friend or supporter. I shall always remember the Dalai Lama's conduct during the spring of 2008 as one of the most profound examples of compassion and respect that I have ever seen.

But this is typical of the Dalai Lama. His Holiness has applied his energy generously and with typical selflessness toward raising the consciousness of his own people, as well as the consciousness of people worldwide. Quite impressively, ever since the 2008 Olympics, His Holiness stated his wish to interact more directly with China's people rather than with her government. In essence, he has recognized that the two are not one and the same. It's another blow to the CCP, who like to presume they speak for the nation when, quite frankly, they don't.

In fact, the Dalai Lama has actualized the struggle for human rights as something far beyond solely a Tibetan issue. He has conceived of it as a struggle that must be addressed by all human beings everywhere if this world is to progress past its current boundaries. I remember a billboard that once bore the image of His Holiness in Times Square, New York City. To paraphrase, the billboard read: Don't just think about peace, do something about it. I challenge anyone to tell me what harm could possibly come from such a viewpoint.

As continued international pressure combines with pressures internal to China, I foresee one possible outcome to the Tibetan struggle for independence: the Chinese government could bestow upon the Tibetan Autonomous Region a status similar to that of current-day Hong Kong— that is, a liberalized zone whose relaxed laws foster rapid and unique development along cultural and economic lines. To my mind, this would be a step in the right direction for both Tibet and China. However, as a guiding principle, I must reiterate my unequivocal belief that Tibet has every right to determine her own fate. To proclaim anything else is not only disrespectful, it also plays into the hands of those who push for a totalitarian and despotic agenda.

By the same token, I believe that the Xinjiang Uyghur should also be granted the right to decide their own fate. For anyone not familiar with it, Xinjiang is the largest administrative division in China. Situated in the northwest of the country, Xinjiang borders several other nations, including India, Pakistan, Afghanistan, Tajikistan, Mongolia, and Russia. In days of old, this region was often referred to as Turkestan. I've actually heard that term used now and again in modern times. Regardless, it's a very large landmass that represents approximately one-sixth of China's total area— and yet, few people live there. Among them can be counted several of China's minority groups, including the Uyghur, Mongols, Hui, Kyrgyz, and Kazakhs.

I could not begin to describe Xinjiang's rich culture by attempting a cursory review of the region's history. Suffice it to say that Xinjiang has long served as a stage for ethnic tensions in China. Of late, the Uyghur, who are predominately Sufi Muslims and peaceful, have been targeted by CCP crackdowns. The Party has labeled the Uyghur "separatists" and "religious extremists," when in fact I believe the truth is that the Uyghur and other groups are being persecuted (sometimes executed) because of their ethnicity, beliefs, and desire to be free from the Party's malevolent control.

In the July 2009 Urumqi riots alone, hundreds of Uyghur people were killed in the streets by soldiers of the Chinese army. Hundreds more disappeared during the crackdown that followed the initial unrest on July 5. The Party, of course, described the situation as one where separatists and violent rebels rose up without cause and had to be suppressed for the good of China. They labeled a woman named Rabiye Kadeer as the rebellion's architect, an assertion that seems both convenient and ridiculous since Kadeer is also the Uyghur freedom movement leader and was out of the country when the attacks took place. She had no idea they had occurred until she heard about them through channels. And, many times previous to July 2009, she had stated her desire to work peacefully toward freedom within the Chinese system.

Frankly, the CCP's relentless drive to secure a region it so often and vociferously disdains smacks of unchecked imperialism. As with Tibet, I feel that the people of Xinjiang Province have every right—certainly the cultural investment and generational wisdom—to govern their affairs however they see fit. Any attempt by the Chinese government to secure the people of Xinjiang through force is yet another travesty of human rights, which brings us to the subject of how the CCP treats Falun Gong practitioners.

No one can deny that Falun Gong presents the biggest human rights issue that China faces today. Falun Gong is a spiritual calling that purports to grant its practitioners greater harmony with the universe. The practice's three central tenets are truthfulness, compassion, and tolerance. It was introduced to the world in 1992 and embraced by individuals around the world.

Many have responded positively to Falun Gong's slow movements and meditation exercises, all of which are based in commonsense morality, qi gong, and ancient peaceful religions such as Taoism and Buddhism. Falun Gong practitioners do not smoke, gamble, or drink alcohol. They believe that they can positively influence the world by first purifying their bodies, minds, and spirits. In short, Falun Gong is a peaceful way of life, and no threat to anyone—unless, that is, you are a totalitarian regime such as the Chinese Communist Party.

By 1998, Party official statistics stated that seventy million people were practicing Falun Gong in China. For various reasons, this number is probably incorrect; the actual number was probably much higher. At any rate, the Party began to grow nervous and critical of Falun Gong's popularity. They ordered the media to publish a series of articles undermining Falun Gong's efficacy. Falun Gong practitioners responded through a series of peaceful protests, the most stirring of which took place when some ten thousand Falun Gong members stood before the steps of *Zhongnanhai*, the Party leadership's residence and central headquarters next to the Forbidden City in Beijing.

By all reports, this large peaceful group of Falun Gong members stayed absolutely silent and still while their leaders beseeched the government to participate in dialogue and learn more about the group's intentions. Predictably, the CCP did not respond well. Personally, I think the Party got scared. Seeing such a large group of citizens organizing in Tiananmen Square must have conjured obvious parallels.

Ever since June 4, the Party tactic has been to nip any and all dissent in the bud as quickly and virulently as possible. And so, three months later in July 1999, the CCP cracked down on Falun Gong, banning its practice and arresting thousands of its leaders nationwide. They branded the practice an "evil cult" and set the media on a course of brainwashing the overall population. Very soon, allegations of Falun Gong members being tortured in and out of prison began to surface. In fact, according to Falun Gong statistics, at least one hundred thousand of their practitioners were detained, and more than three thousand died in jail. The Party was clearly up to its sad little tricks.

I believe I understand the dynamic that exists between the CCP and the Falun Gong community. People and groups hold up mirrors to each other. When faced with people whose sole concern is the cultivation of truthfulness, compassion, and tolerance, the Party beholds its own reflection and sees how ugly it truly is, nothing more than a coven of monsters. And so they react as monsters would. Callously and violent, desperate to maintain control, they lash out and destroy the mirror. They have to. Communist China's control of religion has always stood at the fulcrum of its bid to keep and grow its power.

I do not practice Falun Gong myself, but I have an immense degree of respect for this community. Throughout the course of my work, I have met literally thousands of Falun Gong practitioners. Most have struck me as very kind, peaceful people. Some rank among the most brilliant, enlightened people I've ever met. Moreover, their commitment to freedom extends far beyond their own adherents.

For instance, the Falun Gong community is responsible for developing software programs such as Ultrareach, Dynaweb, Garden Networks, Freegate, and FirePhoenix. These free applications enable web users to circumnavigate Internet blockades their governments might impose, allowing them to read banned or censored material that often contradicts government propaganda. In fact, all the programs listed above are used routinely not only by information-seeking citizens in China but by people living in other autocratic regimes as well, such as Iran, Syria, the United Arab Emirates, and Burma.

Put simply, the Falun Gong movement and I share similar aims. We both seek to improve the human rights condition in China while pursuing democratic reforms. We have worked together, and quite effectively, on numerous human rights issues, including the campaign we began in 2003 to bring former president of the People's Republic of China, Jiang Zemin, to justice, and another campaign launched in 2004 to "Quit the CCP." And yet, sadly, many pro-democracy dissidents ignore the Falun Gong community. Some go so far as to disdain them as openly as the Party does. I find this lack of vision remarkably disappointing, not to mention counterproductive.

In China, we have an old story. When hunters approach a group of monkeys, the monkeys will cast out the weakest among them, hoping the hunters will kill that one monkey and leave the rest alone. In essence, this is the model I see too many pro-democracy dissidents following. Such a simple solution. Each time the hunters come by, they find their weakest link and cast it out so the rest can survive. Falun Gong. Xinjiang. The Dalai Lama. Tibet. Some pro-democracy activists sacrifice these causes, hoping they won't stand out in a crowd, hoping they'll survive a bit longer. But consider the fallacy.

Eventually, your band of monkeys dwindles. Eventually, when the hunters come, you are the one thrown out of the circle. You are the one destroyed. This is not the enlightened or moral approach.

People ask me all the time why I support these so-called unpopular causes. They ask, Why bother? Why make trouble for yourself? I have a simple answer for this: because these causes are just. Because they represent what is right. Human rights.

We must band together, all of us, and face our common enemies. Ignorance. Intolerance. Autocratic regimes. We must put aside petty differences and bind ourselves to a central tenet: that freedom, democracy, and human rights are for everyone, not just some.

I believe— and have always believed—that no true change can come about until the Chinese Communist Party is ousted once and for all by the people of China. When this takes place, I feel confident that important issues such as those concerning Tibet, Xinjiang Province, and the plight of the Falun Gong will resolve themselves peacefully once and for all.

5

For the past two years or so, my colleagues and I have begun to leverage the tremendous power of computer technology in order to reach pro-democracy activists inside China. Wu Fan, president of the Chinese Interim Government, and I use the program called Paltalk to hold two- to three-hour weekly press conferences starting at 8 p.m. Beijing time. Paltalk is a powerful broadcast tool that integrates video, audio, and text capabilities. Each week, our weekly sessions are picked up by some four to five hundred participants inside mainland China. Paltalk gives each of those four to five hundred people the right to rebroadcast our session to listen-only nodes. And our volunteers e-mail and post copies of the broadcasts' transcripts, as well as audio files, to different Internet sites around the world. So in essence, we can't be sure how many people are following us. We estimate the number is in the thousands.

Before going on the air, we make a point to troll the international newswire services. Then we open each session by discussing what happened in China that week. Most of our listeners have no idea what's going on in their own country or even in a neighboring city. The Party controls the media and conveniently bans the transmission of certain facts. Suffice it to say that a lot of the news about China that you and I take for granted comes as a revelation to my listeners.

Once the news is finished, we open the session to questions. Frequently, listeners want to know more about the news clips we've just presented. But once that direction has been exhausted, the questions sort of become a free-for-all. A lot of people ask about how the US system of government works. Some want to know more about the work we do with the China Interim Government or the China Peace and Democracy Federation.

We tell them about the seventy million signatures we've received since starting the Quit the CCP campaign in 2005. We tell them the latest strides our lawyers have made in the campaign to Bring Jiang to Justice. We tell them about a sixty-six-year-old Chinese woman who immigrated to the United States and was recently recognized here for doing something outstanding: she used phone books to cold call people in China and ask them to leave the Communist Party. She did this from 9 p.m. to 12 a.m. each evening for five years straight, and used her own money to pay for the calls. And she is not alone.

A taxi driver in one city called in. He said that he and his colleagues weren't getting their fair share of state benefits from the government, and he asked me, What should we do? I taught him how to organize. To hold meetings with other drivers. Form a union. To elect representatives who could approach the government and hold dialogues. To boycott, if that's what it came to. I told them it could be dangerous. I'll never forget what he said.

"What is more dangerous, really? Taking a stand for what is right? Or giving in to what is wrong?"

A lot of people call in asking about the state of Taiwan and Tibet. Should these regions be recognized as autonomous? I tell them why I think the Tibetans should have the right to choose their own fate. I tell them Taiwan is already functionally autonomous, regardless of what the CCP says. Taiwan has its own government, its own military, its own economy. Taiwan, I say, is doing just fine. It's the CCP who isn't satisfied.

One time a student who had logged onto the chat room urgently requested to cut ahead of the other questions lined up in the queue. He apologized but said that his laptop battery was dying. He said he couldn't go into any of the Internet cafés to plug in because they were all being checked by police. He could only log in from a remote location. We were shocked to know that the CCP treated our press conference so seriously. But actually, it made a lot of sense. The Party doesn't want people to listen. The Party doesn't want people to know.

I'll never forget when a man called in and told me he was a soldier. He said he was sick of the Chinese way, and asked when I thought the time would be right for the people to rise up and overthrow the government. I told him I had no idea. "But whenever it happens," I said, "it must happen without any violence. Violence is the Party's way. To behave as they do solves nothing."

Since we've started our weekly sessions, over a hundred different dissident groups operating inside China have registered as active charters with the China Interim Government. This is highly dangerous for them—an offense that could be punished by death. I urge them all to be careful, and then, when the session is over and we've shut down our computers, I sometimes take a very long walk and think of them, wishing them well. As a Buddhist, I pray for them. May their intentions always be pure. May grace and wisdom, compassion and strength attend to them.

This is such a dangerous game we play. But for me the stakes are low. A new China rises to reclaim the old. Half a world away, on the other end of a satellite link, those brave men and women are waking up. They're starting to come to their senses. They're shaking off doubt and fear and despair, and putting all that they have on the line for their country, their families, their freedom. They are the new breed of patriots. They are the new revolution. They are China's greatest hope. The greatest hope for the world.

Someday, my two Chinas will become one. Until then, we must continue to fight. Forever, if that's what it takes.

6

I've been told that these days, in China, the Party has done an excellent job of censoring information. It's been less than a generation now. Evidently college students in China don't know what occurred at Tiananmen Square. You can show them the pictures of Tank Man, the unknown rebel who halted a line of armored-covered vehicles by standing right in front of them, who—according to witnesses—hopped up onto the first tank's hull, knocked on the hatch, and talked to the driver and crew who came out and asked them to please go home, who said that weapons and soldiers and guns and tanks weren't required to deal with a peaceful protest.

"What is this?" the students apparently say as they snicker and squint at the picture. "When was this taken? Is this a parade?"

It breaks my heart every time.

Felicity and I are still together and very happy, nineteen years by the time this book is released. Between us, there is *xin shang*, which is yet another difficult word to translate into English. In China, to *xin shang* a person goes far beyond liking or loving them. It's more than respect or appreciation. To *xin shang* a person means that they're constantly surprising you with how good they can be, how miraculous, how wonderful. When you find yourself amazed that a person's finer qualities keep growing, when those qualities always soar above the bar of even your great expectations, then you can say that you *xin shang* someone. I wish I could say it more often.

There are two Chinas. I have known them both. One is the global superpower whose rich ancient culture and generous people have already made their influence known in the world of the twenty-first century. The other China is whispered about: a brutal, corrupt autocratic regime whose long list of human rights offenses soils her dignity, brings about shame. To me, this is not enlightened. I have fought to raise my people's hope and fought to raise their consciousness. There is still a long way to fight.

Twenty-one years have passed since June 4, and China is still what it is. Much of the world has forgotten Tiananmen Square. But I remember. I will always remember. I ask that you remember, too, and participate in change.

Someday my people will have their freedom. I *xin shang* my wife. Someday, I will *xin shang* China.

Resources

Since arriving in the United States in 1992, Baiqiao Tang has continued his work as a pro-democracy advocate. Please visit the following websites for more information.

BAIQIAO TANG'S WORK

The China Interim Government: http://www.gdzf.org

China Peace and Democracy Federation: http://www.chinapeace.org

Bring Jiang to Justice: Tel: (617) 293-1030
                                      Fax: (617) 507-5623
                                      http://www.grandtrial.org

The Global Service Center
for Quitting CCP:

4046 Main Street
Suite 201
Flushing, NY 11354, USA
Tel: (818) 338-2883
Fax: (718) 358-8871
http://www.quitccp.org

Baiqiao Tang's Facebook:

http://www.facebook.com/
people/baiqiao.tang/

Baiqiao Tang's Twitter:

http://www.twitter.com/
baiqiaoch (Chinese) or
http://www.twitter.com/
tangbaiqiao (English)

Baiqiao Tang's blog:

http://www.tangbaiqiao
.wordpress.com

CHINA'S PRO-DEMOCRACY MOVEMENT

June 4th Memoir:

China Truth Foundation
PO Box 7265
Fremont, CA 94537, USA
http://www.64memo.com

China Democracy Party:

41-25 Kissena Blvd.
FLR1 #110
Flushing, NY 11355, USA
Tel: (917) 348-5230
http://www.cdpwu.org

Wei Jingsheng Foundation:

PO Box 15449
Washington, DC 20003, USA
Tel: (202) 543-1538
Fax: (202) 543-1539
http://www.weijingsheng.org

Beijing Spring:

PO Box 520709
Flushing, NY 11352, USA
Tel: (718) 661-9977
http://www.bjs.org

China Support Network:

1035 South Main Street
#230
Cheshire, CT 06410, USA
Tel: (203) 640-2715
http://www.chinasupport.net

Human Rights Watch:

350 Fifth Avenue, 34th Floor
New York, NY 10118, USA
Tel: (212) 290-4700
http://www.hrw.org

Initiatives for China:

533 Fifth Street NE
Washington, DC 20002, USA
Tel: (202) 290-1423
http://www.initiativesforchina
.org/

Secret China:

http://www.kanzhongguo.com

RELATED MEDIA

Epoch Times:

34 W 27th Street, 5th Floor
New York, NY 10001, USA
Tel: (212) 239-2808
Fax: (646) 213-1219

Additional regional offices exist in cities throughout the world. Please check the website for listings.

http://www.theepochtimes.com

New Tang Dynasty Television:

229 West 28th Street

Suite 1200
New York, NY 10001, USA
Tel: (212) 736-8535
Fax: (212) 736-8536
http://www.english.ntdtv.com

Sound of Hope Radio: http://www.soundofhope.org

Radio for Free Asia: 2025 M Street NW
Suite 300
Washington, DC 20036, USA
Tel: (202) 530-4900
http://www.rfa.org

FALUN GONG

Falun Gong (alternatively Falun Dafa) http://www.falundafa.org/

World Organization to Investigate   PO Box 84
the Persecution of Falun Gong   New York, NY 10116, USA
Tel: (347) 448-5790
Fax: (347) 402-1444
http://www.zhuichaguoji.org/en

FREE ANTICENSORSHIP SOFTWARE

Dynaweb: http://www.dongtaiwang.com/
loc/about_en.php

FirePhoenix: http://www.firephoenix.edoors
.com/cms/download.html

Freegate: http://www.dit-inc.us/freegate

Garden Networks: http://www.gardennetworks.org

Global Internet Freedom Consortium: http://www.internet freedom.org

UltraReach: http://www.ultrareach.com

TIBET

International Campaign for Tibet:
1825 Jefferson Place NW
Washington, DC 20036, USA
Tel: (202) 785-1515
Fax: (202) 785-4343
http://www.savetibet.org/

The Dalai Lama Foundation:
61 Renato Court #24
Redwood City, CA 94061, USA
Tel: (650) 368-4435
http://www.dalailama
foundation.org

The Official Website of the Central Tibetan Administration:
241 E. 32nd Street
New York, NY 10016, USA
Tel: (212) 213-5010
Fax: (212) 779-9245
http://www.tibet.net

His Holiness the 14th Dalai Lama of Tibet:
PO McLeod Ganj Dharamsala
Himachal Pradesh (H.P.) 176219,
India
Tel: 91 1892 221343 or
91 1892 221879
Fax: 91 1892 221813
http://www.dalailama.com

Students for a Free Tibet:
602 East 14th Street
2nd Floor
New York, NY 10009, USA
Tel: (212) 358-0071
Fax: (212) 358-1771
http://www.studentsforafreetibet
.org

Tibet House:

22 West 15th Street
New York, NY 10011, USA
Tel: (212) 807-0563
Fax: (212) 807-0565
http://www.tibethouse.us

UYGHUR'S HUMAN RIGHTS

Uyghur Human Rights Project:

1701 Pennsylvania Avenue, NW
Suite 300
Washington, DC 20006, USA
Tel: (202) 349-1496
Fax: (202) 349-1491
http://www.uhrp.org

Uyghur American Association:

1420 K Street, NW
Suite 350
Washington DC, 20005, USA
Tel: (202) 535-0037
Fax: (202) 535-0039
http://www.uyghuramerican.org

World Uyghur Congress:

PO Box 310312
80103 Munich, Germany
Tel: 0049 (0) 89 5432 1999
Fax: 0049 (0) 89 5434 9789
http://www.uyghurcongress.org

Acknowledgments

BAIQIAO TANG

Abook like *My Two Chinas* could not have been possible without tremendous support from many people. First thanks go to my good friend Bruce Kivo, who—when we were still strangers—one day introduced himself, said he'd heard about my life story, and wanted me to write about it. Since then, Bruce has become like my older brother. When I need help, he lends a hand without any hesitation. When I encounter difficulty, he urges me not to flinch. Without his encouragement, I don't know if we could have finished writing and publishing this book. Thank you, Bruce.

My coauthor Damon DiMarco and I met because of this book, and I consider it wonderful fate. Writing, as I've learned, can be difficult, but Damon made it a rare and pleasant experience. He kept us on course, was always sincere, and brought humor to the table. I feel like we can talk about anything. Apart from being my collaborator, he has become my manager, minister, partner, and—best of all—my friend. While this work is my story, it is our creation.

My wife, Felicity Lung, is the source of my confidence. To say she is always there for me only scratches the surface of her commitment. She is my safe harbor of love, good judgment, comfort, and sound advice. Without her, I do not know whether I could have persisted in pursuing my ideals. She is the unlisted third author of this book.

I also want to make a special mention of our cat, Xiao Hui, who has lived with Felicity and me these past sixteen years as a steady and cheerful companion. I hope he can one day join me to return to my motherland, China.

Thanks must also go to Frank Weimann, president of the Literary Group International, and his assistant, Elyse Tanzillo, for their constant vision and support. And, of course, to our editor, Linda Regan at Prometheus Books, for her brilliant work, her diligence, and her attentiveness.

The manuscript profited at various stages thanks to valuable suggestions from John Kusumi, Professor XuYi, Dr. Han Lianchao, Li Fengzhi, An Hunqu, Guo Guoding, and Sun Ping.

Many friends and colleagues supported me and allowed me time to finish this book. They include His Holiness the Dalai Lama of Tibet; Mia Farrow; Ronan Farrow; Professor Andrew Nathan of Columbia University; Nicholas Kristof of the *New York Times*; Senator Sam Brownback of Kansas; Congressman Christopher Smith of New Jersey; New York state senator Ruben Diaz; Dr. Zhang Rong; Jeffrey Fiedler, cofounder of the Laogai Research Foundation; Si Tuhua; Yi Rong; Dr. Li Dayong; Wei Jingsheng; Yan Jiaqi; He Qinglian; Dr. Cheng Xiaonong; Bhuchung Tsering; Jeremy Taylor; Wang Jun; Cheng Jianliang; Liu Yan; Yang Wei; and Wu Zhian. The *Epoch Times*, *Secret China*, and the *China Democracy Journal* all provided photos for this book. I appreciate their help.

I feel lucky to have grown up in such a warm and lovely family. Though my father, Tang Rentong, left us after I was arrested, he lives forever in my heart. And to my mother, Luo Huaying, as well as my five sisters: Tang Yanni, Tang Yanzhen, Tang Jiezhen, Tang Yanhong, and Tang Yanfei—you are my most valuable treasures. I love you all so much.

Numerous organizations assisted in helping me escape Hong Kong, stay in Hong Kong, and eventually start a new life in the United States. A partial list would include Human Rights Watch, Open Society Foundation,

Students for a Free Tibet, International Campaign for Tibet, US artist guide, Doctors without Borders, Human Rights First, Taiwan Youth Solitary Association, Hong Kong Alliance for Support of China's Democracy, Hong Kong Chinese University student association, Hong Kong College student association, Amnesty International, China Support Network, campaign to Quit the CCP, Radio Free Asia, New Dynasty TV, Sound of Hope Radio, Secret China, the China Interim Government, the Future China Forum, Human Rights in China, and Global Internet Freedom Consortium.

Countless people have assisted me over the years in too many ways to list. A short list that comes to mind includes Robin Munro, Scott Bellard, Liu Binyan, Sima Lu, Wang Ruowang, Yang Zi, Robert Bernstein, Nie Sen, Zhang Jianjun, Jiang Binrui, Tang Linghua, Fu Yong, Zhang Jianwei, Sheng Zhengyuan, Long Jianhua, Zhen Yan, Xie Changfa, Xie Changzhen, Tan Li, Li Jinhong, Zhou Min, Lian Yufeng, Sun Yanjun, Jiao Guobiao, Li Dan, Chen Kai, Cao Changqing, Xiong Yan, Feng Congde, Zhou Fengsuo, Han Shaohua, Wang Longmeng, Yan Wei, Wu Zhian, Liu Guohua, Bian Hexiang, Lu Yi, Liu Guokai, Feng Ailin, Wang Xizhe, Ling Zhi, Xu Pei, Zeng Jianyuan, Zhang Xiaojun, Xie Tian, Jiang Shizhou, Li Li, Ma Annan, Zhang Derong, Wu Fan, Huang Zhuo, Man Renguo, Li Wenjun, Li Weixun, Sidney Jones, Xiao Qiang, Jennifer Zhou, Zeng Huiyan, Chen Taiying, Zhang Xianzhang, Lu Zhengdong, and Xie Youtian. I would also like to thank all members of China Peace and Democracy Federation, the China Interim government, the founders of Bring Jiang to Justice, the volunteers at the Quit the CCP center, and all audiences of the China Interim government weekly Internet press conference, especially those listeners who currently live in China.

Finally, many more people deserve to be mentioned here, but, unfortunately, their names cannot be spoken in their own security's interest. Many still live in China and work for the Chinese government. They know who they are, and they know what they have done for me. I hope that one day I can thank them all in kind. Until then, they have my undying appreciation. I wish them all safety and happiness.

DAMON DiMARCO

Thanks must go to Frank Weimann and Elyse Tanzillo at the Literary Group, International for all their hard work and support. To Jaimee Gar-

ACKNOWLEDGMENTS

bacik of Footnote Editorial Services, for her invaluable feedback on this project's proposal. To Bruce Kivo, for standing behind such a just cause since this book's inception. To Linda Regan for her keen editorial eye, but also for her constant excitement about this book, which did not go unnoticed. To everyone at Prometheus Books (including Steven L. Mitchell, Chris Kramer, Mark Hall, Jill Maxick, Joe Gramlich, and Julia DeGraf), whose contributions are too numerous to mention. To the staff of Olives at the W Hotel in Union Square, and in particular to the excellent Mr. Mohammad Siraj, for excellent hospitality. To Felicity Lung, for her friendship and wise counsel, to say nothing of translation services far and beyond the call of duty. And to Jessica DiMarco, for helping with photos, encouragement, and her constant, incredible patience.

Finally, to Baiqiao Tang. Your life and spirit continue to amaze and inspire me. Few are given a just cause to fight for. Fewer still rise to the occasion. Thank you for the stand you have made, the privilege of our collaboration, and the gift of your friendship.